Shelter and Society

SUNY Series in Urban Public Policy
James Bohland and Patricia Edwards, Editors

Shelter and Society

Theory, Research, and Policy
for Nonprofit Housing

EDITED BY

C. Theodore Koebel

STATE UNIVERSITY OF NEW YORK PRESS

Published by
State University of New York Press, Albany

© 1998 State University of New York

All rights reserved

Printed in the United States of America

For information, address State University of New York
Press, State University Plaza, Albany, N.Y., 12246

Production by Diane Ganeles
Marketing by Fran Keneston

Library of Congress Cataloging-in-Publication Data

Shelter and society : theory, research, and policy for nonprofit
  housing / edited by C. Theodore Koebel.
      p.   cm. — (SUNY series on urban policy)
    Includes bibliographical references and index.
    ISBN 0-7914-3789-2 (hc : alk. paper). — ISBN 0-7914-3790-6 (pbk.
  : alk. paper)
      1. Poor—Housing—United States   2. Nonprofit organizations—
  United States   I. Koebel, C. Theodore.   II. Series.
  HD7287.96.U6S48   1998
  363.5′8—dc21   97-35890
                                                                CIP

10 9 8 7 6 5 4 3 2 1

Contents

Introduction

Chapter 1

Nonprofit Housing:
Theory, Research, and Policy

C. Theodore Koebel

The Crisis in Housing Policy

American housing policy is stalled at an intersection of several paths. Many believe the path we have been on is in the wrong direction, yet we sit frozen in the face of uncertainties about alternatives. Sitting idle in our indecision, we cut back on what we had been doing without setting a new direction. We seem to be sitting still, running our resources lower and lower.

There is no more poignant image of the failure of American housing policy than the physical dilapidation and social decay that exists in many of our public housing sites. Windows are broken; walls sprayed with graffiti; ground strewn with debris. Men cluster in daily idleness—out of work, out of money, out of hope. Drugs are both an escape and an economy. Women with children struggle to survive, unprepared for the awesome responsibilities of motherhood amid concentrated poverty and untrained for the low-skill jobs that are available. Some cope with drugs and prostitution. Others strive constantly to eke out the best life possible for their children despite overwhelming adversity. In one of the ultimate ironies of public policy, those who forsake housing assistance and devote nearly all their available cash for housing, live in better neighborhoods than those receiving governmental housing assistance (Koebel 1997).

The failure of government to directly provide decent housing for low-income families is now accepted as a given. New housing is rarely developed directly by government. The focus has shifted to demolishing the worst of the existing stock of public housing. Yet the private sector has also failed as a mechanism to produce low-income housing on behalf of government. Many privately owned housing developments that were built and supported with public subsidies are in as despicable shape as the worst public housing. Profiteering and greed can easily join bureaucratic incompetence as whipping boys for our failures.

With a legacy of both government and market failures, housing policy has increasingly turned to the nonprofit sector. The nonprofit housing sector, despite its small size in the United States and serious problems with production and management capacity, benefits in the public eye from the positive aura of nonprofit volunteerism coupled with vague hopes of shifting governmental fiscal burdens to philanthropy and private charity. It is not by accident that the nonprofit sector has escaped the opprobrium heaped on others delivering subsidized housing to the poor. The nation's churches and charitable organizations led the effort to address the shelter needs of homeless adults and families. Nonprofit community development organizations have gained prestige for their redevelopment efforts in distressed neighborhoods. From local grassroots efforts to national organizations, the nonprofit housing sector has become more visible and its successes are routinely touted. Although still providing a much smaller proportion of assisted housing than either government or the for-profit sector, the rising favor of the nonprofit sector can be seen in the preference for nonprofit provision expressed in a variety of federal, state, and local housing programs. In addition to provision of housing services through nonprofit organizations, public-private housing partnerships are universally acclaimed for wedding the complementary capabilities of government, for-profit firms, and nonprofit organizations. Housing advocates point to the hard won successes of nonprofit housing providers and the much larger nonprofit housing sectors in many European countries as evidence that nonprofit housing should be the central building block of domestic housing policy (Goetz 1993; Davis 1994).

The favorable aura of nonprofit housing notwithstanding, governments and housing advocates in the United States display limited understanding about the sector. Notions of substituting voluntarism and philanthropy for government funding are naive at best and intentionally deceitful and manipulative at worst. Half-truths abound in both the rhetoric of politicians who see the sector as solving the nation's domestic problems on the cheap and in the rhetoric of advocates who pay scant attention to the sector's limitations and shortcomings. Meanwhile, advances made in developing theoretical and empirical knowledge about the nonprofit sector in general have been only infrequently applied to housing, depriving policy makers, administrators, advocates, and researchers of much needed models to guide their actions.

The Importance of Theory, Research, and Policy

This book is intended to help advance our understanding of the nonprofit housing sector by addressing theory, research, and policy. An outgrowth of a lecture series sponsored by the Federal National Mortgage Association (Fannie

Mac), the papers were commissioned to provide an in-depth discussion of our current understanding of nonprofit housing. The goal was to move beyond the descriptions that are otherwise available of current nonprofit housing providers and the programs they use. A deeper level of understanding of the nonprofit housing sector requires a dynamic interplay of theory, research, and policy. As a consequence, this is not a "how-to" manual or a description of nonprofit housing programs. Nonetheless, it is intended to provide the policy maker, administrator, and advocate, along with the scholar and student, the theoretical and research grounding from which to develop better policies, practices, and research. At the same time, this is only a start. Current theory is overbroad and needs to be refined to provide insight into the fine-grained texture of nonprofit housing. This book attempts to establish a fruitful direction for the significant work that has to follow.

Theories of the nonprofit sector are of relatively recent mintage. Although the mediating role of voluntary associations was noted by Tocqueville (1840), academic interest in the sector was largely dormant until the 1970s. The prevailing view until then was that the nonprofit sector was reduced to insignificance by the universal coverage of the welfare state. But far from withering, the sector had become a vital partner in the welfare state's provision of social services. Following the introduction in 1971 of the *Journal of Voluntary Action Research* (now *Nonprofit and Voluntary Sector Quarterly*) and the creation of the Association for Research on Nonprofit Organizations and Voluntary Action, academic interest in the sector was further promoted by Weisbrod's (1975) introduction of an economic theory of the nonprofit sector in response to government failure and Berger and Neuhaus's (1977) work on mediating structures. Simultaneously, the Filer Commission (Filer 1975) drew public attention to the importance of philanthropy and the need for continued research on the "independent" or nonprofit sector. In the 1980s, the concepts of contract failure, voluntary failure, and third-party government were introduced and developed by Hansmann (1980) and Salamon (1987), among others.

Increased interest in the sector has been both scholarly and normative. Berger and Neuhaus promoted the sector as a positive counterbalance to the coercive and impersonal powers of the state, thus making the sector's mediating role a desirable goal to maximize. Similarly, the nonprofit sector was seen as a mechanism of reasserting grass-roots democracy and local autonomy in response to the centralization of power at the national level, leading to calls for "devolution" of power and responsibility back to groups closest to the problem being addressed. Putnam's (1993) study of democracy in Italy identified a rich variety of voluntary associations promoting cooperative endeavors as the necessary currency for creating social capital and "making democracy work." Social capital links the associational life of the community to its overall ability to mount effective collective action.

Although the term *social capital* appears to have been first introduced by Jane Jacobs in the 1960s, it has recently received widespread attention due to the work of Putnam. Putnam found that the effectiveness of democratic government in Italy was closely associated with the vitality of "networks of civic engagement." These networks were largely nongovernmental, voluntary associations of people brought together to pursue mutual interests and respond to community problems. For Putnam, social capital refers to features of "social organization, such as trust, norms, and networks, that can improve the efficiency of society by facilitating coordinated actions" (167). It is the mortar that binds individuals in collective action.

Putnam attributed the social capital benefits of voluntary associations to their horizontal organization and reliance on reciprocity, which help create networks of civic engagement. According to Putnam (1993: 173–74) "networks of civic engagement increase the potential costs to a defector in any individual transaction"; "foster robust norms of reciprocity"; "facilitate communication and improve the flow of information about the trustworthiness of individuals"; and "embody past success at collaboration, which can serve as a culturally-defined template for future collaboration." Further, these benefits supposedly are restricted to horizontal organizations, rather than the vertical structures of government: "A vertical network, no matter how dense and no matter how important to its participants, cannot sustain trust and cooperation" (174). Social capital is increased through its use—the more we devote to voluntary association, the more trusting, reciprocal, cooperative, and effective we become. Communities with a more active associational life will be more effective communities because of the trust established, the availability of networks for responding to community problems, and the reduction in uncertainty surrounding joint ventures.

American advocates of nonprofit housing have looked with envy on the much larger and well-established nonprofit housing sectors in many countries of western Europe, where the concept of *subsidiarity* has provided strong normative underpinning for nonprofit delivery (Mierlo 1990). A similar but much richer concept than devolution, subsidiarity emphasizes national funding of local responses to social problems, often through the nonprofit sector. Subsidiarity, however, places priority on responses that are organized closest to the individual needing service, favoring a progression from the family, the church or association, the locality, up to the national government. More remote levels can fund the services of those closer to the individual, but would provide those services directly only when a closer level has clearly failed to do so. Consequently, the subsidiarity principle has provided a strong normative justification for nonprofit provision of public services throughout western Europe. Rooted in Catholic theology and European tradition, subsidiarity has never gained currency as an American norm (Wolfe 1995).

Lacking the normative justification of the subsidiarity principle, justifications for nonprofit provision in the United States and England have been a more diverse interweaving of democratic principles and economic concepts. Expanding on Tocqueville, nonprofit organizations are believed to be "agents of democracy" in several ways (Ware 1989). They countervail the powers of the state and the market; provide avenues for participation in collective activities; facilitate social and political integration; promote diversity of opinion; mobilize minority interests and demands; provide goods not provided by the market or the state; and provide such goods more effectively or more trustworthy than the market or the state. Justifications of nonprofit provision specific to housing are its permanence; better maintenance; neighborhood stability and development; leveraging of governmental subsidies, philanthropy, and volunteerism; constancy of tenancy; and greater concern for client needs (Adams 1990; Fallis 1993). These assertions have been only partially addressed by theoretical and empirical investigations.

Much of the public attention and academic research on nonprofit housing organizations (NHOs) in the United States has been on community development corporations (CDCs). CDCs are distinguished by being indigenous to the distressed communities they serve; located in low-income neighborhoods; comprehensive in approach; and productive of tangible results (Steinbach 1995). Other nonprofit housing organizations include those that produce and manage low-income housing in several areas of a city or broader region; provide homeless shelters and related services; provide housing counseling and fair-housing services; and those that provide intermediary technical and financial assistance. The field is very diverse. Most organizations have multiple functions and are difficult to classify with precision.

Significant research has been done on nonprofit housing describing the size and functions of the sector, evaluating output and, to a lesser extent, evaluating the management performance of the sector. This research has been done primarily on nonprofit builders rather than providers of homeless shelters, housing counseling, fair housing programs, and related nonconstruction programs. When housing services are studied, nonprofit provision is rarely questioned or a subject of examination. Instead, such studies focus on the problem being addressed (e.g., homelessness), program outputs, or the relative effectiveness of treatment options.

Nonprofit housing cannot be discussed without attention to its interorganizational context, its involvement with neighborhood redevelopment, and its role in advocacy and policy formation. NHOs do not operate in isolation. They depend on a variety of funding, technical assistance, and political networks. Sometimes these networks are formally identified as *partnerships*, a term of great favor but often little precision. Without its own resources other than perhaps voluntary service and philanthropy, the nonprofit sector is reliant on government and to a lesser extent on the for-profit sector for the funds necessary to provide services. This is particularly the case with housing and neighborhood redevelopment, which are extremely capital intensive. Consequently, implicit or explicit public-private partnerships are the norm. Interpersonal and interorganizational networks are the essence of the implementation structures that are increasingly required to "set goals, mobilize resources, coordinate . . . actions," and provide the expertise to produce services (Porter 1990).

Even within the contracting relationship that binds many nonprofit organizations to government, the relationship is not simply hierarchical. Putnam's assertions notwithstanding, these vertical relationships are often rooted in bargaining and trust, with the potential for stable contracting to evolve as an implicit partnership. Indeed, Salamon (1989) describes the relationship between government and the nonprofit sector in the United States as the "paradigm of partnership":

> Government-nonprofit cooperation appears . . . as a productive adaptation of the traditional welfare state that takes advantage of government's peculiar strengths in raising resources and ensuring equity through a democratic political process and the voluntary sector's advantages as a deliverer of services in a more informal, smaller-scale fashion than large government bureaucracies frequently make possible. (44)

Unfortunately, this partnership has never been integrated into a sustaining ideology or popularly understood principle such as subsidiarity. Consequently, recent responses to the complexities of managing public-private partnership have been distorted by misunderstandings that "threaten to throw out the baby with the bath water. . . . These changes seem likely to change the character of the voluntary sector in fundamental ways and remove the partnership between government and the nonprofit sector from its place as the central organizing principle of the American welfare state" (Salamon 45).

Salamon identifies five recent changes affecting this partnership: government retrenchment and budget cuts; shifting from categorical aid to universal entitlements (including shifting from low-income categorical funding to middle-class entitlements); shifting from producer to consumer subsidies; demographic shifts (such as aging, higher female participation in the labor force, changes in family structures, and the emergence of an urban underclass); and erosion of support for social services as a response to poverty.

The shift away from production to consumer subsidies is particularly notable in housing. This shift has not so much reduced the role of NHOs as changed that role. Under consumer subsidies, the service NHOs offer becomes marketized. In order to maintain income, NHOs operate increasingly as commercial businesses in competition with for-profit firms. The distinctiveness of nonprofit housing can be eroded as competition forces NHOs to look more and more like for-profit firms. Voluntary and charitable support lapse in importance. The rise of "commercial nonprofits" has led to proposals for the elimination of favorable tax treatment of all nonprofit organizations or at least those that are not clearly supported by donations (Hansmann 1989).

Recent threats to the government-nonprofit partnership relationship that underpins the welfare state illustrate the dynamic nature of partnerships. Partnerships are inherently built on trust and performance—delivering the goods, so to speak. Painstakingly difficult to establish, partnerships have certain self-sustaining forces. For one, the time invested in establishing partnership relationships and the reduction in partnership maintenance costs over time help keep partnerships in place. Additionally, the economic and political rewards from partnership accomplishments provide incentives to continue the partnership. Partnerships are, in these ways, very similar to Stone's urban regimes (1989). Although they are not necessarily part of such regimes, their potential role in urban governance broadly understood is illuminated by regime theory.

An urban regime is defined by "*the informal arrangements by which pubic bodies and private interests function together in order to be able to make and carry out governing decisions*" (Stone 6). These governing decisions manage conflict and adapt to social change rather than exercise extensive control over the city. Although the informal arrangements characterizing the urban regime vary, they always attend to institutional scope and cooperation. Institutional scope reflects "the need to encompass a wide enough scope of institutions to mobilize the resources required to make and implement governing decisions," whereas cooperation is required for "the diverse participants to reach decisions and sustain action in support of those decisions." Two arenas of community leadership are central to governing regimes: popularly elected community leaders and business leaders. The reasons for including elected leaders are obvious. The centrality of business leaders, although often assumed, warrants some explanation.

Business investment is essential for the economy of any area. If governing regimes excluded business leaders, they would risk disfavor in decisions affecting location and expansion. Few areas, particularly central cities, have such strong economic pull that elected leaders would not automatically seek to include business leaders in the discussions and deliberations that influence the city. Additionally, "businesses control politically important resources and are rarely absent totally from the scene" (7). Certain businesses, such as banks and the real estate sector, are directly affected by community decisions and engage in civic affairs out of self-interest. Their engagement includes political contributions but ranges well beyond. It is a rare community where the elected leadership can implement its economic agenda without the resources and assistance of the business community.

Urban regime theory also provides insight and normative guidance into a central function of many NHOs—community development. Housing is inherently associated with place and space, thus the real estate chestnut that its three most important features are "location, location, location." This has naturally led NHOs to address the problems of place, which are substantial for many low-income households. Building a few new or rehabilitated houses does little to overcome the multiplicity of physical, social, and economic problems faced in old, poor neighborhoods. These NHOs (mostly community development corporations) are confronted squarely with the dilemmas of neighborhood redevelopment.

The issues of equity and economic redistribution are inevitably joined in neighborhood redevelopment. One school of thought attributes neighborhood decay to capitalist exploitation. It argues that CDCs should attend to political organization and opposition rather than to building a few structures and participating in inherently unequal partnerships that produce co-optation instead of progress (Stoecker 1996; Twelvetrees 1989; Kantor 1995). Even when a radical agenda is not articulated, the underlying ideology of most community developers assumes that the current managerial and capitalist city alienates the individual from himself and his neighbors (Steinberger 1985: 88). Thus a community approach rooted in communalism (a less volatile term than socialism) is required to liberate these neighborhoods. The communalist approach would limit action to organizing neighborhoods in opposition to exploitation and waiting for the demise of capitalism and the evolution of a new social order. This is not a very appealing agenda for most NHOs and clearly not a basis for the development of improved intersectoral networks within the current culture and economy. Nonetheless, this perspective contributes a valuable emphasis on the importance of politics and the need for community organizing to obtain political influence.

Steinberger identifies two other ideologies that are pertinent to neighborhood redevelopment—*managerialism* and *possessive-individualism*. Managerialism approaches neighborhood redevelopment as a rational "engineering" problem rather than a problem that is fundamentally political. The focus is on finding the right technical solutions, such as improved infrastructure, nonprofit housing, or public-private partnerships. The managerialist approach will continue as the siren's call to the professional leadership of NHOs. Although its political perspective is patently naive, it's central tenet is virtually a truism. NHOs have to be competent producers of outcomes that are seen by most citizens as beneficial. The production of affordable housing requires technical skill and know-how; the production of redevelopment even more so. A technically incompetent NHO is probably as damaging as a politically naive one.

The dominant American ideology is possessive-individualism. In the economy, this is expressed as capitalism and competitive markets. It is hard to ignore that competitive markets have produced a level of housing quality in America that pleases the vast majority of consumers. Competitive housing markets and the exercise of consumer choice should be tapped whenever possible in redressing contemporary housing and neighborhood problems. It is equally hard to ignore that competitive markets have left many poor families ill-housed in deteriorated neighborhoods. NHOs exist to redress this inequity and must somehow blend capitalism, managerialism, and communalism in order to achieve their ends. This is obviously difficult and it may be impossible, but there is evidence to suggest otherwise.

Stone's (1989) study of redevelopment in Atlanta, and more particularly Monti's (1990) study of redevelopment in St. Louis, point to the potential for progressive redevelopment that does not necessarily exclude the poor (also see Stone and Sanders 1987). Stone's regime politics and Monti's description of successful redevelopment politics are very similar. Monti suggests that urban regimes:

> Can be responsive to the demands of groups often excluded from the redevelopment process. . . . Pluralism became an important goal. Developers were encouraged to find ways to include low-income persons in their plans. Representatives of these same low-income people were much more involved in helping to fashion a place for themselves in the city. They did not always get everything they wanted, but their interests no longer were ignored. (40–41)

According to Steinberger, CDCs are the embodiment of communalism's principles of self-rule and empowerment (76). NHOs, however, do not need to advocate neighborhood democracy. They are eminently compatible with the market ideology of possessive-individualism and to managerialism's emphasis on performance. NHOs are naturally tied to the central elements of development coalitions participating in many governing regimes—banks, developers, contractors, and city hall. The argument for nonprofit provision reflects a view of both government and profit-motivated private action as limited in their abilities to deliver certain goods and services. It will always appear to be intellectually weaker than the arguments for communalism and individualism, because it is a blend of both. Consequently the lines are not clearly drawn and neither ends of the spectrum are rejected. NHOs are quasi-governmental and quasi-market. However unappealing this might be to those who like clear lines drawn in the conceptual sand, it might better reflect the experience of those working to improve housing for those who are inadequately served by government and the market.

The requirements of political action are more of a challenge for NHOs. They are dependent on the resources of others, as are their clients, and can hardly risk being strident in their advocacy. At the same time, they routinely engage in advocacy at the policy and program levels. They can help give their clients greater voice through their own influence. They should also promote the political organization and activism of their clients, so that they can exercise power directly, including the power of political protest. A more powerful client constituency could provide NHOs a counterweight to disproportionate power and coveted resources of their for-profit and government partners. Encouraging client protest to gain bargaining power is a difficult and potentially dangerous task. If such actions are recognized by others in their network, NHOs risk damaging the very trust that enables partnerships to work. It is probably better for NHOs to recognize the importance of politically empowering the poor and to advocate it, but not directly encourage political protest.

Even if NHOs can avoid the political land mines surrounding client organization and protest, there are other risks. The social capital of NHOs requires performance and delivering on promises. Once deals are struck, they cannot be easily rejected. NHOs are expected to deliver their constituents. If an organized clientele rejects its intermediaries and continues to protest, the intermediaries breech their partnership agreements and risk being seen as ineffectual. In some instances, knowing what is at stake could modify behavior. But there are no guarantees. By any stretch of the imagination, this is not an easy business to be in.

Organization of the Book

Despite the importance of the nonprofit sector and public-private partnerships in the delivery of housing services, little attention has been paid to developing theories of nonprofit housing and public-private partnerships. The first step toward a theory of nonprofit housing and of public-private partnerships is to locate these within the context of existing descriptions and theories of the nonprofit sector. Theories of nonprofit provision have largely addressed why nonprofit provision would occur in place of for-profit or government provision (see, for example, Weisbrod 1975; Hansmann 1980; Salamon 1987) and its contributions to democracy (Putnam 1993). Modern studies of the nonprofit sector originated with sociologists, who focused on why people volunteer, an interesting sociological question, but not a foundation for broader understanding of the nonprofit sector. Contemporary theoretical speculation was prompted among economists and political scientists by the continued existence of nonprofit provision. Economists wondered why nonprofit provision would coexist with profit provision in a market economy, and political scientists wondered why nonprofit provision would coexist with the welfare state. Consequently nonprofit theory has been preoccupied with explaining the existence of the nonprofit sector and its democratic benefits (employing such concepts as market failure, contract failure, government failure, mediating structure, and social capital). Detailed theories about the performance of the sector remain to be developed. Much of what is considered nonprofit theory is devoted to description and prescription rather than explanation.

Although nonprofit theory is still very rudimentary, the available theoretical constructs such as contract failure, government failure, and the contract state, provide significant insight into nonprofit housing. A broad conceptual understanding of the role of nonprofit housing is provided in the first section of this book, consisting of chapters 2, 3, and 4. It is beyond the scope of this book to develop a unified theory of nonprofit housing. But these chapters lay the groundwork for future theoretical work and provide a loose framework for guiding empirical research and the development of concepts and norms to support public policies for the provision of housing through nonprofit networks. The second section, consisting of chapters 5 through 10, provides historical, descriptive, and evaluative research on nonprofit housing provision. These chapters allow a deeper understanding of the historical development of nonprofit housing in the United States and Europe, as well as the contemporary performance of the nonprofit sector in the delivery of housing. Reflective of the nascent state of nonprofit theory, these chapters echo the conceptualizations of nonprofit provision presented earlier rather than having derived research explicitly from theory. Research on nonprofit housing has been based primarily on description and performance evaluation rather than theory. By itself, this is not a problem, since the study of nonprofit housing is obviously a very pragmatic, applied field. But the ability of research to instruct and inform policy is seriously limited without broader, theoretical conceptualizations of the nonprofit sector. The last section of this book is devoted to furthering the development of nonprofit housing policy. Policy prescriptions are inherently a blend of explicit and implicit conceptualizations and norms, as well as pragmatic knowledge derived from experience and research.

Chapters 2, 3, and 4 apply general theories of the nonprofit sector to nonprofit housing, the extension of nonprofit theory to public-private partnerships, and the political context of intersectoral cooperation. Richard Steinberg reviews the general theories of the nonprofit sector and demonstrates their application to housing in chapter 2. Koebel, Steinberg, and Dyck develop a taxonomy of intersectoral cooperation ranging from competitive contracting to public-private partnerships in chapter 3. Although rhetorical attention to partnerships is greatest in the U.S., this chapter finds more evidence of true partnership in the intersectoral networks for delivering social housing in several European countries than in the contracting and franchise relationships that dominate in the United States. Bishwapriya Sanyal addresses the importance of political imperatives in understanding the relationship between government and nonprofit organizations in chapter 4. Sanyal criticizes the general theories of the nonprofit sector for overlooking "the political character of a place." Looking at the long-standing promotion of partnerships between government and nonprofit organizations (NPOs) in providing employment and shelter in developing countries, Sanyal questions why such partnership takes root in some settings but not in others. The answer is found in an all too often overlooked factor: politics matters.

The next six chapters present research on intersectoral cooperation in the delivery of publicly assisted housing. Peter Drier (chapter 5) provides a detailed historical perspective of the past 100 years of housing philanthropy in the United States, starting with the housing reforms of the Progressive Movement. Particular attention is paid to the recent roles of charitable foundations in fashioning responses to homelessness and to neighborhood redevelopment. Evidence of government and market failure, as well as nonprofit response, can be found throughout this history. The historical development of nonprofit housing in the U.S. is further examined by Rachell Bratt in chapter 6. The perception of a linear progression from the reform movement of the turn-of-the-century to current nonprofit development is challenged. Reflective of Sanyal's emphasis in chapter 3 on political economy, Bratt's "central argument is that at each period during which NHOs have arisen, the decision by government to use NHOs is the outcome of a series of political, economic, and social needs. The NHOs, themselves, are not the key actors in the story and federal initiatives have generally not been concerned with how to make these organizations and the nonprofit sector work more efficiently. NHOs, it is argued, are a subplot." The lack of a "nonprofit-centric housing policy" is identified as a key flaw in the provision of housing in the United States. Lacking such a policy, NHOs risk potentially disastrous reactions by accepting and supporting a policy framework that uses but does not promote the nonprofit sector.

In contrast to the U.S., nonprofit housing sectors are historically well developed in several European countries. In chapter 7, Boelhouwer and Heijden place the evolution of housing policy in western Europe and its reliance on the nonprofit sector through four historical stages: I, addressing housing shortages; II, increasing housing quality; III, strengthening private markets; IV, the return of housing shortages. The role of the nonprofit sector in resisting the marginalization and stigmatization of social housing is addressed.

William Rohe provides a comprehensive review of research conducted on the performance of the nonprofit housing sector in the United States in chapter 8. Several claims have been made about the nonprofit housing sector. Nonprofit housing organizations (NHOs), particularly community development corporations (CDCs), are frequently expected to exceed either government or for-profit firms in responding to community needs, applying a comprehensive approach to development, committing to community capacity building and leveraging funds. They are also claimed to be more efficient and effective than government agencies. Many of these claims have been addressed in the several descriptive and evaluative studies reviewed by Rohe.

The efficiency of NHOs and the comparative cost of nonprofit housing development are examined by Wallace and Hebert in chapter 9. One of the fundamental questions about nonprofit housing provision is the efficiency of the sector in comparison with profit-motivated developers. Some nonprofit housing developers operate only as general contractors and do not maintain their own construction capacity. These NHOs contract with for-profit firms for construction. Other NHOs provide all or some construction with in-house crews. (The degree of mixed nonprofit and for-profit contracting has not been documented.) Operating without attention to profit and without the attention to minimizing costs that is forced by competition, NHOs are often suspected of being inherently inefficient and wasteful organizations.

The existing production subsidy system used for nonprofit housing in the United States requires the use of multiple sources of funding. Although nonprofit housing corporations have emerged as successful packagers of various subsidy programs, the time required and complexity involved with this system can be overwhelming. Koebel (chapter 10) provides a detailed case study of one such development, the conversion to a single-room only (SRO) facility of a previously renovated but unmarketable inner-city hotel. The development project was in many ways typical of current nonprofit housing production, with a multiyear predevelopment period, multiple funding sources, and numerous crises that would push many organizations to failure.

Based on the performance of current U.S. policies for low-income housing, the performance of the nonprofit housing sector, as well as the achievements of nonprofit housing sectors in Europe, Robert Whittlesey presents a detailed critique of U.S. housing policies in chapter 11. The requirements for a simpler, more efficient system to produce low-income housing are identified, including financing, equity, per-unit costs, asset management, and institutions.

The concluding chapter (Koebel) identifies critical issues facing the nonprofit housing sector in the United States. While most of the current discussion about nonprofit housing centers on the reduced funding of federal housing programs and promotes nonprofit provision as the foundation of progressive housing policy, the fundamental empirical and normative issues raised in this chapter must be addressed before nonprofit housing can live up to such high expectations.

A Note on Terminology

When possible, this book refers to nonprofit housing organizations (NHOs), but related terms are impossible to avoid. Community development corporations (CDCs) are NHOs with a commitment to improving specific neighborhoods and are often rooted in those neighborhoods. The term nongovernmental organization (NGO) or nonprofit organization (NPO) is frequently used in the literature to refer to NHOs and other nonprofit organizations. These terms are used to refer to a broader set of organizations that include but are not limited to NHOs. The unhyphenated "nonprofit" is preferred, as is its hyphenated counterpart "for-profit." "Nonprofit" is typically used as an adjective, but at times is used as a noun, but only in the plural (i.e., "nonprofits"). Although subtle distinctions are occasionally made, the terms "nonprofit sector," "voluntary sector," and "third sector" are generally interchangable.

"Social housing" or "social rental sector" is used to refer broadly to governmentally assisted housing. "Public housing" is restricted to the American housing program of the same name, wherein federal subsidies are used for social housing owned and operated by a local housing authority.

References

Adams, Carolyn T. 1990. "Nonprofit housing producers in the U.S.: Why so rare?" Urban Affairs Association Annual Meeting, Charlotte, N.C.

Berger, Peter L., and Richard J. Neuhaus. 1977. *To empower people: The role of mediating structures in public policy.* Washington, D.C.: American Enterprise Institute.

Davis, John E., ed. 1994. *The affordable city: Toward a third sector housing policy.* Philadelphia: Temple University Press.

Fallis, George. 1993. "On choosing social policy instruments: The case of nonprofit housing, housing allowances or income assistance." *Progress in Planning* 40. 1–88.

Filer, John H. 1975. "The Filer Commission report." *Giving in America: Toward a stronger voluntary sector.* Washington, D.C.: National Commission on Private Philanthropy and Public Needs.

Goetz, Edward G. 1993. *Shelter burden: Local politics and progressive housing policy.* Philadelphia: Temple University Press.

Hansmann, Henry B. 1980. "The role of nonprofit enterprise." *Yale Law Journal* 89. 835–98.

———. 1989. "The two nonprofit sectors: Fee for service versus donative organizations." In *The future of the nonprofit sector,* Virginia A. Hodgkinson et al. San Francisco: Jossey-Bass.

Kantor, Paul. 1995. *The dependent city revisited.* Boulder: Westview Press.

Koebel, C. Theodore. 1997. "Housing conditions of low-income families in the private, unassisted housing market in the United States." *Housing Studies.* 12. 201–213.

Mierlo, Hans J. G. A. van. 1990. "Privatization and the third sector of the economy: A public choice perspective." *Annals of Public and Cooperative Economics* 61. 537–60.

Monti, Daniel J. 1990. *Race, redevelopment and the new company town.* Albany: State University of New York Press.

Porter, David O. 1990. "Structural pose as an approach for implementing complex programs." In *Strategies for managing intergovernmental policies and networks,* Robert W. Gage and Myrna P. Mandell, eds. New York: Praeger.

Putnam, Robert D. 1993. *Making democracy work: Civic traditions in modern Italy*. Princeton: Princeton University Press.

Salamon, Lester M. 1987. "Of market failure, voluntary failure, and third-party government: Toward a theory of government-nonprofit relations in the modern welfare state." *Journal of Voluntary Action Research* 16. 29–49.

———. 1989. "The changing partnership between the voluntary sector and the welfare state." In *The future of the nonprofit sector*, Virginia A. Hodgkinson et al. San Francisco: Jossey-Bass.

Steinbach, Carol F. 1995. *Tying it all together: The comprehensive achievements of community-based development organizations*. Washington, D.C.: National Congress for Community Economic Development.

Steinberger, Peter J. 1985. *Ideology and the urban crisis*. Albany: State University of New York Press.

Stoecker, Randy. 1996. "The political economy of the community development corporation model of urban redevelopment." Revised version of a paper presented at the 1995 American Sociological Association Annual Meeting.

Stone, Clarence N. 1989. *Regime politics: Governing Atlanta, 1946–1988*. Lawrence: University Press of Kansas.

Stone, Clarence N. and Heywood Sanders, eds. 1987. *The politics of urban development*. Lawrence: University Press of Kansas.

Tocqueville, Alexis de. 1840. *Democracy in America*, vol. 2. New York: Alfred A. Knopf.

Twelvetrees, Alan. 1989. *Organizing for neighborhood development*. Aldershot, England: Avebury.

Ware, Alan 1989. *Between profit and state: Intermediate organizations in Britain and the United States*. Princeton: Princeton University Press.

Weisbrod, Burton A. 1975. "Toward a theory of the voluntary nonprofit sector in a three-sector economy." In *Altruism, morality, and economic theory*, Edmund S. Phelps, ed. New York: Russell Sage Foundation. 171–95.

Wolfe, Christopher, 1995. "Subsidiarity: The 'Other' ground of limited government." In *Catholicism, liberalism, & communitarianism*, Kenneth L. Grasso et al. Lanham, Md. Rowman & Littlefield Publishers.

Part I

Theory

Chapter 2

The Theory of the Nonprofit Sector in Housing

Richard Steinberg

This chapter reviews general theories about the nonprofit sector and the behavior of nonprofit organizations. Four conditions are identified where nonprofit organizations can outperform for-profit firms: contract failure, public goods, externalities, and income redistribution. The trustworthiness of the nonprofit provider is an essential element when conditions of contract failure exist. The potential for nonprofit provision to be inferior to for-profit firms or to government is also identified and attributed to higher costs and inefficiencies associated with possible mismanagement, excessive managerial perks, insufficient resources, particularism, paternalism, and amateurism.

Introduction

Although many scholars have studied the role and functioning of nonprofit organizations and many have studied housing markets, there has been relatively little interchange between these scholarly communities. This is unfortunate, for those housing specialists who assess the proper role of nonprofit organizations in housing provision could learn much from the study of those nonprofits that provide other services (day-care centers, nursing homes, foster homes, hospitals, soup kitchens, dance companies, research charities, religious institutions). Housing may be different in some details, but much of the learning on nonprofits is broadly applicable. In turn, nonprofit scholars may learn generalizable lessons from the study of housing partnerships between nonprofit organizations, government agencies, and for-profit firms that may apply to partnerships that provide other social services. One question permeates the research: What kinds of tasks do we wish to assign to nonprofits, for-profits, and governments, and how should we structure relations between these three sectors?

In this chapter, I first review the general theories of nonprofit organizations and detail how the sector is distinctive from for-profit firms and from governmental agencies. I then discuss the idiosyncratic qualities of housing markets that make the nonprofit form useful. I conclude by surveying the advantages, disadvantages, and power structure of nonprofit organizations when they form partnerships with the public and private for-profit sectors.

First, a few facts about the role of the nonprofit sector in U.S. housing markets. The best available statistics on the subject, as reported in the Hodgkinson et al. (1992), come from the informational tax returns filed by formally incorporated tax-exempt nonprofit organizations. These statistics are far from reliable (Steinberg 1993a), but are nonetheless informative. In 1989, there were about 8,500 nonprofit organizations involved in "housing and shelter." The average organization spent $1.1 million, but this average confounds a few large organizations with the vast majority of smaller organizations. Thus, median expenditures were only $292,000. Housing and shelter organizations are generally smaller than other tax-exempt nonprofits eligible to receive tax-deductible donations, which averaged spending $2.7 million in 1989. The average value of assets held by housing and shelter nonprofits was not particularly large either, at $3.2 million, and is presumably skewed from the median value like all other statistics on this industry.

Although we often think of nonprofits as primarily supported by voluntary donations, donations are a relatively small source of housing and shelter nonprofit income. The average amount of "gifts, grants, and contributions" (including contributions from government sources) was $218,000 (the median was $32,000). Most of the income received by nonprofit housing organizations comes from sales to the public (often using a sliding fee scale) and purchase-of-service contracts with government.

The number of organizations increased rapidly between 1987 and 1989. There was a 35 percent increase in the number of nonprofits concerned with housing and shelter, compared with an 18 percent growth rate for the nonprofit sector as a whole during this period. It is likely that this trend will continue or even accelerate, as the 1990 National Affordable Housing Act favors targeting federal aid to the nonprofit sector.

What Makes Nonprofit Organizations Distinct from For-Profit Firms?

Nonprofit organizations can and do make profits. Often, profits are used to finance subsidized care, so that in other activities, nonprofit firms may wish to maximize their profits (fund-raising, unrelated commercial activities, investment returns, sale of property). In fact, the average profit rate for a nonprofit organization in this country is about 10 percent, the same as the profit rate among for-profit firms (Steinberg 1987a). This is all perfectly legal and as it should be, for the key defining characteristic of the sector is not the absence of profit, but a prohibition on *the distribution* of profits to those in control of the organization.

This "nondistribution constraint" (Hansmann 1980) is the ultimate source of all inherent differences between these two sectors. First, it implies that there are no stockholders, hence no equity capital or takeover bids. Second, it explains why nonprofit firms receive substantial donations of time and money, unlike their for-profit competitors. Third, it explains why management and worker attitudes differ across sectors. In addition to these inherent differences, there are differences due to current public policies such as differential taxation across the sectors. Each of these factors is discussed below.

For-Profit Firms and Stockholder Control

For-profit firms distribute their profits to those in control (the shareholders) in the form of dividends, and the prospect of future dividends determines the price of a share of stock (at least in the long run). If a publicly held for-profit firm deviates too much from managerial strategies that maximize future profits, the stock price will fall. In response to this fall, either current stockholders will demand a change in management or there will be a successful hostile takeover bid by new stockholders. In either case, stockholders are motivated by the improvement in share prices that follows from the change in regimes.

EQUITY CAPITAL. Stockholder control of for-profits leads to the first distinguishing characteristic between the sectors: nonprofits cannot secure equity capital. Stock certificates issued by nonprofit firms would hold no value because future dividend payments are prohibited by the nondistribution constraint. This raises the cost of capital for nonprofit firms, slowing the growth of the nonprofit sector (Hansmann 1981) and, in particular, hampering the ability of nonprofit organizations to finance major housing projects. On the other hand, for-profits rarely receive substantial donations, government grants, or foundation grants, and must pay a plethora of taxes from which nonprofits are generally exempt. Overall, nonprofit organizations can obtain some low-cost capital, but clearly do not have enough to solve the problem of housing for all the indigent in this country under current governmental policies. A major expansion of the non-profit role would require the cooperation of banks (for-profit) and a major increase in public subsidies, grants, or purchase-of-service contracts.

ABSENCE OF TAKEOVER BIDS. The second distinction follows from the first: because there is no takeover market for nonprofits, they have the latitude to pursue goals other than profit maximization in at least some of their activities. There can be no hostile takeover bids or stockholder revolts against current management because there are no shares to sell.

Private Goods and Public Goods

The profit imperative has both positive and negative effects on the social performance of organizations. When the buyer and seller or producer are symmetrically informed about the quality of a traded, purely private good, the positive effects surely dominate. The for-profit institutional form is ideal in these cases. However, there are many goods and services where the seller has an informational advantage over the buyer, or where the exchange process between buyer and seller has side effects on those with no voice in the way that exchange is conducted. Here, the nonprofit and public institutional forms are more appropriate, either alone, or in combination with for-profits, for reasons detailed below. This is the "market failure" school of thought on the role of nonprofits.

A pure private good is one that does not affect anyone other than the buyer and the seller, such as a cake. In contrast, a pure public good affects everybody, whether or not they personally buy the good (such as national defense). In between are goods with external effects—goods that affect the buyer and seller but also affect some other parties, either positively or negatively. Electricity generation produces the harmful external effect of pollution; urban renewal produces the beneficial external effects of reduced crime and enhanced property values for bordering nonrenewed communities. Profit maximizing producers of purely private goods under conditions of symmetric information must pay attention to purchaser needs and tastes, and must not waste scarce resources by producing the good inefficiently. These are the types of goods that should clearly be produced and sold by for-profit firms.

Nonprofit Inefficiencies

Nonprofit organizations might waste resources through mismanagement or excessive managerial perks. They may intend to operate efficiently, for if they can cut their costs for, say, providing a unit of low-income housing, they can build more units and help more of the indigent. Cost minimization is the flip side of output maximization. However, there is no external market for control to assure that good intentions are intelligently translated into performance. Alternatively, nonprofit managers may have little interest in charitable outputs and circumvent the intent of the nondistribution constraint by distributing profits to themselves in the form of nonfinancial perks. Either way, nonprofit costs may be higher than for-profit costs for producing intended housing outputs.

To be sure, those that supply revenues to nonprofits (governments, foundations, united fund-raising organizations, and major donors) care about efficiency and provide an external check on performance. The matter has not, to my knowledge, been carefully studied, but many believe that major funders are less successful than stockholders in overseeing performance. Too much generality here may be harmful, for the market for stockholder control will vary in effectiveness in response to national policies regulating takeovers, access to corporate information, and perhaps cultural proclivities. In turn, oversight by nonprofit funders may vary in quality and intensity across funders, industries, and availability of alternative revenue sources.

There is some statistical evidence that higher nonprofit costs are common from the hospital, nursing home, day care, and health insurance industries, but the estimated differences are not large. However, data and estimation limitations severely restrict the persuasiveness of the conclusions from these studies (Pauly 1987; Steinberg 1987a; Weisbrod 1988; Knapp 1989).

Nonprofit Trustworthiness and Contract Failure

The profit imperative may lead to harmful organizational behaviors when the seller is better informed than the buyer. Hansmann (1980) extended and popularized the theory of "contract failure," which he later (1987, p. 29) described as follows:

> Nonprofits . . . typically arise in situations in which, owing either to the circumstances under which a service is purchased or consumed or to the nature of the service itself, consumers feel unable to evaluate accurately the quantity or quality of the service a firm produces for them. In such circumstances, a for-profit firm has both the incentive and the opportunity to take advantage of customers by providing less service to them than was promised and paid for. A nonprofit firm, in contrast, offers consumers the advantage that, owing to the nondistribution constraint, those who control the organization are constrained in their ability to benefit personally from providing low-quality services and thus have less incentive to take advantage of their customers than do the managers of a for-profit firm. Nonprofits arise (or rather, have a comparative survival advantage over for-profit firms) where the value of such protection outweighs the inefficiencies that evidently accompany the nonprofit firm, such as limited access to capital and poor incentives for cost minimization. Because this theory suggests, in essence, that nonprofits arise where ordinary contractual mechanisms do not provide consumers with adequate means to police producers, it has been termed the "contract failure" theory of the role of nonprofits.

There are several ways in which contract failure might apply to low-income housing markets. The "buyer" that is shortchanged may be either the government that purchases housing services for the indigent, or the indigent themselves (under a housing allowance or voucher scheme that fosters resident choice). Obvious and verifiable defects are no more likely in for-profit provided housing than nonprofit—provided housing, for the usual mechanisms of contract protection are adequate to insure for-profit performance (guarantees, civil suits, payments to escrow funds, etc.). Subtler shortfalls in the promised quality of housing stock, including hidden defects that lower the safety or durability of facilities, are more likely with for-profit providers. This is especially likely if profit margins are low (Chillemi and Gui 1990; Kim 1992) or industry turnover is rapid, for then the for-profit firm has less reason to care about its reputation. Maintenance can also be less than promised, and residents can be treated so discourteously when they ask for repairs that they give up reporting their problems. For-profit rental agents may not be so careful about screening out people who would be dangerous to the other residents, and may be less than diligent in verifying the eligibility of residents for public subsidies. For-profit contractees may pad expenditures when operating on a cost-plus contract. For-profits may adjust their tolerance for late payments at their convenience and violate implicit understandings with residents.

Contract failure can occur even if product quality can be observed by the purchaser, provided that such observation is sufficiently costly. Although for-profit performance will be the same as nonprofit performance when the firm is intensely monitored, the purchaser could reduce the cost of monitoring and enforcing contract compliance by dealing with a nonprofit organization (Ferris and Graddy 1991). Finally, the desired housing outputs are complex and difficult to put into contract language. If the purchaser and provider share similar goals and trust each other, the costs of negotiating the contract will be lower (DeHoog 1984).

One bit of evidence that contract failure is important in low-income housing is provided by two surveys of residents in Canadian nonprofit and cooperative housing projects. Both found significantly higher reported levels of client satisfaction than with previous residences. (Serge 1981; Hulchanski 1983). Evidence from other industries where the nonprofit and for-profit forms coexist suggest that contract failure is widespread (see the survey in Steinberg and Gray 1994). There are several studies on hospitals, facilities for the mentally handicapped, facilities for psychiatric care, nursing homes, and day-care centers, and they generally show that nonprofit organizations are more trustworthy in subtle ways. One study (Weisbrod and Schlesinger 1986) looked at differences in nursing homes between Wisconsin-based nonprofit and for-profit facilities. There was no difference across the sectors in violations of the state code, which covers easily observable factors such as doctor availability and square footage per resident. However, for-profits had substantially higher complaints about the harder-to-observe factors not mentioned in the state code. This is a market where trust is especially important, because it is difficult for the elderly to move if they discover shortfalls after establishing residence.

Weisbrod and Schlesinger also found that for-profit nursing homes administered substantially more sedatives to their residents, even though there was no sectoral difference in percentage of residents with sedative prescriptions. Perhaps this just proves that for-profits know how to use sedatives properly, unlike their nonprofit competitors. One suspects other factors predominate—a desire to lower care costs and provide happy smiling faces for prospective customers, rather than to provide appropriate care in the residents' interest.

Finally, Gray (1991) surveyed several studies that concluded that for-profit hospitals charged third-party payers anywhere from 8 to 29 percent more than their nonprofit competitors in the early and mid-1980s, before retrospective cost-based reimbursement systems were replaced by other forms of payment. This difference exceeded the value of tax breaks given to nonprofit hospitals, and illustrates the potential for abuse when governments contract for housing services.

Contract failure remains an important theme in nonprofit research, but more needs to be done to define the limits of the paradigm. When should one expect exceptions, where nonprofits are no more trustworthy than for-profits? Is there any evidence that nonprofit-provided or nonprofit-managed housing for the indigent is of higher quality per dollar of buyer expenditure (as would occur if the trust advantage outweighed the productive efficiency disadvantage of the nonprofit form)? Would nonprofits remain trustworthy if there was a major increase in public subsidies to the sector? If contracting with nonprofit organizations is the cheaper alternative under current policies, are there changes in government contracting or regulatory policies that would reverse the balance of sectoral costs and benefits?

Public Goods, Externalities, and Income Redistribution

The second beneficial thing that nonprofits can do because they are not beholden to stockholders is to provide those things that are worth providing but which cannot be profitably sold. These include pure public goods and private goods with external benefits. As mentioned above, housing improvements in run-down neighborhoods provide external benefits. Because the homeowner only gets some of the benefits of home improvement (a nicer home, but not an increase in neighbor's property values) but must pay all of the costs, for-profit markets provide too little urban renewal. For-profit firms would not survive stockholder wrath if they consistently sold home improvements at prices below cost to correct this externality (although they may do so on a small scale to earn good will from paying customers, gain political advantages, or reduce the costs of recruiting top management by improving the image of the firm). Public and nonprofit actions can be helpful here. However, this factor alone does not elim-inate a for-profit role, for either of the other two sectors can contract out with for-profits to make provision of beneficial externalities profitable.

A third way in which nonprofits can beneficially differ from for-profits is to support socially motivated private income redistribution. For-profit firms may use sliding fee scales to increase their profit margin by increasing their business volume. Superficially, these fees may look pro-poor—a discount for the indigent will certainly help sales. However, profit maximizing firms would not charge a rate that was below costs for any customer group unless it provided ancillary profit (as with corporate support of goods with external benefits). In contrast, a nonprofit housing service agency might charge some customers at a rate above costs and use the profits from these customers to provide below-cost services to others. Alternatively, wealthier customers may be charged a rate equal to the costs of providing their housing, and indigent consumers receive a lower rate financed through donations, grants, and volunteer efforts. This too would look, superficially, like the price discrimination practiced by for-profit firms, but we would judge its intent and effects quite differently.

There is some overlap between the second and third beneficial distinction. In a society of altruists, if anyone helps the indigent, all others who care about the poor will benefit. Even without altruism, redistribution may provide external benefits (lowered crime rates, enhanced growth rates, and the like).

Speed of Adjustment

There is another possible distinction, but it is unclear whether this is socially beneficial or harmful. Nonprofits can be slower to respond to changing market opportunities. They are not forced by the stockholders' interest in profit to pay attention to changes in the market. However, some feel that for-profit firms pay too much attention to changing market conditions, sacrificing long-term profits for short-term gain. Housing is a very long-term proposition, especially rental housing, and a short-term orientation may not serve the public interest in housing very well. On the other hand, government policy and internal governance procedures can make for-profit managers more attentive to the future consequences of their decisions. For example, if executive bonuses are tied to a moving average of past performance and continued after the executive leaves, there is an incentive to look toward the future. Little is known about the importance of this distinct behavior and whether it is inherent in the corporate form.

Limits to Distinct Nonprofit Performance

Competition limits the extent of performance differences between the sectors (Steinberg 1987a, 1993b). If there are many coexisting for-profit or nonprofit firms driving down the sales price, and many competing charities limiting the net returns available through fund-raising, then nonprofits will have to pay attention to costs and market opportunities, limit their provision of goods with external benefits, and eschew socially motivated income redistribution. Consumers might be willing to pay more for the services of a nonprofit organization because it is more trustworthy, but a few "for-profits-in-disguise" (organizations which claim to be nonprofits but somehow sneak around the nondistribution constraint) could degrade consumer confidence in the sector, reducing prices to a level below that necessary to support trustworthy behavior.

Donations

Contract failure also explains why nonprofit firms, but rarely for-profit firms, receive donations of time, assets, and money. It would be difficult to verify whether a contribution given to a for-profit firm for, say, low-income housing would actually assist the poor. Even if the company provided some housing services for the indigent, the individual donor would not be able to distinguish whether the firm was spending more on these services than they otherwise would in response to their own donation. For-profit stockholders would insist that donations be diverted to dividend payments wherever possible, so that donors are rightly distrustful of for-profit charitable intermediaries. A donation to a nonprofit organization might be wasted on managerial inefficiencies and perks, but at least there is not the strong positive incentive to divert donations to dividends. This enhances donor trust so that they will contribute to nonprofit organizations even though they cannot verify directly that their donation was used appropriately.

Donors can be even more confident that their gifts of time will be helpful (Schiff 1990). As volunteers, they can observe firsthand whether the nonprofit organization is well run and determine whether their monetary donations would be well-spent by the recipient nonprofit.

Donations provide a cushion that allows nonprofit organizations to function distinctly despite competition that erodes their ability to cross-subsidize using profits from sales of goods and services. On the other hand, the costs of fund-raising absorb some of the donated resources, and as competition grows for the donated dollar, it becomes harder and harder to cross-subsidize with donations (Rose-Ackerman 1982).

It has also been argued that nonprofit organizations are better contractees because they can use donations to leverage government funds. Governments often use implicit and explicit matching requirements to encourage nonprofit contractees to supplement contract money with donations. However, I argue elsewhere that the leveraging effect can be either a disadvantage or an advantage, depending not on the level of donations but on how that level responds to a change in government contracting dollars (Steinberg 1997).

Entrepreneurial Sorting

There are many possible ways in which nonprofit organization's functioning will be distinguished from that of for-profit firms. What governs whether a particular nonprofit will devote its surplus to managerial perks, maximal output, sliding scale fees, financing trustworthiness, or financing external benefits? Young

(1981) proposed that the answer lay in the type of entrepreneur attracted to found or manage the nonprofit organization. In turn, entrepreneurial sorting across fields or industries is determined by four factors: the intrinsic character of services produced, the degree of control by professions, the degree of economic concentration, and the social priority attached to the field. Within a field or industry, entrepreneurs sort among the sectors (for-profit, nonprofit, and government) on the basis of income potential, bureaucratic structure, service ethic, and opportunities for postemployment-choice sector mobility. Clearly, both the inherent structural difference between the sectors (nondistribution and fair compensation) and the noninherent tax and regulatory differences affect industry and sectoral sorting and so the character of the nonprofit sector. Several analysts have begun to formulate formal models of aspects of this sorting (reviewed in Steinberg 1993b).

There is little evidence on sorting of entrepreneurs across sectors, but a bit more on the sorting of workers and managers. Mirvis (1992) and Mirvis and Hackett (1983) found differences in educational attainment, gender, social attitudes and ideals, job satisfaction, and work attitudes across the sector in two national samples. Rawls, Ullrich, and Nelson (1975) found that graduate management students from Vanderbilt University who subsequently worked in the nonprofit sector placed high value on being cheerful, forgiving, and helpful, whereas those who worked in the for-profit sector placed high value on prosperity, ambition, neatness, obedience, and dependability. Weisbrod, Handler, and Komesar (1978) found that lawyers at nonprofit public-interest law firms were more likely to be liberal, politically-involved, Jewish, and to have grown up in a large city than lawyers in private practice. Despite substantially lower pay, 97 percent of the nonprofit lawyers reported satisfaction with their career choices.

Noninherent Differences Between the Sectors

Nonprofit organizations receive different tax and regulatory treatment from for-profits, and this may lead to differences in behavior and performance. Most nonprofit organizations are exempt from the federal corporate income tax, although their earnings from certain nonmission-related commercial activities may be subject to a special unrelated-business income tax. Nonprofits are also exempt from state and local income, property, and sales taxes in many jurisdictions. Licensing requirements and terms for bidding for government contracts often differ across sectors, and government grants are rarely given to for-profit firms.

The generally favorable tax treatment given to nonprofits has three types of effects. First, the nonprofit gets an implicit subsidy from the state (exemption from a tax becomes a subsidy if competitors are not exempt), allowing the organization to finance its distinct activities. Second, the subsidy is not linked to the value of these activities to the broader society, so it creates secondary distortions (Clotfelter 1988–89). There is no tax break that is closely linked to the external benefit content, trustworthiness, or redistributive aspects of service provision. Instead, the subsidies are linked to usage of specific inputs and outputs, and so distort the choices made by the organization. For example, exemption from the property tax gives nonprofit firms a bigger advantage over competitors if they locate in high rent districts. Exempt organizations may use more land (and hence less labor and capital) to produce their outputs. Neither distortion serves society well. Third, differential tax treatment affects entrepreneurial sorting, either in favorable or unfavorable ways (depending on specified factors) (Eckel and Steinberg 1995). The balance of costs and benefits from these three factors is the subject of much current research.

What Makes Nonprofit Organizations Distinct from Governments?

Most economics students learn that when the market fails, the government acts and that is the end of the story. Governments fail too—they don't provide every nonmarketed service that is worth providing, they don't remedy every remediable case of asymmetric information, and they don't satisfy every constituent when mandating income redistributions through progressive taxes and welfare programs. Thus, we have the theories of market failure and government failure, and also the theory of "voluntary failure" which has been hinted at for years but has been developed and popularized by the work of Lester Salamon (1987). Each sector steps in for the failures of others and it is a simultaneous process.

What is the true difference between nonprofit organizations and governments? Both serve "public purposes." Both are legally bound by a nondistribution constraint: the president of the U.S. cannot receive a bonus based on the national budget surplus. Both sometimes violate this nondistribution constraint—self-dealing, embezzlement, and the promise of future high-paying jobs for former regulators in the regulated industry can compromise the trustworthiness of governments. Both have oversight mechanisms that are not based on financially-motivated takeover bids.

The first (perhaps) inherent difference is that governments can raise taxes, whereas nonprofits must ask for funds. The reason I am not certain that this difference is inherent is because nonprofits in other countries can raise taxes from members or adherents, and utilize the full range of government enforcement mechanisms for tax evaders. For example, in Germany, declared members of certain religious faiths must pay a church tax. It is not entirely compulsory, for German citizens can always declare that they are atheists, but strong social pressures keep even most agnostics from taking this route. Nonprofits in the U.S. rely on weaker social pressures, with "give five" campaigns, reference point pitches (your neighbor gave more; your fair share is . . .), or pressure from the boss to sign up for a payroll deduction plan. Nonprofit organizations in this country are sometimes accused of fostering coerced contributions, although this is contrary to their stated policies and does not have the civic legitimacy of state sanctions for nonpayment of taxes.

The second difference is in the structure of ultimate responsibility and accountability. The government (at least in democracies) is responsible and accountable to an electorate. Political systems vary, and no doubt the electoral details have an impact on the division of activities between the state and private nonprofit sectors, but whoever wins an election (generally by securing only a plurality of public support) gets to declare policies affecting the entire electorate. A government is answerable to a majority; a nonprofit can be answerable to a minority. The nonprofit sector allows the expression of civic values that do not achieve a sufficiently broad consensus for government action and follows from the impulse to volunteer.

Weisbrod (1975) noted the well-established theory of majority voting that political outcomes tend to be that most preferred by the median preference voter. This is true for two reasons. First, in direct referenda, a proposal consistent with the median voter's preferences will secure a majority victory over any counterproposal, so a sequence of votes tends to converge on the median preference. Second, in representative democracy, vote maximizing politicians will select platforms based on their best estimate of the median voter's preferences, and vote maximizing politicians often win. There are known exceptions and limitations to this theory, but the general point is valid regardless—someone will almost always wish that public outputs were at a level other than the one selected by the political process. Those who wish to see less spent on these goods are out of luck. Those that want to see more, according to Weisbrod, band together to form and support a private voluntary alternative such as a nonprofit organization.

We do indeed see "high demanders" as the force behind such voluntary initiatives as Habitat for Humanity. In this context, high demanders include both those with means who care about housing for others (Jimmy Carter and Jim Rouse) and those without means who care about housing for themselves and others. Because the indigent either pay a small or a zero share of taxes resulting from the public programs they vote for, they may be high demanders despite their lack of purchasing power. Sometimes, however, the high demanders form a successful lobbying group to alter political equilibrium (and the financially indigent may be rich in time for organizing), but there are limits as to what they can do and leadership (defined as elected officials altering voter preferences to make "the right thing" survivable rather than passively voting for whatever the public opinion polls say is popular) is a lost art these days. Thus, there is still room for private supplementation of public outputs (Ben-Ner and Van Hoomisen 1991).

Weisbrod's approach emphasizes how nonprofits step in when governments fail. Salamon (1987) emphasizes the insights provided by alternative sequencing: governments step in where nonprofits fail (voluntary failure). Historically, this sequencing may be more accurate in many industries: day care, soup kitchens, shelters for battered women, hospices for AIDS victims, and nursing homes were invented in the nonprofit sector long before governmental support and direct provision followed. Salamon emphasizes that the nature of accountability is behind the often slow initiative shown by government. In order for government to act, officials must recognize that there is a problem, arouse the public and assemble the information necessary to build a consensus of support, then set up an implementing bureaucracy with labor rules (civil service) and other bureaucratic structures that also have consensus political acceptability. In contrast, a few like-minded individuals can set up a nonprofit organization in an afternoon. If someone else opposes the private initiative, the founders may seek to convert their opinions gradually, but this does not stop them from getting started.

The voluntary sector may act first, but there are four sources of "voluntary failure" that limit the private response. These failures lead to calls to transfer responsibility for these initiatives to the government, either in the form of direct government provision or of government grants and contracts to finance provision through the voluntary sector ("third-party government"). First, there is philanthropic insufficiency: nonprofits lack taxing authority, rarely have the ability to deficit spend, and can't sell stock. Donations are limited by the incentive to free-ride: some potential donors hope they can enjoy viewing a charitable service paid for by other donors without themselves contributing. Thus, the voluntary sector is unlikely to raise, by itself, the kind of financial resources necessary to make a major dent in the problem of indigents' housing.

Second, there is philanthropic particularism: we are much more likely to see, say, a Methodist old age home or orphanage than we are to see a private initiative for anyone who needs it. This is inherent in the structure of governance and the problem of securing resources. Nonprofits do not need to forge a consensus from a constituency enjoying universal suffrage, so their particularist impulse will be supported by those to whom the organization is accountable. It is also easier to overcome the free-rider problem if you solicit from a community of donors who know, trust, and identify with each other, and ethnic, religious, and community-specific service orientation attracts such a community of donors. This is a shortcoming of the voluntary approach, because not every needy clientele will find a coherent community of donors ready to act, so there will be gaps in coverage.

Third, there is philanthropic paternalism (or, as I prefer, parentalism). The like-minded individuals who decide to help the poor may volunteer because they believe they know how to help the poor live better lives. They need not listen to the desires of their clientele, nor even meet them, so parentalism is common. Parentalism also occurs in governmental services for the poor, but at least the poor have a voting voice in governmental service provision, even if it is hard for them to exercise political power.

Finally, there is philanthropic amateurism, although I think this is less clearly a disadvantage of the voluntary sector. The reason amateurism is a mixed blessing is that although service provision may be impaired, the voluntary impulse is fostered when extensive training is not a prerequisite, and freedom to express the voluntary impulse enhances the legitimacy of a civil society.

In my own research, I have taken a third approach, emphasizing the simultaneity and dynamic interadjustments of sectoral provision levels. Rather than looking at the voluntary sector as a response to government failure, or the government sector as a response to voluntary failure, I look at the simultaneous choice of voters who are also potential donors and how these choices are altered in a community (joint crowding out) when a higher level of government changes its level of grants to the community (Steinberg 1987b, 1991).

Because nonprofit organizations receive tax expenditures (the buzzword that is used to describe the tax revenues not collected from exempt organizations and itemizing donors), government grants, and purchase-of-service contracts, there are increasing calls for public accountability. Organizations must open their books to the public, at least in part, by providing anyone who requests one a copy of the informational tax return filed by exempts. Grants and service contracts impose layers of frequent and multiple reporting in mutually inconsistent formats, auditing requirements, and sometimes requirements that government bureaucratic structures be grafted onto the contractee (rules for subcontracting, affirmative action, citizen participation on boards of directors, and the like) (Gronbjerg 1993). Service contracts often include such tight specifications that there is no evident difference between public and private provision.

Certainly, patrons (suppliers of resources, either through purchases, grants, donations, or tax expenditures) have some rights to see that their money is well spent by recipient organizations. Indeed, nonprofit contractors are often hired because of their perceived trustworthiness, so that reporting requirements and other elements of accountability can enhance the primary asserted nonprofit advantage. However, there is a real danger of carrying public accountability too far—if a nonprofit organization is accountable in all its activities to the entire democratic electorate, it is no different than a branch of government and contracting out becomes mere window-dressing (related points are made in Salamon 1987).

What Makes Housing Services Different
from Other Goods and Services?

Mishra (1990) lists five factors that distinguish housing from other goods, some of which bear on sectoral choice. First, in housing, we are not really interested in providing equality of outcomes, we are just interested in providing a minimum standard of occupancy for everybody. If the public role is simply to provide a minimum standard, then governments are still necessary to fill in gaps (and gaping holes) but philanthropic particularism causes no concerns that some groups get more help than others.

Second, housing is rife with externalities. There is the well-known NIMBY (not in my backyard) syndrome that inhibits the siting of low-income housing or housing for AIDS patients. Here, the nonprofit sector may play a special role because of what Salamon thought of as a failure—philanthropic particularism may help overcome NIMBY objections. One might object to a government project for low-income housing, but a project sponsored and managed by one's church and restricting entry to residents who share your faith might achieve a local consensus.

Third, there are long lags in supply adjustments. Here, the role of nonprofit housing institutions requires more study. As I noted earlier, it is unclear whether nonprofits take a socially beneficial longer view of housing needs or are less responsive to market opportunities than other sectors.

Fourth, there is an ownership/rental choice in housing, a characteristic of durable goods that is absent from goods like bubble gum. Clearly, there is more need for initial trust when property is owned, more need for continuing trust when it is rented. However, the implications of this observation for sectoral choice of providers has not, to my knowledge, been explored. Finally, Mishra notes that housing policy is used to regulate the overall economy. Government tries to cure recessions by lowering interest rates and thereby stimulating housing (and other investment). There is no evident application of this distinction to this chapter.

Conclusion

Nonprofit, for-profit, and government providers of housing services differ from each other. Housing partnerships may create synergistic benefits and costs, providing a whole different from its parts. However, the institutional choice tradeoffs are not unique to low-income housing services, so that housing policy specialists have much to learn from the emerging community of scholarship on the role and functioning of the nonprofit sector. In turn, careful study of housing markets can inform and enrich the developing theories of nonprofit organizations. Both communities of scholars and policy makers would benefit enormously from increased dialogue and interdisciplinary partnership.

References

Banting, Keith G. 1990. "Social housing in a divided state." In *Housing the homeless and poor: New partnerships among the private, public, and third sectors.* George Fallis and Alex Murray, eds. Toronto: University of Toronto Press. 115–63.

Ben-Ner, Avner, and Theresa Van Hoomissen. 1991. "Nonprofits in the mixed economy: A demand and supply analysis." *Annals of Public and Cooperative Economics* 62. 519–50.

Chillemi, Ottorino and Benedetto Gui. 1990. "Product quality in trust type nonprofits: An expository evaluation of three economic models" In *Towards the 21st century: Challenges for the voluntary sector.* Proceedings of the 1990 AVAS Conference. London.

Clotfelter, Charles. 1988–89. "Tax-induced distortions in the voluntary sector." *Case Western Reserve Law Review* 39. 663–94.

DeHoog, Ruth Hoogland. 1984. *Contracting out for human services: Economic, political and organizational perspectives.* Albany: State University of New York Press.

Eckel, Catherine, and Richard Steinberg. 1995. "A deeper look at the tax preferences given nonprofit organizations." Working Paper, Dept. of Economics, Indiana University-Purdue University at Indianapolis.

Ferris, James, and Elizabeth Graddy. 1991. "Production costs, transaction costs, and local government contractor choice." *Economic Inquiry* 29. 541–54.

Gray, Bradford H. 1991. *The profit motive and patient care: The changing accountability of doctors and hospitals.* Cambridge: Harvard University Press.

Gronbjerg, Kirsten A. 1993. *Understanding nonprofit funding.* San Francisco: Jossey-Bass.

Hansmann, Henry B. 1980. "The role of nonprofit enterprise." *Yale Law Journal* 89. 835–98.

———— 1981. "The rationale for exempting nonprofit organizations from the corporate income tax." *Yale Law Journal* 91. 54–100.

———— 1987. "Economic theories of nonprofit organization." In *The nonprofit sector: A research handbook.* Walter W. Powell, ed. New Haven: Yale University Press. 27–42.

Hodgkinson, Virginia Ann, Murray S. Weitzman, Christopher M. Toppe, and Stephen M. Noga. 1992. *The Nonprofit Almanac 1992–1993.* San Francisco: Jossey-Bass.

Hulchanski, J. David. 1983. "Shelter allowances and Canadian housing policy: A review and exploration." Manuscript prepared for the Canadian Housing Federation.

Keyes, Langley. 1990. "The private-sector role in low-income housing." In *Housing the homeless and poor: New partnerships among the private, public, and third sectors.* George Fallis and Alex Murray, eds. Toronto: University of Toronto Press. 164–96.

Kim, In-Gyu. 1992. "On the use of selective tendering in the procurement market." Blacksburg: Virginia Polytechnic Institute and State University Dept. of Economics.

Knapp, Martin. 1989. "Intersectoral differences in cost effectiveness: Residential child care in England and Wales." In *The nonprofit sector in international perspective*. Estelle James, ed. New York: Oxford University Press. 193–216.

Mirvis, Philip H. 1992. "The quality of employment in the nonprofit sector: An update on employee attitudes in nonprofits versus business and government." *Nonprofit Management and Leadership* 3. 23–42.

Mirvis, Philip H., and E. J. Hackett. 1983. "Work and workforce characteristics in the nonprofit sector." *Monthly Labor Review* 106. 3–12.

Mishra, Ramesh. 1990. "The collapse of the welfare consensus? The welfare state in the 1980s." In *Housing the homeless and poor: New partnerships among the private, public, and third sectors,* George Fallis and Alex Murray, eds. Toronto: University of Toronto Press. 82–114.

Pauley, Mark. 1987. "Nonprofit firms in medical markets," *American Economic Review* 77, 257–62.

Rawls, James R., Robert A. Ullrich, and Oscar T. Nelson Jr. 1975. "A comparison of managers entering or reentering the profit and nonprofit sectors." *Academy of Management Journal* 18. 616–23.

Rose-Ackerman, Susan. 1982. "Charitable giving and excessive fundraising." *Quarterly Journal of Economics* 97. 193–212.

Salamon, Lester. 1987. "Of market failure, voluntary failure, and third-party government: Toward a theory of government-nonprofit relations in the modern welfare state." *Journal of Voluntary Action Research* 16. 29–49.

Schiff, Jerald. 1990. *Charitable giving and government policy: An economic analysis.* New York: Greenwood Press.

Seibel, Wolfgang. 1989. "The function of mellow weakness: Nonprofit organizations as problem nonsolvers in Germany." In *The nonprofit sector in international perspective: Studies in comparative culture and policy.* Estelle James, ed. New York: Oxford University Press. 177–92.

Serge, Luba. 1981. *Assessment of organization of third sector groups: Milton Parc.* Ottawa: Canadian Mortgage and Housing Corporation.

Steinberg, Richard. 1987a. "Nonprofit organizations and the market," In *The nonprofit sector: A research handbook.* Walter Powell, ed. New Haven: Yale University Press. 118–38.

———. 1987b. "Voluntary donations and public expenditures in a federalist system." *American Economic Review* 76. 24–36.

————. 1991. "Does government spending crowd out donations? Interpreting the evidence." *Annals of Public and Cooperative Economics* 62. 591–618.

————. 1993a. "On the financial structure of the U.S. nonprofit sector." *Voluntas* 4 (2). 199–204.

————. 1993b. "Public policy and the performance of nonprofit organizations: A general framework." *Nonprofit and Voluntary Sector Quarterly* 22 (1). 13–32.

————. 1997. "Competition in contracted markets." In *The Contract Culture in Public Services: Studies from Britain, Europe and the USA.* Perri 6 and Jeremy Kendall, eds. England: Ashgate Publishing Limited. 181–99.

————. and Bradford Gray. 1993. "The role of nonprofit enterprise in 1993: Hansmann revisited." *Nonprofit and Voluntary Sector Quarterly* 22(4). 297–316.

Weisbrod, Burton A. 1975. "Toward a theory of the voluntary nonprofit sector in a three-sector economy." In *Altruism, morality, and economic theory.* Edmund S. Phelps, ed. New York: Russell Sage Foundation.

————. 1988. *The nonprofit economy.* Cambridge: Harvard University Press.

————. and Mark Schlesinger. 1986. "Public, private, nonprofit ownership and the response to asymmetric information: The case of nursing homes." In *The economics of nonprofit institutions: Studies in structure and policy.* Susan Rose-Ackerman, ed. New York: Oxford University Press. 133–51.

————. Joel F. Handler, and Neil K. Komesar. 1978. *Public Interest Law.* Berkeley: University of California Press.

Wolfe, Jeanne M., and William Jay. 1990. "The revolving door: Third-sector organizations and the homeless." In *Housing the homeless and poor: New partnerships among the private, public, and third sectors.* George Fallis and Alex Murray, eds. Toronto, University of Toronto Press. 197–226.

Young, Dennis R. 1981. "Entrepreneurship and the behavior of nonprofit organizations: Elements of a theory." In *Nonprofit firms in a three-sector economy.* Michelle White, ed. Washington, D.C.: The Urban Institute. 135–62.

6, Perri. 1992. Private communication with the author.

Chapter 3

Public-Private Partnerships for Affordable Housing:
Definitions and Applications in an International Perspective

C. Theodore Koebel, Richard Steinberg, and Robert Dyck

*This chapter explores the ranges of intersectoral networks for delivery of housing in the
United States, England, and west Europe. Particular attention is paid to housing partnerships, which are placed in a continuum of intersectoral cooperation ranging from single sector provision through contract provision to public-private partnership. Appropriately
structured partnerships may enhance the legitimacy, efficiency, quantity, and quality of
service delivery. Partnerships may, however, also prove to be unwieldy, dilute the benefits
of pluralism, and diminish accountability. The public-private provision of social housing
through nonprofit housing associations in England and several west European countries
is placed toward the full partnership end of this continuum. In the United States, the
network providing homeless shelters comes closer to partnership, while most other public-
private networks are more in the category of contract provision. Two impediments to the
development of a national public-private housing partnership for social housing in the
United States are identified: the lack of an integrated nonprofit housing sector in
the United States and the absence of a prevailing norm (such as subsidiarity) guiding
the relationship between government and nonprofit providers.*

Introduction

The delivery of government housing assistance through nonprofit housing
organizations and public–private partnerships has been a central tenet of contemporary housing policy in many west European countries and has recently
received increased attention in the United States. As with other social services
where nonprofit delivery mechanisms are prominent, housing services are frequently delivered in a complex system that ranges from direct provision through
intergovernmental networks to indirect provision through various degrees of

cooperative, intersectoral networks. This chapter focuses on *housing partnerships* and charts them on a continuum of intersectoral cooperation ranging from competitive contracting to full partnership. Rather than treat nonprofit housing and partnerships in isolation, we place them squarely within the context of the larger intersectoral networks discussed in the literature on nonprofit theory, policy, and management.

Placing current housing delivery mechanisms within the context of intersectoral cooperation and the broader literature on the nonprofit sector has several benefits. It highlights the variety and complexity of intersectoral cooperation that exists, which in turn can contribute to the development of more stable housing policies, more refined research on housing delivery mechanisms, and improved theories of housing and the nonprofit sector. Discussing nonprofit housing and public-private partnerships as singular constructs inhibits our understanding of the various approaches possible for the delivery of housing. Little attention has been paid to the development of conceptual constructs of these delivery mechanisms, contributing to overblown testimonies of both success and failure.

The lack of a deeper understanding of intersectoral networks for the delivery of housing has contributed to the instability of housing policy and its derived programs in the United States. Indeed, it has been rare for specific housing programs to last more than ten years. Heretofore, the exception has been the intergovernmental (federal-local) delivery of public housing owned and operated by government agencies, a network that has been in existence for over forty years. However, the stability of this arrangement, which is now under intense review, does not reflect a philosophical commitment to direct government provision. Quite the contrary, the public housing program is routinely criticized for the quality of housing provided, inefficiency and waste, federal micromanagement and interference, and local management failures and malfeasance. Its stability attests more to the permanence of buildings than policy: built and owned by government, public housing necessitates an ongoing federal program until government ownership of this stock of housing is terminated through sale or demolition. Although greater policy stability is evidenced in other countries, the past decade has witnessed substantial changes in social housing networks in most postindustrial countries.

In addition to the federal-local system that provides public housing, various delivery models have been used in the U.S. for the production of subsidized housing. Until recently the most widely used model was contracted supply through the for-profit sector, but even this has had several variations (e.g., mortgage insurance, interest subsidies, rent subsidies). Currently, housing policy is increasingly implemented through intersectoral networks that involve nonprofit housing organizations. The public delivery of housing services for the homeless has largely been the result of nonprofit initiation, advocacy, and delivery. Similar roles have been played by nonprofit organizations in the development and management of housing for persons with disabilities. Community development corporations, which have focused their energies to a large extent on housing, have been the most visible and effective organizations addressing neighborhood revitalization. Nonprofit corporations created to develop and manage low-income housing have become important producers of assisted housing during the past twenty years. Various forms of public-private housing partnerships have been created at local and state levels. Intermediary and sponsor organizations like the Enterprise Foundation, the Local Initiatives Support Corporation (LISC), and the Neighborhood Reinvestment Corporation have received widespread praise as public-private partnerships.

The network for delivery of publicly supported housing has become a complex amalgam of government agencies, profit-motivated firms, and nonprofit organizations. Public-private partnerships are frequently touted as the best method for providing low-income housing and urban redevelopment. In much of western Europe, partnerships between government and the nonprofit sector have been a central feature of post-WWII housing policy. Public-private partnerships are promoted as solutions to problems encountered in the exclusive provision of housing through the public, profit, or nonprofit sectors. If adequate provision for all groups was provided by these sectors working independently or with crosssector funding, partnerships would be unnecessary, except perhaps as coordinative mechanisms. In order to more fully understand the potential benefits and disadvantages of partnerships, it is necessary to identify not only their role in housing markets and how they are defined, but how they respond to failures in public, profit, and nonprofit provision.

The Role of Partnerships

A clear demarcation between the public and private sectors has probably never existed. The purpose and functions of the public, profit, and nonprofit sectors often overlap and the contemporary delivery of public services is frequently through a complex network involving all three sectors. The development of the nonprofit sector operating to provide public services through private organizations is well advanced in western Europe, the United Kingdom, Canada, and the United States, although each setting provides significant differences. In some instances, nonprofit corporations are mere extensions of state provision of public services and operate with limited discretion in policy, practice, or funding. In other cases, the third sector operates more independently of the state and reflects the private provision of collective goods to constituent groups.

Public-private housing partnerships are examples of the development of hybrid organizational forms in mixed economies. In many instances, they involve representatives from all three sectors: profit, nonprofit, and public, as well as multiple levels of government. By definition, public-private partnerships are intersectoral, but decentralization of services and the need for coordination have led to many intergovernmental and intragovernmental cooperative efforts that could be considered public-public partnerships, particularly in countries with federal governments. Canada has decentralized many housing programs to the provinces, but retains national funding and regulatory oversight. National funding and local implementation have been characteristic of many housing programs in the United States and it is not uncommon to have these programs described as partnerships. Intragovernmental coordination of housing and of related social benefits also has elements of public-public partnerships.

Understood broadly, *partnership* can be used to describe virtually all housing programs in a mixed economy. It is rare to find purely public or purely private housing. But used as a synonym for any form of intersectoral cooperation, partnership loses its usefulness to identify anything more specific than cooperation. In this view, subsidies for private production of social housing and reliance on private capital markets for funds would constitute partnerships, even though there is no joint decision-making or common responsibilities among the parties. Indeed, the participants probably do not think of themselves as partners. In contrast, there are partnerships that are distinguished by shared responsibilities, joint decision-making, and mutual commitment of resources—characteristics that might distinguish full partnerships. Broad applications of the term do little to promote better understanding of the diversity of public-private partnerships.

The task of defining public-private partnerships even within the context of a single country is difficult. Doing so internationally is extremely complex, given the differences in legal, governmental, economic, and social systems among nations. There are federal and nonfederal governments, varying orientations to the use of public power, substantial differences in the sizes and historic roles of the three sectors, and numerous important historical developments specific to each country. Although there has been a general trend away from housing production subsidies toward consumer subsidies as population growth pressures have eased, Germany faces significant housing shortages associated with postunification migration. France, too, is concerned about housing shortages. The United States has a small third sector in housing, however it is the basis for much of this country's housing partnerships. The Netherlands has a very large public sector and a strong commitment to third-sector provision of housing as an extension of government. The third sector in England has been heavily involved in social housing production and the privatization of council housing, but is being pushed toward greater reliance on private financing. Although there are signs of convergence of housing policies across national lines, there is also evidence contradicting a convergence thesis (Boelhouwer and Heijden 1992:295; and chapter 6 herein).

Amid such diversity, it is important to define terms and to discuss conceptual boundaries. We readily admit to a U.S. perspective on public-private partnerships, but have scanned a variety of international materials and conducted several interviews with housing experts in other countries in an attempt to identify international commonalities in partnership arrangements. Not everything being called a partnership is one (except perhaps in the most general sense), and not all partnerships are identified as such. Although reference to partnerships is most prevalent in the United States, there are many important examples of housing partnerships in countries that do not refer to them as such. The case for the historical importance of public-private partnerships cannot yet be made, but the apparent success of some partnerships suggests that the form is likely to survive.

Partnership definitions[1] have been aptly described as "neither conceptually neat nor empirically rigorous" (Haider 1986:139). Blurred boundaries between public and private sectors, the variety of paragovernment organizations that might be considered partnerships, and the rhetorical appeal and overuse of the term work against clarity and precision in discussions of partnerships. Wylde (1986:111) has offered perhaps the most detailed and expansive definition of public-private housing partnerships, associating partnership with shared responsibility, risk, and reward.

The sharing of responsibilities for a mutual venture implies participation in decision-making, rather than simply reacting or responding to the directions set by others. Sharing and participation are key terms in most descriptions of partnerships. Usually participation is through membership in the governing board, but informal negotiations are likely to be highly important. Many partnerships are not formally organized and cooperation is an ongoing informal process (Gage and Mandell 1990). But even among incorporated partnerships, the informal processes of influence, exchange, and decision-making are the richly textured backdrop to formal decision-making.

Shared funding responsibilities are likely to be a feature of partnerships, particularly when the goal is to leverage private investment (Keyes and DiPasquale 1990: 5; Lyall 1986; Wylde 1986:112). The capital requirements of housing may well be an impediment to philanthropic donations. Donors would probably require both government funding and private investment or financing capital. Similarly, government faces its own fiscal constraints and would prefer to commit its funding to required subsidies, rather than creating equity or providing financing.

Partnership can also imply equity participation—sharing in expenses, profits and losses. However, equity participation is probably too strict a standard to apply to public-private partnerships, at least for government. Some governments are legally barred from investing in private business ventures, although broader funding participation is usually allowed. Public co-ownership of redevelopment projects has been acclaimed as the beginning of the entrepreneurial city (Cummings et al. 1989) but also criticized as an intolerable compromise of a city's regulatory responsibilities (Babcock 1990; Siemon 1990; Squires 1989).

In addition to mutual benefit, shared responsibility for decision-making, and joint funding, community agenda building is characteristic of many public-private partnerships. With participation from leaders of all three sectors, a partnership can obtain commitments from important institutions in each sector and can help "insulate projects from political instabilities and at the same time assure lenders, developers, and the public that private sector commitments will be sustained" (Lyall 1986:12). Although this community "log rolling" has been very important in urban redevelopment partnerships, which often include housing, it is not as apparent in smaller partnership programs that focus exclusively on housing. In addition, urban redevelopment partnerships have often excluded nonprofit organizations and neighborhood groups, with the result that redevelopment ignored displacement and other issues of political equity (Stone 1989; Fainstein 1994).

There are inherent dangers in this aspect of public-private partnerships, since private benefit can be disguised as public interest. Unequal (asymmetrical) access to information between the private and public sectors can leave the latter at a disadvantage in partnership negotiations. Large-scale urban redevelopment partnerships have been criticized as serving foremost the aims of the private sector (see e.g., Squires 1989; Fainstein 1994). This criticism, however, has not been directed at housing partnerships, perhaps because these partnerships are more often between the public and nonprofit sectors, with the profit sector in an assisting role. Nonetheless, the imbalance of power between government and nonprofit partners has led Smith and Lipsky (1993) and Stoecker (1996) to criticize these arrangements for displacing the original goals of the nonprofit partner, shifting emphasis away from volunteerism to professional management, and preventing the nonprofit from pursuing an ambitious reform agenda.

It is important to recognize a mix of altruism and self-interest in any public-private partnership, as well as the more powerful position of the profit sector in local partnerships. Stone (1989) identifies local governing coalitions as informal partnerships between the elected leadership, their supporters, and the business community. Although such coalitions do not exercise hegemonic control, the participation of the profit sector is highly favored because of the importance of business investment to the local economy and the slack resources that businesses can apply toward local civic agendas.

Partnerships also vary in the duration and breadth of their interests. Project partnerships are temporary, single-purpose, or single-product agreements, while program partnerships are longer-term, multipurpose, or multiproject agreements requiring an ongoing organizational arrangement (Suchman 1990:1). Program partnerships are more likely to be affected by the ongoing need for cooperation among partners and less susceptible to pursuit of narrow, short-term interests. They have potential for becoming part of a local governing coalition, or at least augment such coalitions.

To recap, public-private housing partnerships must include intersectoral sharing of decision-making and resources for the finance, production, renovation, or management of affordable housing or the provision of related housing services (e.g., fair housing). Shared responsibility for the selection and implementation of partnership activities is essential, although sharing in equity and legal liability are not likely. Partnerships can be formally organized as corporations (usually nonprofit) or informally constituted as coalitions, but require mutual participation in decisions. Participation in decision-making is most often achieved by board membership, but other forms of formal and informal participation in decision-making are equally important.

Theory of Intersectoral Partnerships

Partnerships as a Response to Sector Limitations

Although much has been written on how particular partnerships are performing, there has been little attention to developing a general theory of public-private partnerships. The circumstances that lead to the formation of such partnerships and the special competencies and drawbacks of this institutional form have to be documented. Our review of the respective theories of the separate roles of the three sectors suggests a rudimentary framework for a deeper understanding of partnership. Appropriately structured partnerships may enhance the legitimacy, efficiency, quantity, and quality of service delivery. Partnerships may, however, also prove to be unwieldy, dilute the benefits of pluralism, and diminish accountability. Each of these issues is considered in turn.

Public-private partnerships may enhance the legitimacy of political action in two ways. First, they spread the credit for solving housing problems to all sectors of society. This enhances civic participation levels, provides a benefit for intersectoral cooperation, and creates political indebtedness. This is the essence of coalition building (Stone 1989). Since many contemporary social problems have resisted solution by any one sector acting alone, effective partnerships require benefits that can be delivered to each partner. In addition to providing these necessary benefits, housing partnerships could enhance the legitimacy of the partnership's actions, making it easier to solve the not-in-my-backyard (NIMBY) syndrome that limits many housing initiatives for the disadvantaged. One of the contributions of local government to housing and redevelopment partnerships is streamlining local regulations. Thus, Keyes (1990) found that the Massachusetts Housing Partnership sped the local zoning, permit, and approval processes. Keyes also found that private-sector involvement fostered the critical mass of political support needed for negotiating special-needs housing programs.

Second, partnerships provide another layer of interest groups and thereby enrich pluralism. For example, Banting (1990) found that Canadian housing partnerships between the central government and nonprofit organizations altered the balance of power between the federal and provincial governments. The provinces countered by forming partnerships of their own. Both the central and provincial partnerships improved housing for the indigent in Canada.

Partnerships aid efficiency by providing a coordinating structure that can eliminate needless duplication and achieve economies of scale. It is quite common for both the public and voluntary sectors independently to address housing problems due to the respective shortcomings of each, but there is no need to duplicate the entire administrative structures in both sectors. Partnerships can coordinate record keeping, standardize eligibility verification, provide a central repository for technical expertise, share overhead, and coordinate buying plans to achieve quantity discounts. Each of these actions can improve the efficiency of the partnership.

Governments rarely receive monetary donations and obtain far less volunteer time than nonprofit organizations. Partnerships can serve to leverage public funds, as resources volunteered to nonprofit organizations can be combined with tax revenues to increase the quantity of service provided.

Partnership coordination may also enhance the quality of services. Government agencies, for-profit contractees, and nonprofit organizations tend to focus on one problem at a time when acting independently. Thus, one agency may be interested in securing temporary shelter, another in providing long-term shelter, a third in providing counseling, a fourth in employment assistance, a fifth in providing day-care, a sixth in analyzing community security concerns and a seventh in addressing substance abuse. Responses to these various social problems are rarely coordinated by independent agencies even though they are all essential parts of a comprehensive program to eliminate housing problems. Further, it is difficult to share the information necessary for appropriate remedies when transients move from one shelter to another within a community. Partnerships can deliver higher-quality services because they can deal with clients holistically as people rather than as a series of specific problems to be solved. This is by no means automatic and will depend in part on the comprehensiveness of the partnership. Urban redevelopment partnerships, for example, have been criticized for being too narrowly oriented to enhancing the investment security and profit of the private partners.

Finally, partnerships can provide a forum for negotiating among the inherently contradictory objectives of the various sectors when the sectors must work together. For-profit firms (or, more generally, producer-managed organizations) have objectives that are distinctly opposite from those of consumers:

firms want high prices, consumers want low prices; firms want low quality (in order to cut costs), consumers want high. Ben-Ner and Van Hoomisen (1991) view nonprofit firms as a special form of consumer-controlled organization that can resolve this problem, but the problem goes beyond what can be accommodated within any sector separately. Government objectives to satisfy politically powerful interest groups may conflict with the objectives of some firms and nonprofit organizations. Consumer control within nonprofit organizations does not always eliminate the need to work with producer-controlled and electorate-controlled entities.

Partnerships can provide a forum for discussing internal conflicts and a structure for addressing them. By creating a new organizational loyalty for the respective partnership members, necessary information is shared with less suspicion and manipulation, and both the efficiency and quality of services will improve. The continuation of a partnership is based on accomplishment and implementation—getting things done. This depends in part on commitment and loyalty to the partnership. Information sharing and trust are key ingredients to maintaining the partnership and to enhancing implementation.

Public-private partnerships have unique disadvantages in three areas: they are unwieldy; they confuse accountability; and they dilute the benefits of pluralism. Partnerships are unwieldy because it is hard to structure a partnership agreement that can secure the continuing cooperation of sectors with such diverse goals. Sometimes partnerships flounder over matters as seemingly simple as who gets public credit for accomplishments (Banting 1990). In any case, considerable resources must be invested in creating and maintaining the partnership superstructure, although maintenance costs should decrease as a record of trust and accomplishment is built. Partnerships where maintenance requirements remain high probably will be unstable.

Partnerships confuse accountability in two ways. First, responsibility is so widely shared that the electorate cannot know whom to blame and punish when things go wrong (Banting 1990). Smith and Lipsky (1993) noted the confusion of public accountability as one of the major drawbacks to the use of nonprofit organizations to deliver public services. Second, partnerships can become fronts for claims of massive accomplishments when little, in fact, can be fixed given political and practical constraints. Housing partnerships have publicly celebrated relatively small accomplishments, with even the completion of a single house prompting "ribbon-cutting" media events. Seibel (1989:187), in noting this problem for German nonprofits acting alone, suggested "the competitive advantage of nonprofit organizations, then, is not to do things better but to disguise better how poorly things are being done." The co-opting function of public-private partnerships has been noted in general by Smith and Lipsky (1993) and in the particular case of community development corporations by Stoecker (1996). It would seem partnerships are uniquely equipped for performing this role. The need to widely spread credit fosters rhetorical excess and makes it difficult for nonmembers to press for a clearer accounting of performance. Seibel finds some social value in this charade, for smokescreens can provide symbols that enable complex societies to cope with social and political problems that prove intractable. Nonetheless, co-optation of nonprofit partners can dilute the creative tensions that make pluralism effective. Wolfe and Jay (1990:214) ask "How are [nonprofit organizations] to strike the appropriate balance between providing service to the population while providing a source of criticism of statutory welfare services? When, in practice, does a watch-dog become a lap-dog?"

The multiple veto points created in partnership agreements may slow innovation, as occurred in intergovernmental pension agreements in Canada (Banting 1985). Partnership agreements can also eliminate the competitive spur to efficiency. Finally, partnerships can lead to overstepping of bounds, as nonprofits succumb to vendorism or governments become "captured" by for-profits. Relative to the hazards facing nonprofit organizations by participation in government programs, Salamon (1987:44) concludes:

> Involvement can also put a strain on other important features of the organizations, such as their reliance on volunteers, their sense of independence, their frequently informal and nonbureaucratic character, and their direction by private citizens along lines that these citizens think appropriate. Since many of these features are the ones that recommend nonprofit organizations as service providers in the first place, it would be ironic if government programs seriously compromised these features. What this suggests is the need for . . . structural features that help to strengthen rather than weaken the distinctive elements of the nonprofit sector.

A Taxonomy for Public-Private Partnerships

This discussion suggests three critical dimensions on which to classify these hybrid structures: the extent to which decision-making is shared, the duration of the agreement, and the division of responsibilities across partners. Collaboration between the sectors spans a spectrum from co-equal partnerships through hierarchical contracting to coincident involvement in related housing activities with incidental coordination. This spectrum constitutes the governance dimension of our taxonomy. (See Figure 3.1.)

At the full power-sharing pole of this spectrum, we include partnerships that require the unanimous consent of members on all substantive issues. Unanimity partnerships foster the greatest degree of political legitimacy and the broadest participation by citizens and interest groups, but are the most unwieldy. Some sort of majority or plurality rule is a more common power-sharing arrangement. Under such arrangements, those partners who lose on some votes will nonetheless wish to stay in the partnership if they expect they can win on

Figure 3.1

The Governance Dimension of the Partnership Taxonomy

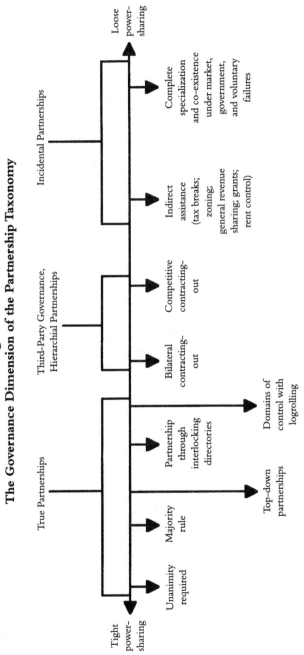

other important votes. Looser still is a partnership agreement in which each partner is given responsibility to make unilateral decisions in specified domains, but
partners logroll (that is, promise to compromise on issues within their domain of
control if the other partner compromises within its domain).

Two other forms of tight power-sharing belong at this end of the spectrum, although their exact placement within this range is debatable: top-down
partnerships and partnerships through interlocking directorates. In top-down
partnerships, a lead organization persuades, coerces, or cajoles client organizations into a partnership, with power-sharing among the subordinates. Some
U.S. partnerships initiated by the Enterprise Foundation appear to fit this mold.
Directorates designed to represent various multisectoral constituencies form an
implicit partnership that is quite similar to an explicit majority-rule partnership.
If there are reserved slots on the nonprofit board for representatives of government and the private sector, then, in effect, the nonprofit organization becomes
a majority-rule partnership.

In the middle of the spectrum are two forms of hierarchical relationships:
bilateral and competitive contracting-out. In bilateral contracting-out, governments write service-provision contracts with specified nonprofit and/or for-
profit firms, either because there are no alternative contractees or because of
special efficiencies created by ongoing contract relationships ("relationship-spe-
cific capital" in the law and economics jargon). Although the relationship is formally hierarchical, it has some elements of a true partnership for two reasons.
First, the contractee has substantial negotiating power over the terms of the
contract. Second, the contractee has some discretion over the implementation
of the contract and can demand renegotiation. The careers of government
bureaucrats are advanced if their contractees perform well, contractees know
this, and can demand concessions in return for performance (Saidel 1989).

In competitive contracting situations, where there are alternative contractees and little relation-specific capital to preserve, the hierarchical structure
is more definitive. Contract terms can be set on a like it or leave it basis, and
government bureaucrats can threaten to turn to alternative contractees if the
original terms are not properly implemented.

At the loose power-sharing end of the spectrum, we find vaguer hierarchical and incidental coordination structures. Thus, governments might provide
indirect assistance to nonprofit housing organizations in the form of tax breaks,
earmarked grants, or preferential zoning in return for which the organization
supports the government's housing objectives. Even looser is the complete spe-
cialization and coexistence predicted by the theories of market, government,
and voluntary failure with only incidental coordination and no explicit partnership agreements.

There is no generally accepted definition of a public-private partnership,
and various authors have implicitly drawn the line at different places along the

governance spectrum. For example, Salamon's (1987) paper mostly talks about bilateral and competitive contracting-out, but claims to cover public-private partnerships in general. We prefer to restrict the rubric "true partnerships" to hybrids with tighter and more equal power-sharing than this, but for many purposes, "third-party governance" or "hierarchical partnerships" deserve to be included as partnerships. Some authors (e.g. Salamon 1992) include a portion of those organizations at the loose power-sharing pole of the spectrum within their definition, but such "incidental partnerships" represent a different phenomenon.

The second dimension of our taxonomy is the duration of the agreement. Partnerships are typically structured on a program or a project basis. It is easier to negotiate a project partnership agreement because the interests of the partners need to be harmonized only for one project, but the disadvantages of such a relationship loom large relative to a program partnership. Once the partnership infrastructure is established and trust relationships are built, it is inefficient to start over again on every project. The explicit duration of the agreement is not the only element of this dimension. Contract design can affect the ease with which partnerships dissolve or are broken. For example, if payments are held in escrow or partners must be bonded, parties will remain in contract agreements during times of controversy and conflict.

The third dimension of our taxonomy is the division of responsibilities across partners. Partnerships differ in the types of partners involved and in the assignment of principal responsibilities to partners. Of course, the major types of partners are governments, for-profit firms, and third-sector organizations, but a finer set of distinctions is desirable for assessing partnership structures.

Governments can be categorized by level of government within a federated structure, or as a nonfederated government or crossnational government (such as the European Economic Community). For-profit partners are divided into the categories of banking/financial institutions, legal/realtor, construction/maintenance/housing-service delivery, and two kinds of other firms: those with strong community ties (which will presumably have a profit interest in improving their community) and "footloose" firms (which do not, and would rarely involve themselves in partnerships). Third-sector organizations can be labor-managed, consumer cooperatives, or nonprofit institutions. Nonprofits can be further classified by their secular versus religious orientation, by whether they are self-help, member serving, or client serving, and by whether they are direct services providers or pass-through intermediaries (including United Fund organizations, foundations, and corporate foundations).

The principal responsibilities of the partnership are often assigned to one partner or another. These responsibilities include funding, housing-service provision, auxiliary-service provision, and administration/regulation/governance. One can crosstabulate partnership members and assignments of principal roles to form the third dimension of our taxonomy. For example, a typical partnership would have two levels of government as funders, for-profit firms as builders, and nonprofit organizations as auxiliary service providers and administrators.

This taxonomy of partnerships helps to clarify the diversity and dimensions of partnerships. By providing a structured conceptualization of partnerships, the taxonomy can be used to identify key components of partnerships and relate these components to partnership functions. For example, the requirements of partnership maintenance are likely to vary according to the size and complexity of the partnership, as well as the duration of the partnership. Size and complexity should increase maintenance requirements, making it easier to establish smaller, project-oriented partnerships than larger, program or community agenda-building partnerships. Thus it is probably easier to have program and community agenda-building partnerships evolve from the successful experiences of smaller, project partnerships. The latter can provide the "small opportunities" that Stone identifies as the glue that binds urban regimes. As experience is gained from small successes, partnerships endure, decreasing partnership maintenance requirements. Experience and trust acquired over time should diminish the amount of communication and negotiation needed to maintain the partnership.

The taxonomy also suggests a broadening spiral of partnerships building from project to community levels. Indeed, one of the difficulties that nonprofit housing and community development groups face in many cities is that they have remained isolated from community governing regimes. Impediments exist in both directions. Governing regimes can be narrowly drawn coalitions of public and business elites. If the ability to "get things done" is compromised by expanded membership, there will be obvious disincentives to broaden the coalition. However, in Stone's investigation (1989:202) of redevelopment in Atlanta, the exclusiveness of the governing regime resulted in "substantial social costs. . . . A more inclusive form of decision making surely would have resulted in less social disruption." But inclusiveness is only likely when the included groups can also deliver accomplishments that otherwise are outside the ability of the governing regime. In the domain of social housing, such groups are likely to be members of program or project partnerships.

Examples of Housing Partnerships in Europe
and the United States

The research record on housing partnerships to date is primarily descriptive and there is little published evidence available to advance our understanding quickly. The following review is thus necessarily cursory and abbreviated. In addition, in order to provide examples of national housing partnerships that have emerged over several decades, it is necessary to look outside the United

States. Despite significant rhetorical promotion of housing partnerships in the U.S., its nonprofit housing sector is still relatively undeveloped. Nonprofit housing in much of western Europe stands in stark contrast to the U.S. experience. A detailed review of the differences in governments, housing finance systems, and subsidy programs is well beyond the scope of this chapter. The discussion focuses, instead, on how intersectoral networks in a variety of countries provide examples of various levels of housing partnerships.

Housing Partnerships in Europe

The networks responsible for social housing in several European countries have evolved into institutionalized partnerships between government and the nonprofit sector. With some prewar antecedents, the current partnerships are rooted in the severe housing shortages facing these countries after World War II. Commercial and residential redevelopment required massive governmental commitments and subsidies. Given the severity of housing shortages, the involvement of government in the provision of housing for a significant portion of the population was a necessary condition of redevelopment. Under the widely accepted principle of subsidiarity (enabling persons, groups, and institutions closest to the problem to respond to problems first), national governments designed programs to work through local organizations to produce social housing. These countries faced chronic housing shortages and balanced markets would not be established for years. Consequently, profit-driven firms were an unlikely choice to implement social housing programs. In some cases, implementation involved local governments, such as with council housing in England. More often, it involved nonprofit housing associations.

These approaches went well beyond contracting for the delivery of housing, even on a preferred supplier basis. Rather, the relationship was established as an implicit partnership, with government subsidies flowing through nonprofit housing organizations to provide much needed rental housing. Strong, national representation of the nonprofit partners emerged as a central element of the overall housing partnerships in England, the Netherlands, France, Denmark, and Sweden. These national organizations participate in the development and implementation of housing policy. As the national voice for numerous local nonprofit housing organizations, they represent a significant portion of each nation's housing stock. To some extent, the partnership between government and the nonprofit sector has become so close that their identities and purposes are inseparable. The nonprofit housing sector became "governmentalized," operating as a branch of the public sector with little independence, but also with virtually no exposure to risk. At the same time, government has little independence either and the national housing organizations can extract substantial subsidies to maintain the partnership.

The social housing partnerships in these countries are now changing in response to the emergence of balanced housing markets and unbalanced national budgets. Housing shortages have been substantially eliminated for most groups, but housing subsidies have become a serious fiscal burden for national governments. Consequently, there is a well-established trend to privatize the middle-class portion of the social housing stock and to transfer more financial risk to the nonprofit sector. There is greater emphasis on using market mechanisms within the delivery of social housing and on creating "autonomy" for the nonprofit housing sectors.

THE NETHERLANDS. Dutch housing associations are "authorized institutions" active "solely in the interests of housing" (Lundqvist 1992:61). Although they are publicly regulated and are dependent on public subsidies, they remain private institutions. There are approximately 850 housing associations, covering two million housing units—30 percent of the total housing stock. Governmental policy has encouraged the transfer or reorganization of the relatively small supply of local authority housing to housing associations in order to consolidate the nonprofit sector into one category. Housing associations are organized along the established pillars of Dutch society—Catholic, Protestant, socialist, and liberal—which create the country's governing coalitions. The principle of subsidiarity provides the ideological basis for a passive but generous welfare state, wherein the state pays for expansive social welfare programs that are implemented by nonprofit organizations aligned with the primary pillars.

Housing associations are represented by two national umbrella organizations, the National Housing Council and the Netherlands Christian Housing Institute, which are regularly consulted by the Ministry of Housing. In addition, housing policy in the Netherlands is developed in consultation with "an independent housing advisory body: the Raad voor de Volkshuisvesting (RAVO)" (Boelhouwer and Heijdan 1992:55). The RAVO represents housing organizations and experts and is required to be consulted by the minister for housing on any changes in housing regulations.

The Dutch have had a complex mixed-subsidy system for social housing, which virtually eliminated any exposure to risk among housing associations. The level of government subsidy became a major topic of debate when housing expenditures increased more rapidly than total governmental expenditures despite a decreased emphasis on production. A steady progression of recent changes in policy has attempted to reshape the Dutch housing partnership to contain costs by establishing greater autonomy for the government and the nonprofit housing sector. In 1984 the government, housing associations, and local authorities set up the Guarantee Fund "to improve access to capital markets by housing associations" by providing governmental guarantees of repayment, leveraging favorable interest rates and loan conditions from the private sector (Boelhouwer and Heijden 1992:54). The 1987 Housing Act created the

Central Housing Fund, which provides assistance to weaker housing associations through mandatory cross-subsidization from stronger associations. The Guarantee Fund and the Central Housing Fund were created to promote greater independence among Dutch housing associations (Primeus 1995) and have been accompanied by greater fiscal autonomy as well. In 1988 the government eliminated direct loans and loan guarantees for housing associations. The government is phasing out new construction subsidies and cashing out operating subsidies in the "grossing and balancing" operation whereby housing associations are paid the present value of future subsidies and repay their outstanding government loans (Primeus 1995; Dieleman 1994).

A 1989 policy memorandum, the so-called Heerma memorandum, set the direction for a major restructuring of housing policy and expenditures during the 1990s. Current policy directions promote increased decentralization and autonomy for the nonprofit rental sector; increased home ownership; greater emphasis on market mechanisms; rent increases set 1 percent above inflation; attempts to limit distortions in the distribution of housing subsidies; and decreases in production subsidies (Priemus 1990; Boelhouwer and Heijden 1992). The 1993 social renter sector management order advanced sector independence further by stipulating performance criteria for housing associations in terms of scope of operations, tenants served, housing quality, and financial stability.

According to Priemus (1995:150) these reforms have "strengthened the bargaining position of central government in respect of the national umbrella organizations of the housing corporations" but have created a "strongly independent housing corporation sector on which central government has little grip." But this is at the expense of commercializing the nonprofit sector, whereby "housing corporations will increasingly proceed to behave like commercial landlords, who sell parts of their property, undertake too little new construction in unfavorable times, demolish parts of their property and vigorously engage in commercial property development."

FRANCE. The social rented sector in France (17 percent of the housing stock) consists of units built and operated by Habitations a Loyer Modére (HLM) with roots in a nineteenth-century philanthropic movement that produced housing for the working class. There are about 1,200 HLM with 3.14 million housing units. HLM also have constructed more than one million owner-occupied units in the social sector. HLM institutions include nonprofits and limited liability companies that are allowed limited profits. The latter mainly involve low-income, owner-occupied units developed under the so-called 1 percent scheme, which is a program financed by a one-percent surcharge on an employer's payroll. The 1 percent scheme involves businesses with ten or more employees in an employer-assisted housing construction program, which requires that a significant percentage of vacant units go to employees of the enterprises that financed the building (Boelhouwer and Heijden 1992:208). This program now surpasses construction subsidies from the state and constitutes an increasing majority share of the social housing sector.

HLM units are targeted to low-income groups under governmental income criteria (a 25 percent rent to income standard is applied at time of lease). However, there is no subsidy for operating losses, so the HLM "refuse to accept tenants who . . . are unable to meet their financial commitments in the long term" (Boelhouwer and Heijden 1992:208). Consequently, persons earning less than the minimum wage have trouble renting HLM units. As with several other countries, French social housing faces problems with vertical equity in the distribution of units: "poor, elderly, handicapped, single parent, and large families are forced into poor-quality, rented private-sector housing, while many HLM tenants are relatively well off and able to afford higher private sector rents" (Boelhouwer and Heijden 1992: 209).

HLM institutions are either at the regional or municipal levels and are managed by councils appointed by the prefect of the department and by other organizations (municipalities, saving banks, tenants). In 1987 tenant and local authority representation was increased. This multisectoral control of HLM institutions gives them strong partnership characteristics and political influence. According to Boelhouwer and Heijden, 700 of the 800 members of the French Parliament are council members of HLMs. The umbrella organization for HLM (Union Nationale des Fédérations d'Organismes d'HLM, or UNFOHLM) is "well organized and has considerable influence on government housing policy" (208). HLM tenants are represented by the Confédération Nationale du Logement (CNL) and HLM institutions are legally required to negotiate each year with tenant representatives.

DENMARK AND SWEDEN. The Danish and Swedish nonprofit rental sectors are also large (approximately 650 and 300 housing associations with 17 percent and 21 percent of the housing stock, respectively), heavily subsidized, and represented by strong national organizations. Perhaps the most interesting characteristic of the Danish housing partnership is the participation of tenants. Nonprofit housing corporations, of which there are two types, are required to have at least 50 percent representation by tenant election. Consequently, the National Federation of Nonprofit Housing Associations can legitimately represent tenant interests as well as the interests of nontenant sponsors. Swedish social housing is implemented through a partnership of national and local governments. Housing associations are managed by boards composed of members of the municipal council. The national umbrella organization for housing associations (SABO) is involved in annual negotiations over rents with the national government along with tenant associations.

ENGLAND. Housing policy in England is administered through the Department of the Environment, which is responsible for redevelopment programs and the funding of council housing (municipally controlled public housing) and the Housing Corporation, which in turn funds third-sector provision of social housing through housing associations. Although the Housing Corporation is chartered to promote the housing association movement, it also regulates housing associations and its policy direction is set by the government (Housing Corporation 1989). The interests of housing associations are independently advocated by the National Federation of Housing Associations.

Social housing is a large portion of the overall market (24 percent) and accounts for three-fourths of the rented housing sector. Municipal authorities provided the initial response to postwar housing shortages and have been extremely important in the delivery of housing, providing about 20 percent of the overall housing stock and 90 percent of social rented housing. Reducing their role is the focus of much of the recent privatization thrust of the Conservative government. Consequently, housing associations have been promoted as the private-sector alternative to council monopolies in social housing.

The housing policy direction under Conservative government since 1979 has been the "demunicipalization of rented housing" (Kemp 1990a). This has primarily meant shifting power from local government to the central government while simultaneously converting council houses to owner occupancy and shifting local responsibilities for social housing to the third sector. Municipal authorities are now seen as "enablers" rather than producers of housing, but they remain the country's largest landlords and still dominate the supply of social housing (Boelhouwer and Heijden 1992: 175).

The third sector was first promoted as a counter to council housing starting with the Housing Acts of 1961 and 1964, with the latter creating the Housing Corporation in response to an innovative project run jointly by the National Federation of Housing Societies and the national government (Housing Corporation 1989:7). Originally working with a limited production subsidy and, after 1972, controlled rents, the corporation became "the promotional and funding body for the voluntary housing movement to achieve 'a substantial expansion of rented homes' " (19). In 1973 the production of housing associations was targeted to expand to 30,000 homes a year and the 1974 Housing Act provided a new capital subsidy (the Housing Association Grant, or HAG) and a Revenue Deficit Grant (RDG) to offset operational deficits due to development cost overruns. The HAG covered 85 to 100 percent of capital costs and the RDG covered any risk exposure due to cost overruns. Although housing associations remained as private-sector corporations, they had to be registered and regulated by the Housing Corporation to receive public funds, on which they became totally dependent. Under the 1974 Act, housing associations were effectively governmentalized: "housing associations have only been able to expand substantially by being virtually incorporated into the public sector" (Kemp 1990b:796).

Under the current privatization movement, some tenanted estates have been sold to housing associations (usually newly created) at the initiation of municipal authorities. These so-called voluntary transfers have had a significant impact on the expansion of the stock controlled by housing associations, but they are more reflective of the complexities of current policies that favor associations over councils than of either privatization or partnership. After review of these issues, Kleinman (1991:16) concluded that these "transfers are essentially about re-financing *within* the social sector." Municipal authorities have in some instances astutely continued their control of this housing through control of the housing association receiving the property.

Current policy is also forcing the privatization of housing associations. Rents are no longer controlled and associations have had to cope with market pressures to increase rents or to shift their service population to higher incomes. The HAG has been reduced to 75 percent of capital costs and the RDG is being eliminated. Housing association developments are now required to be "mixed-funded," but the mechanism for efficient provision of loans from private lenders has not been established. From an environment where government protected housing associations from any exposure to risk, private sector criteria now dominate the decisions of housing associations. This has changed housing associations from "development driven" to "finance driven" organizations and has shifted decision making to bottom-line concerns of cash flow and financial risk (Pryke and Whitehead 1995). This commercialization of housing associations has made them more attentive to cost containment and the requirements of financing and less innovative in production schemes. The asset base of the association, its reserves, and the ability to cross-subsidize developments are important factors in determining access to financing. The new environment favors larger associations and those dominated by finance professionals. It also favors new construction over rehabilitation and suburban sites over inner-city sites.

Under the new social housing regime in England, local authorities exercising their "enabling role" are creating a quasi market through competition among housing associations for new development (Pryke and Whitehead 1995; Dolling 1995). Housing associations are required to bid on new social housing development and local authorities bargain for the best deal for particular sites. This competition has accelerated the commercialization trend among housing associations. Although housing associations have had a larger share of social housing production, overall production levels have been substantially reduced. Additionally, commercialization has been accompanied by a decreased income mix in social housing (residualization) and increased problems with homelessness.

GERMANY. Housing policy in Germany followed a substantially different scheme than the public-nonprofit partnerships that exist in other western European countries. Although the size of the German social rented sector (16 percent of total units) is comparable to that in some other countries, German housing policy is sector-neutral and subsidies for social housing are available to profit or nonprofit organizations. Financing is largely through the private sector. Social housing can be profitably developed by the private sector and 38 percent of the social rented stock is controlled by for-profit landlords (Boelhouwer and Heijden 1992:115).

Registered, nonprofit institutions producing social housing include member co-ops and large, nonprofit organizations associated with trade unions, national employers like the post office, churches, state and local governments, and manufacturers. The latter nonprofit organizations lost their tax advantages in 1988. Member co-ops account for two-thirds of registered institutions, but only 30 percent of the units held by such institutions. Nonprofit housing corporations are required to be registered and audited, but otherwise operate at their own risk. Third sector consultation is not required. However, a committee of housing experts with broad representation is used for negotiation over controversial policies.

Instead of pursuing multisectoral partnerships, German housing policy encourages competition by treating profit and nonprofit landlords the same in the production of social housing. Nonprofit housing organizations are expected to be entrepreneurs and accept exposure to risk. This was expected to indirectly encourage the transfer of half the units under nonprofit control in 1984 to for-profit ownership in the private rented sector by 1995. Under the "interchangeable subsidy," states and municipalities are given the flexibility to negotiate several aspects of the subsidy and to select the developer proposing the lowest level of subsidy for the units proposed. This quasi market established for social housing production constitutes a competitive bidding partnership, an important alternative to the tighter partnership arrangements between the third sector and government elsewhere in Europe.

Housing Partnerships in the United States

In the United States, the explicit use of public-private partnerships is most prevalent for commercial redevelopment projects. Public-private partnerships for urban economic development had their origins in this country immediately after World War II. Several of these partnerships (e.g., in Baltimore, New York, and Pittsburgh) remain prominent examples of the lasting contributions of organized intersectoral cooperation. In the 1980s, the intersectoral partnership was rediscovered in the face of mounting public sector fiscal problems, regional economic transitions, and the relative intractability of many urban problems. The success of several commercial redevelopment projects supported by public-private partnerships, particularly a few prominent "festive marketplace" developments, boosted the popularity of partnerships, but has prompted closer inspection of the distribution of their private and public benefits (Lasser 1990; Frieden and Sagalyn 1989; Squires 1989).

Unlike the experience in western Europe where post-WWII housing shortages and the subsidiarity principle created an environment favoring government implementation of social housing production through a regulated nonprofit sector, social housing in the U.S. has been primarily implemented through direct public provision through municipal authorities and through publicly subsidized, private, for-profit provision. Nonprofit housing has had a relatively minor role in producing social housing, although the nonprofit sector dominates the provision of social housing for special populations, such as the poor elderly, the handicapped, and the homeless.

HOMELESS SHELTER PARTNERSHIP. The provision of shelter for the homeless comes closest to a full partnership between the national government and the nonprofit housing sector. The initial response to the homeless problem that emerged in the 1980s was by the third sector, which then brought the issue to national public attention and lobbied for funding from the national government. Unlike the otherwise highly fragmented nonprofit housing sector, the response to homeless was led by several nonprofit organizations with strong national representation: e.g., the United Way of America, American Red Cross, the Salvation Army, the Council of Jewish Federations, the Catholic Church, and the National Council of Churches.

The coalition of these organizations is the only national representation of nonprofit housing that is even remotely comparable to the national organizations in Europe. This coalition was not only instrumental in fashioning the national government's response to homelessness, it became the primary conduit for the flow of federal funds under the Emergency Food and Shelter Program (Moskowitz 1989; Housing and Development Reporter 1993). The program is nationally administered by the Federal Emergency Management Agency (FEMA) and a national board comprised of the FEMA director and representatives from the coalition's secular and religious nonprofit organizations. Local administration of the program is also under the jurisdiction of a board dominated by the third sector. The hegemony of the nonprofit sector in responding to the housing problems of the homeless probably reflects the problems of contract failure and opportunism encountered with profit-seeking organizations. These problems are not as clear for most low-income households targeted by federal housing assistance (except perhaps for the elderly and the handicapped).

ABSENCE OF BROAD NATIONAL PARTNERSHIP. The lack of nonprofit hegemony in the primary arenas of social housing makes bi-sector, government-nonprofit partnerships much more unlikely. Until recently, a national tri-sector coalition supporting subsidized housing production consisted of trade unions, cities, public housing authorities, and for-profit builders. This coalition was heavily committed to for-profit production and viewed most public and nonprofit production as an inappropriate interference with the private sector. Once for-profit production subsidies were eliminated, the national coalition evaporated.

A new coalition centered on the nonprofit sector emerged during the 1980s and was instrumental in promoting the National Affordable Housing Act of 1990, the first omnibus housing legislation since 1976. The 1990 act made supporting public-private housing partnerships a national goal and provided several preferential set-asides for nonprofit housing. The nonprofit coalition, however, was not influential enough to withstand the emerging political priority of deficit reduction and the snipping and cutting of housing programs resumed. Instead of a strong, national housing partnership for nonprofit housing production, three looser forms of partnership have emerged for the production of social housing: the franchise model used by the Neighborhood Reinvestment Corporation, the finance and technical assistance partnerships that support the use of the Low Income Housing Tax Credit, and the community development corporation model.

NEIGHBORHOOD REINVESTMENT CORPORATION. In 1978 the federal government launched a national effort to foster public-private housing partnerships under the Neighborhood Reinvestment Corporation (NRC), a quasi-governmental corporation created by Congress in 1978 based on a model developed by Pittsburgh's Neighborhood Housing Services and the Urban Reinvestment Task Force established by the Federal Home Loan Bank Board and the U.S. Department of Housing and Urban Development. The Neighborhood Reinvestment Corporation provides seed money, technical assistance, and on-going financial support for local Neighborhood Housing Services (NHS), Apartment Improvement Programs, and Mutual Housing Associations. NRC-sponsored local nonprofit corporations are designed to bring the local housing-finance community, the city, and the neighborhood into a partnership to reverse decline in older neighborhoods (Neighborhood Reinvestment Corporation 1991).

Once a NRC franchise is started in a local community, it must rely on a network of primarily local funding relationships that are encouraged by its board structure. Although residents constitute a majority of the local board, it must also have representatives from business (particularly insurance companies and financial institutions) and local government. In addition to providing expertise and leadership, private sector members of the partnership agree to provide loans and insurance coverage to residents through the NHS programs, as well as contribute to the operating budget. Local government partners provide public services, code inspections, capital improvements, and support a revolving loan fund for housing loans for otherwise "unbankable" residents. Today, NRC works with over 160 local organizations active in over 140 towns and cities.

The NRC franchise model was too narrowly designed and insufficiently funded to include a large portion of the existing nonprofit housing sector, thereby restricting its representation. Additionally, it did not emerge as the conduit for other federal housing programs. Rather than becoming a unifying focus for nonprofit housing, NRC became a specialized partnership model with limited coverage.

INTERMEDIARY PARTNERSHIPS. Intermediary partnerships evolved in response to the fiscal pressures of the 1980s and to federal retrenchment in social housing. The national emphasis shifted from production subsidies for the for-profit sector to less costly consumer subsidies, substantially slowing the pace of social housing production. Direct federal production subsidies were eliminated and previous tax incentives were replaced by the Low-Income Housing Tax Credit. Without a federal production subsidy program to provide sufficient support for low-income housing, social housing production became a complex mix of intersectoral funding (see chapters 10 and 11). It is now common to layer several sources of support and the lexicon of low-income housing has expanded to include syndication of tax credits, soft seconds, and a variety of other creative financing techniques.

To help make this inordinately complex and inefficient funding system work, various intermediary organizations emerged to provide technical and financing assistance to the nonprofit housing sector. The Local Initiatives Support Corporation (LISC) was established by the Ford Foundation in 1980 to provide local CDCs seed money, technical assistance, and expertise in securing investment financing (Government Information Services 1980). The Enterprise Foundation was established in 1982 to provide technical assistance and funding for development of local housing partnerships (a top-down partnership), obtaining the money to do so from the federal government, donations, and a social investment fund. The foundation works with a local nonprofit, which has the responsibility for housing construction, administration, and maintenance. Local nonprofits are only helped if the local municipal government and private firms enter into the partnership. Local intermediaries, such as the Boston Housing Partnership and the Massachusetts Housing Partnership, provide similar functions within their designated areas (Boston Housing Partnership 1991).

The emergence of these national, state, and local intermediaries supporting nonprofit housing production was "the single most important story of the nonprofit development sector in the 1980s" (Walker 1993). Intermediaries like the Enterprise Foundation, LISC, and local housing partnerships provide valuable technical and financial assistance, particularly for nonprofit housing organizations working with the Low Income Housing Tax Credit (LIHTC) program. The complexity of developing social housing under the LIHTC, particularly for poor renters, has created a niche market for nonprofit housing developers. The average development has six to eight subsidy sources and requires substantial predevelopment planning and negotiations (Walker 1993; Hebert et al. 1993). The cost of such protracted planning and negotiating is apparently borne by foundations, government grants, and cross-subsidization among income producing properties held by nonprofit developers.

Since for-profit developers are ineligible for most foundation and government grants, and cross-subsidization would reduce profits, there is little incentive for these developers to pursue subsidized housing production for very low income households. The bulk of LIHTC support goes for units available for households with somewhat higher incomes, for whom additional subsidies are not necessary. These units are almost exclusively produced by for-profit developers. Consequently, for the production of subsidized housing overall, the nonprofit sector accounts for only 14 percent of the total (Walker 1993).

COMMUNITY DEVELOPMENT CORPORATIONS. Numerous neighborhood-based redevelopment efforts were stimulated through the War on Poverty's Office of Economic Opportunity (OEO) and the Community Development Block Grant Program (CDBG), which initially placed heavy emphasis on targeted redevelopment of low-income neighborhoods. Community Development Corporations, neighborhood-based nonprofits addressing their community's redevelopment problems, found that housing redevelopment was an essential complement to economic development and was often a more immediately obtainable goal. Although many CDCs created with OEO or CDBG support were not able to survive when OEO was eliminated and CDBG was substantially reduced, several have become well-established nonprofit development organizations.

The Council for Community-Based Development (a national nonprofit that promotes CDCs) reported in 1991 that "community-based development is a full-fledged national movement." Walker (1993), Goetz (1992), and NCCED (1991) report annual production of approximately 23,000 units, mostly funded through the Section 202 (elderly housing) program and the CDBG program. The sector had a total cumulative production of approximately 736,000 units between 1960 and 1990 (Walker 1993). Nonetheless the sector remains small and fragmented. Average production below 25,000 units per year pales in comparison with a total annual housing production in the U.S. of well over one million units.

Public Policy and Partnerships

The range of intersectoral networks employed for the delivery of social housing illustrate the three dimensions on which to classify public private partnerships: the extent to which decision-making is shared, the duration of the agreement, and the division of responsibilities across partners. Several European countries have implicit partnerships between government and the nonprofit sector at the full partnership end of the spectrum. These partnerships have a high degree of shared decision-making, with the nonprofit housing sector represented by strong, national organizations. Changes in housing policy and administration of programs are negotiated between the national government and the organizations representing the nonprofit sector.

The vertical integration of the nonprofit housing sector in these countries allows stronger participation in national housing partnerships. The relative influence of the third sector on housing policy is greatly enhanced through government certification of the third sector and national organization of that sector. In several instances these partnerships had essentially governmentalized the nonprofit housing sector, spurring efforts to increase the sector's independence from government. In the Netherlands and England, for instance, current efforts promote increased autonomy for the nonprofit housing sector through exposure to risk and greater reliance on for-profit investment and lending. National representation and vertical integration of the nonprofit housing sector have been critical in fashioning the degree and direction of autonomy.

Some European housing partnerships also extend to local government and to tenants. Several countries stipulate sectoral representation in the governance of third sector housing associations, which helps integrate the third sector as a partnership between local and national governments, tenants, and (on occasion) the profit sector. Inclusion of local government has been achieved through representation of local, elected officials on the boards of housing associations, giving these associations direct access to governing regimes. Tenant representation has occurred through national tenant organizations and requirements for annual negotiations on rent and management policies.

Another striking feature of the European housing partnerships is their longevity. For the most part, the partnerships between national governments and the nonprofit sector were rooted in efforts to redress chronic and severe housing shortages after World War II. These partnerships are now entering their sixth decade. Housing shortages have eased, particularly for the middle class, and greater emphasis is now being placed on the fiscal implications of partnership policies that place significant portions of the housing stock outside private, profit-motivated markets.

The division of responsibilities within these partnerships has been split between funding and implementation. National governments, until recently, have been responsible for subsidizing both nonprofit organizations and the housing they provide, while housing associations have been responsible for producing and managing social housing. The sheer magnitude and security of public funding isolated housing associations from financial risk and contributed to their lack of autonomy. As noted, these funding agreements are being renegotiated to reduce government's cost, increase the risk exposure for the nonprofit housing sector, and expand the participation of the for-profit sector.

Examples of other housing partnership relationships are available in Germany, England, and the United States. Germany's explicit policy of competitive contracting and neutrality between for-profit and nonprofit bidders is at the opposite end of the partnership spectrum. The competitive bidding now encouraged among housing associations in England is an example of bi-lateral contracting. The implications of competitive contracting partnerships for housing are unclear, but the evidence on competition between nonprofit and for-profit hospitals points to convergence on the behaviors and motivations of the for-profit sector. Forced to compete with for-profit providers, the nonprofit sector will emphasize the "bottom-line" concerns of that sector. Under this arrangement, the nonprofit sector remains so in name only and loses its distinctive commitments to charity and service. Although incipient, the bottom-line emphasis of England's housing associations and the increased marginalization of poor tenants suggest competitive bidding within the sector is already diminishing some of the sector's distinctive characteristics.

A variety of housing partnerships exist in the United States, but the national level is dominated by competitive or preferential contracting. The distinctiveness of many nonprofit housing corporations is maintained by their ability to layer subsidies from different programs and to attract the support of philanthropic foundations and volunteers. This has resulted in a complex and costly system of housing production (see chapter 11). The emergence of national intermediaries provides important support for making this system work (as well as rationalizing it), but this has not provided any significant vertical integration of nonprofit housing providers. Consequently, the lack of national organization of the nonprofit housing sector in the U.S. continues as one of the main impediments to any larger scale national housing partnership.

Examples of more complete housing partnerships at the national level exist, but these are limited to homeless shelter providers and the franchise partnership of the Neighborhood Reinvestment Corporation. The difficulties inherent in establishing full partnerships between the national government and the nonprofit housing sector in the United States have been apparent in the provision of services to homeless populations. The nonprofit sector built a strong coalition to help define and promote a national legislative response. The obvious threat of contract failure and potential for opportunistic behavior by the for-profit sector point to continued preeminence of the nonprofit sector in delivering homeless programs. A full partnership was established to implement the first wave of programs, but this effort failed to provide an organizational structure for subsequent programs, partly due to problems surrounding separation of church and state. Consequently, the contracting partnership model replaced full partnership.

Public policy generally extols the virtues of intersectoral partnerships while avoiding any direct specification of the legitimate roles of each sector, the reasons for partnerships, the expectations held of partnerships, and the policies promoting partnerships. A case in point is the United States, where intersectoral housing and community development partnerships appear to enjoy widespread political support. Partnerships are promoted through numerous programs, but the purpose and organizational character of partnerships are left undefined, the number of partnerships created and the level of funding for partnerships are not systematically available, and there is no office specifically responsible for the development of policies to promote partnerships (USGAO 1989 and 1990).

Several public policy issues are raised by intersectoral partnerships. The most important and fundamental questions address the appropriate role of intersectoral partnerships in responding to failures in each sector and in utilizing the strengths of each sector. Both public policy and research need to address the relative merits of shared decision-making (what we have characterized as true partnerships) and third-party governance through bilateral or competitive contracting-out. The benefits of partnerships need to be assessed relative to their risks: increased political legitimacy can be endangered by lack of representation and avoidance of democratic processes; increased efficiency due to coordination and economies of scale in technical expertise, purchasing, and access to capital markets can be offset by the costs of unwieldy and overcomplex organizations; the potential to leverage public and private funds requires sustainable commitments of public subsidies and private investments; increased corporate philanthropy for housing can be offset by reductions in giving to other sectors. And lastly, there is the ongoing need to improve our understanding of the mechanics of intersectoral partnerships within the context of a given country's political, social, and economic environment.

Notes

1. Definitions of public-private partnerships come almost exclusively from the U.S., except for Mierlo's (1990) discussion of "neo-corporatism" and discussions of public-private partnerships in Canada in Fallis and Murray (1990) and Canada Mortgage and Housing Corporation (1991).

References

Babcock, Richard F. 1990. "The city as entrepreneur: Fiscal wisdom or regulatory folly?" In *City deal making,* T. J. Lasser, ed. Washington, D.C.: ULI-the Urban Land Institute. 9–44.

Banting, Keith G. 1985. "Institutional conservatism: Federalism and pension reform." In *Canadian social welfare policy: Federal and provincial dimensions.* J. Ismael, ed. Kingston and Montreal: McGill Queen's University Press.

———. 1990. "Social housing in a divided state." In *Housing the homeless and poor: New partnerships among the private, public, and third sectors.* George Fallis and Alex Murray, eds. Toronto: University of Toronto Press.

Ben-Ner, Avner and Theresa Van Hoomissen. 1991. "Nonprofits in the mixed economy: A demand and supply analysis." *Annals of Public and Cooperative Economics* 62(4).

Boelhouwer, Peter and Harry van der Heijden. 1992. *Housing systems in Europe: Part I, A comparative study of housing policy.* Delft, the Netherlands: Delft University Press.

Boston Housing Partnership. 1991. *A catalogue of local housing partnerships.* Boston: Boston Housing Partnership.

Canada Mortgage and Housing Corporation. 1991. *"Partnership Courier."* 1.1.

Cummings, Scott, C. Theodore Koebel, and J. Allen Whitt. 1989. "Redevelopment in downtown Louisville: Public investments, private risks, and shared risks." In *Unequal partnerships: The political economy of urban redevelopment in postwar America.* G. D. Squires, ed. New Brunswick, N.J.: Rutgers University Press. 202–21.

Dieleman, Frans M.. 1994. "Social rented housing: Valuable asset or unsustainable burden?" *Urban Studies* 31 (3). 447–63.

Dolling, John. 1995. "British housing policy: 1984–1993." *Regional Studies* 27,6: 583–88.

Fainstein, Susan S. 1994. *The city builders.* Cambridge, Mass: Blackwell.

Fallis, George and Alex Murray, eds. 1990. *Housing the homeless and poor: New partnerships among the private, public, and third sectors.* Toronto: University of Toronto Press.

Frieden, Bernard J., and Lynn B. Sagalyn 1989. *Downtown, Inc.: How America rebuilds cities.* Cambridge, Mass: MIT Press.

Gage, Robert W. and Myrna P. Mandell, eds. 1990. *Strategies for managing intergovernmental policies and networks.* New York: Praeger.

Goetz, Edward G. 1992. "Local government support for nonprofit housing." *Urban Affairs Quarterly* 27,3. 420–35.

Government Information Services. 1980. "Private corporation set up to aid neighborhood revitalization." *Local government funding report* VIII(23). June 9.

Haider, Donald, 1986. "Partnerships redefined: Chicago's new opportunities." In *Public-Private partnerships: Improving urban life.* P. Davis, ed. Proceedings of the Academy of Political Science, vol. 36, no. 2. New York: Academy of Political Science. 137–49.

Hebert, Scott, et al. 1993. *Nonprofit housing, costs and funding, final report: Volume I—findings.* Washington, D.C.: U.S. Department of Housing and Urban Development, Office of Policy Development and Research.

Housing Corporation. 1989. *The first twenty-five years.* London: The Housing Corporation.

Housing and Development Reporter. 1993. *Reference File Volume 1.* Washington, D.C.: Warren, Gorham, and Lamont.

Kemp, Peter. 1990a. "Shifting the balance between state and market: the Reprivatization of rental housing provision in Britain." *Environment and Planning A.* 22. 793–810.

————. 1990b. "Income-related assistance with housing costs: A cross-national comparison." *Urban Studies* 27(6). 795–808.

Keyes, Langley C., 1990. "The private-sector role in low-income housing." In *Housing the homeless and poor: New partnerships among the private, public, and third sectors.* George Fallis and Alex Murray, eds. Toronto: University of Toronto Press.

Keyes, Langley C. and Denise DiPasquale. 1990. "Housing policy for the 1990s." In *Building foundations: Housing and federal policy.* D. DiPasquale and L. C. Keyes, eds. Philadelphia: University of Pennsylvania Press. 1–24.

Kleinman, Mark P. 1991. "Large-Scale transfers of council housing to new landlords: Is British social housing becoming more 'European'?" London: London School of Economics, mimeo.

Lassar, T. J., ed. 1990. *City deal making.* Washington, D.C.: ULI-the Urban Land Institute.

Lundqvist, Lennart J. 1992. *Dislodging the welfare state? Housing and privatization in four European nations.* Delft, the Netherlands: Delft University Press.

Lyall, Katharine. 1986. "Public-Private partnerships in the Carter years." In *Public-Private partnerships: Improving urban life,* P. Davis, ed. Proceedings of the Academy of Political Science. 36(2). New York: Academy of Political Science. 4–13.

Mierlo, Hans J. G. A. van. 1990. "Privatization and the third sector of the economy: A public choice perspective." *Annals of Public and Cooperative Economics* 61. 537–60.

Moskowitz, Jack. 1989. "Increasing government support for nonprofits: Is it worth the cost?" In *The Future of the nonprofit sector.* Lyman Hodgkinson and associates. San Francisco: Jossey Bass. 275–84.

NCCED. 1991. *Tying it all together: The comprehensive achievements of community-based development organizations.* Washington, D.C.: National Congress for Community Economic Development.

Neighborhood Reinvestment Corporation, 1991. *Into the '90s: 1990 annual report.* Washington, D.C.: Neighborhood Reinvestment Corporation.

Priemus, Hugo. 1990. "Housing policy in the Netherlands: Changing priorities." *International Journal of Urban and Regional Research.* 687–96.

————. 1995. "How to abolish social housing? The Dutch case." *International Journal of Urban and Regional Research.* 19(1). 145–155.

Pryke, M. and C. Whitehead. 1995. "Private sector criteria and the radical change in provision of social housing in England." *Environment and planning C: Government and policy* 13. 217–52.

Saidel, Judith. 1989. "Dimensions of interdependence: The state and voluntary-sector relationship." *Nonprofit and Voluntary Sector Quarterly* 18(4).

Salamon, Lester. 1987. "Of market failure, voluntary failure, and third-party government: Toward a theory of government-nonprofit relations in the modern welfare state." *Journal of Voluntary Action Research* 16. Jan.–June.

———. 1992. *America's nonprofit sector: A primer.* New York: The Foundation Center.

Seibel, Wolfgang. 1989. "The function of mellow weakness: Nonprofit organizations as problem nonsolvers in Germany." In *The nonprofit sector in international perspective: Studies in comparative culture and policy.* Estelle James, ed. New York: Oxford University Press.

Siemon, C. L. 1990. "Public/Private partnerships and fundamental fairness." In *City deal making.* Lasser, T. J. Washington, D.C.: ULI—The Urban Land Institute. 139–54.

Smith, Steven R. and Michael Lipsky. 1993. *Nonprofits for hire: The welfare state in the age of contracting.* Cambridge: Harvard University Press.

Squires, Greg D., ed. 1989. *Unequal partnerships: The political economy of urban redevelopment in postwar America.* New Brunswick, N.J.: Rutgers University Press.

Stone, Clarence N. 1989. *Regime politics: Governing Atlanta, 1946–1988.* Lawrence: University Press of Kansas.

Stoecker, Randy. 1996. "The political economy of the community development corporation model of urban redevelopment." Revised version of a paper presented at the 1995 American Sociological Association annual meeting.

Suchman, Diane R. 1990. *Public/Private housing partnerships.* Washington, D.C.: ULI-the Urban Land Institute.

USGAO (United States General Accounting Office). 1989. *Partnership projects: Federal support for public-private housing and development efforts.* Washington, D.C.: USGAO (GAO/PEMD–89–25FS).

———. 1990. *Partnership projects: A framework for evaluating public-private housing and development efforts.* Washington, D.C.: USGAO (GAO/PEMD–90–9).

Walker, Christopher. 1993. "Nonprofit housing development: Status, trends, and prospects." *Housing Policy Debate* 4(3) 369–414.

Wolfe, Jeanne M. and William Jay. 1990. "The revolving door: Third-sector organizations and the homeless." In *Housing the homeless and poor: New partnerships among the private, public, and third sectors.* George Fallis and Alex Murray, eds. Toronto: University of Toronto Press.

Wylde, Kathryn, 1986. "Partnerships for housing," In *Public-Private partnerships: Improving urban life.* P. Davis, ed. Proceedings of the Academy of Political Science 36(2). New York: Academy of Political Science. 111–21.

Chapter 4

Beyond the Theory of Comparative Advantage:
Political Imperatives of the Government-Nonprofit Relationship

Bishwapriya Sanyal

This chapter investigates why government and nonprofit organizations cooperate. Nonprofit theory is found to provide little guidance on structuring relationships between government and nonprofit organizations (NPOs). Understanding the historical and political context of the government-NPO relationship is necessary to appreciate the politics surrounding this relationship. Case studies of this relationship in Bangladesh and India reveal the importance of the prevailing political system, the political affiliation of NPO leaders, the degree of decentralization of political management, and the political coherence of the ruling regime. The underlying message is that political structures and politics shape the relationship between government and nonprofit organizations.

Introduction

Public-private partnerships, and the role of nonprofit organizations (NPOs) in such partnerships are probably the two most popular notions to dominate any discussion of social problem-solving these days. Yet, beneath the popular rhetoric, there is not much wisdom about why public-NPO partnership is not widely practiced, even though it is such a good idea. When practiced, it takes different forms in different places. This is not to say that there are no theories about why NPOs emerged or why governments and NPOs should cooperate. The theories of market failure, state failure—and, for that matter, voluntary failure—are widely known. So is the notion of comparative advantage, which guided much of our thinking about why governments and NPOs should cooperate. But, when confronted with programmatic questions, such as whether and how to facilitate NPO-government cooperation in a particular setting to provide a particular good or service, these theories do not provide adequate answers.

71

Part of the problem of inadequate theories stems from our rather ahistorical understanding of the phenomenon of government-NPO relationship. We know very little about why and when such cooperation was proposed, who proposed it, and, more importantly, why it was implemented in some places but not in others. If one were to pursue these questions with regard to any specific context, one would surely come up with some related questions about another set of issues generally overlooked—namely, the political character of a place. How frequently do studies explain why certain political regimes are more willing than others to support government-NPO cooperation? In probing the NPO potential to initiate economic development, how many studies analyze the implications of such initiative for the political system? Unfortunately, our understanding of both the historical and the political aspects of the government-NPO relationship is very limited. These limitations, I will argue, reduce the analytical as well as the practical power of our theories.

My objective in this chapter is to address this shortcoming. I do not claim, however, to have a historical-political theory of the government-NPO partnership. Nor do I have the sort of empirical evidence necessary to build such a theory. Rather, I will try to provide a glimpse of what a historical-political approach to the government-NPO relationship may involve. I will do that by relying upon my limited work and research experience in India and Bangladesh. In articulating my position on the topic, I will first give a very brief history of how NPOs emerged as key institutions capable of fostering "development from below." Although the term *development* is broad enough to encompass virtually all activities, my focus in this section will be restricted to employment creation and shelter provision by NPOs in developing countries.

I will follow this with a brief analysis of why cooperation between NPOs and governments became important in developmental discourse and will describe the most popular argument about why such cooperation is to be encouraged. I will then discuss the limitations of this argument, highlighting its normative nature—meaning that it emphasizes why government *should* cooperate in practice. It is only fair that I follow this with a brief summary of some institutional reasons for government-NPO partnerships. In the last section of the chapter I argue that even the institutional reasons are not adequate to explain the variations in government-NPO relationships in different political contexts. To make this point, I provide three specific examples from India and Bangladesh. A few concluding comments remind the reader of what I consider to be my key points.

NPOs and Development from Below

Although NPOs existed in most developing countries prior to the 1970s, they increased in number significantly during that decade (Gorman 1984; Drabek 1987). This period was also marked by a strong critique of state-led industrialization, and a whole range of slogans embodying that critique appeared in development discourse during this time. In advocating an alternative development model that would shift the emphasis away from the state and to the people development was intended to aid, social scientists, planners, and international donor institutions coined slogans such as development from below, bottom-up development, grassroots development, and development as if people mattered. The alternative model was to counter the "top-down/trickle-down" approach of the 1950s. Its central objective, the critics argued, had been to achieve state-led accelerated industrialization. The top-down model had failed, the critics claimed, because the institutions that were created to foster development from the top had themselves become the greatest hindrances to development.

The primary target in this criticism was, of course, the state. But others were blamed too. For example, market institutions, such as large private firms, were criticized for taking advantage of various types of state protection, which made them capital-intensive and inefficient. Established political parties were criticized for merely seeking power by manipulation of the poor and collusion with the army and the elite. Trade unions were chastised for protecting the interests of only the "labor aristocracy," and for being incorporated by the state in "the system."

To initiate broad-based development, the proponents of the alternative paradigm suggested a different constellation of actors, issues, values, and modes of action. In contrast to the top-down model's central objective of accelerated industrialization and economic growth, the bottom-up model advocated new emphasis on rural development and distributional issues. Instead of the state-administered, large-scale infrastructure projects central to the top-down model, it advocated small-scale, bottom-up projects that directly involved the urban and rural poor in income-generating schemes. Typically, these projects involved small groups of poor families who had neither any assets nor a steady source of income. Subsidized credit was made easily available to these families for starting small business enterprises. The assumption was that these activities would generate profit, savings, and investment at the bottom, thereby eliminating the need for income to trickle down through the social hierarchy.

Housing and Development from Below

To address the housing needs of the poor, the new paradigm suggested a move away from public housing, constructed, managed, and owned by the government, to self-built housing by the poor. There were many arguments against public housing projects (Rodwin and Sanyal 1987). First, they were shown to be too costly, and the rate of their supply was too slow compared with the rapidly increasing housing needs of the urban poor. Second, public housing was badly managed because the highly subsidized rents did not generate sufficient revenue for maintenance work. Third, some argued that the subsidies involved in the provision of this housing were regressive in nature—meaning they benefited not the poor, but the relatively better off families who gained access to these homes because of their personal relationship with public officials. Fourth, many criticized the architectural design of these houses, which were high-rise buildings, for ignoring the spatial and cultural needs of the poor.

John Turner's research in Peru was probably most influential in discrediting public housing and directing public policies toward the encouragement of self-built housing by the poor (Turner 1976). Prior to Turner, self-built housing by the poor who squatted on public land was considered a major problem because of its illegal status and low standards. These houses lacked even basic services, like water, sewerage, and electricity. As a result, public authorities considered these squatter settlements a major threat to public health. Many considered the residents of these areas social and political threats as well. They were known to be unemployed, making a living through illegal business or theft. And politically, they were seen as a potentially violent class of people who were likely to disrupt the modernization process. Many of these assumptions proved to be myths (Perlman 1978).

Turner's and others' research helped to alter the image of these people from "peasants in the cities" to self-supporting urban workers who built their own homes, created their own employment, and socially constructed their own communities (Hart 1973; McGee 1976; Peattie 1980). Governments were urged to assist these people by legalizing their housing status, which required that they receive title to the land and also public services. In line with this new spirit of development, governments were not to construct and manage the infrastructure. The poor were to build and manage the infrastructure, incrementally—as they had built their houses, step by step—by pooling communal resources and through mutual aid programs considered central elements of the new development initiatives from below.

The bottom-up approach to development was expected to have a political impact as well (Ralston et al. 1983; USAID 1985). It was commonly believed that by building their own homes, creating their own jobs, and upgrading the infrastructure of their own communities, the poor would also be politically empowered. These efforts were to enable the poor to break away from traditionally exploitive relationships with local moneylenders, middlemen, landlords, and politicians.

To break away from these exploitive relationships, the argument went, the poor had to be organized into small "solidarity groups," which were to function independently of the political process. The need for the solidarity groups' autonomy was justified on the ground that the mainstream political process, controlled and manipulated by the state, the political parties, the elite, and in some cases the army, was not responsive to the needs of the poor. Hence, the poor needed to organize themselves, not as another political party that could be co-opted by the system, but as small, territorially based, autonomous groups. Some thought that these groups would eventually function as "democratic cells," culminating in a system of self-governance.

NPOs: The New Agents of Development

Although self-governance and economic self-sufficiency of the poor were the central objectives of "development from below," proponents of this paradigm argued that to achieve these objectives the poor needed the assistance of NPOs (USAID 1985; Frantz 1987, May 1989). There were three arguments in support of NPOs (Ralston et al. 1983; Gorman 1984; Korten and Klauss 1984; Fernandes 1981). First, it was assumed that NPOs were the most appropriate catalytic agent for fostering development from below, because their priorities were diametrically opposite to those of institutions at "the top." Unlike state and market institutions assumed to be driven by the need for social control and profit-making, respectively, NPOs were assumed to be interested primarily in community building. And to pursue this objective, it was assumed, NPOs had to function independently of both the state and the market institutions. The need for NPO relative autonomy was argued in the following manner. If NPOs were to work jointly with the state, they would either be controlled or co-opted by the state, thereby losing their legitimacy and effectiveness. If NPOs were to work with market institutions, they would be influenced by profit-seeking motives, which would cause community solidarity to degenerate into market-based exchange relationships. Thus, autonomy of NPOs from both state and market institutions would encourage self-sufficiency, self-reliance, and social innovation on their part, thereby enhancing the chances of self-reproduction of this grassroots-based institutional form.

Second, it was also argued that NPOs operated very differently from either state or market institutions. NPOs were less bureaucratic than the state, and being less bureaucratic, they were more responsive to specialized needs, more efficient in their operation, and more innovative in their response to local problems. And, as an extension of that argument, it was also assumed that NPOs relied on decentralized forms of management sustained primarily by voluntary local participation. This, coupled with their small size, allowed NPOs to learn rapidly from their actions. That explained the NPO ability to continuously fine-tune their organizational strategies.

A third assumption about NPO effectiveness was the notion that their relative autonomy from political parties and their distance from the corrupt political process was key to their success. Underlying this assumption were two other assumptions: that the NPOs could organize the poor into "solidarity groups" without alienating the local elite or local political parties. The solidarity groups would better represent the interests of the poor than local political parties because the latter were dominated by the local elite.

The Limits of Bottom-Up Projects and NPOs

By the beginning of the 1980s hundreds of bottom-up development projects had been implemented by various NPOs around the world. As these projects began to be assessed by development scholars, it became increasingly apparent that their projects had not lived up to expectations (Tendler 1989; Bromley 1985; Cohen 1983; Mayo et al. 1988). Neither did the income generation projects increase income and employment significantly for a large number of people. Nor did the upgrading of squatter housing prove to be an effective strategy to meet the acute housing needs of the poor. There were many reasons for this disappointing outcome and three key reasons are directly relevant for the concerns of this chapter.

First, the projects suffered because they were based on the assumption that the economy and polity at "the top" were disconnected from the economy and polity at "the bottom." This misperception ruined many income-generating projects that had not taken into account the generally low national growth rate of the economies in which they were situated. Similarly, high rates of inflation and high domestic interest rates had adversely affected the housing sector, reducing the supply of housing. The slum upgrading projects were too few in number to counteract this market failure. As a result, their impact on the housing situation of the poor was negligible at best and, in some cases, even counterproductive (Keare and Parris 1982). As a result of upgrading, the rents in the project areas increased, making it more difficult for the poorest of the poor who are predominantly renters. As a result, many of them moved out from the upgraded areas and began renting in other nonupgraded areas.

Second, the political impact of bottom-up projects was even less striking than their economic impact. The "solidarity groups" of five to ten households set up by the NPOs served mainly as social pressure groups to ensure monthly payments by the group members who had received small business loans. In the upgraded housing areas, payments for services, such as for water or electricity, were also collected by using the "solidarity groups." Although, in this case, the social pressure system did not work as well (Sanyal 1987). The solidarity groups, or the community groups formed in some of the upgraded areas, did not have much impact beyond that. They did not function as alternative political units to the traditional party structure. Nor were they used as an institutional mechanism to challenge the local government's resource allocation policies.

The lack of political impact of bottom-up projects was, in part, due to the lack of institutional linkages between the NPO and political parties. As mentioned earlier, this lack of linkage was not an oversight on the NPO part: they consciously avoided such linkages on the grounds that it would reduce their autonomy and, hence, their effectiveness. Some even argued that linkages with corrupt and opportunistic political parties would require compromises regarding the ends as well as the means of bottom-up development. As a result, the NPOs functioned without any political backing. Ironically, this made them even more vulnerable to pressure from the local elite and strongmen.

Third, the NPO inability to cooperate with one other contributed to their political vulnerability. This is particularly surprising since the NPOs are thought to represent models of cooperation. In reality, though, the NPOs were extremely competitive with each other and rarely formed institutional linkages among themselves. This was primarily due to the dependence on donations and grants, which made every NPO claim that its particular organization was the most effective in helping the poor. To support such claims, each NPO tried to demonstrate to the donor community how it alone had succeeded at designing and implementing innovative projects (Sanyal 1990).

The lack of cooperation among the NPOs and their unwillingness to forge institutional linkages with the government greatly limited the impact of their activities. At best, their efforts created small, isolated projects that lacked the institutional support necessary for large-scale replication. The NPOs were particularly effective in managing small projects away from the official eye, yet they also recognized that unless their scale of operation was expanded, they could not make a significant impact on the problem they wanted to solve.

Most NPOs tried to resolve this dilemma not through cooperation with other NPOs, but by expanding their own operations. In the process, they lost the comparative advantages of being small and focused on one activity or one geographic location. Typically, they fell apart as either the scale and the array of problems became unmanageable, or the original leaders were challenged by others who broke away from the parent organization, taking with them some of the best workers. This, in turn, made cooperation among the NPOs even more difficult, thus undermining their ability to create a unified, broad based institutional form independent of the government.

There were a few other surprises for the proponents of NPOs who had envisioned them as leading from below an alternative approach to development. For one, the efficiency of NPOs did not turn out to be as high as was expected. Evaluation studies indicated that the NPO-managed projects relied on intensive supervision, which was very time-consuming (Tendler 1982). On the issue of equity, too, there was a surprise: NPOs were found to concentrate their efforts not on the poorest of the poor but on groups above the lowest income decile. That was the only way NPOs could respond to the donors' pressure to show results quickly. As for the claim that NPOs are more responsive and accountable than the government, the evidence indicated that, indeed, NPOs were more responsive in the sense that they were better at finetuning projects to suit local needs, but this required a good amount of flexibility in project operation, which could only be ensured by relaxing the procedures for accountability. In other words, NPOs were more responsive but probably less accountable than government organizations (Lipsky and Smith 1988).

NPO-Government Partnership

In development planning discourse the issue of NPO-government relationship emerged in the early 1980s, partly in response to the findings described in the previous section. It became clear to even the NPO staunch supporters that the starkly contrasting good guy/bad guy image of NPOs and government was incorrect. In reality, neither are NPOs all good nor is the government all bad. This, in turn, led to a more sophisticated redefinition of development strategy, which went beyond the popular rhetoric of either "trickle-down" or "bottom-up" development. It indicated that as development does not trickle down from "the top," neither does it effervesce from "the bottom." Development requires a synergy between efforts made at "the top" as well as "the bottom." It requires a collaborative effort between the government and NPOs that uses the good qualities of each while neutralizing or eliminating the drawbacks of both (Stearns and Otero 1990).

In taking the new stance, the development theorists relied on the notion of "comparative advantage," proposing that the government and NPOs should work in ways that draw on their distinctly different institutional strengths (Cernea 1988). For example, the government alone could create the policy environment necessary for maximizing NPO effectiveness. Only government has the administrative machinery for large-scale implementation of projects and policies. Although NPOs lack this potential, their comparative advantage over government is in their ability to reach citizens who are beyond the reach of the formal administrative apparatus of the governments. NPOs are also better than the government at ensuring citizens' participation in the development process by engaging them in learning environments, as opposed to the rules-driven, hierarchically structured institutional setting common to government projects. Development efforts should draw on the comparative advantage of both institutions and, also, that of the market, the argument went, so as to maximize the synergistic effect of partnership.

The problem with the comparative advantage approach is that it is normative in orientation. It prescribes why the three types of institutions *should* interact. It does not explain why they actually interact, and why they often do not interact the way they should. This shortcoming of the comparative advantage approach first became clear to me while I did fieldwork on the government-NPO relationship in Bangladesh. I came to realize, as a result of extensive interviews with both government officials and NPO leaders, that the government-NPO relationship in Bangladesh at that particular historical moment could best be described as antagonistic cooperation, shaped more strongly by the different institutions' current interests than by their comparative advantages. I could also see that the interests of both groups changed over time in response to changes in the structure of the economy, the institutional environment of laws and regulations, and, most importantly, the political situation at the local and national levels (Sanyal 1991).

Institutional Motivations for Interaction

In pursuing this line of thinking, it may be useful to go beyond the normative theory of comparative advantage and, instead, probe the question: Why would the government and NPOs be willing to cooperate, particularly to ensure housing and employment for the poor? There could be a range of answers to this question. For example, the government as the protector of law may be more inclined to work with NPOs than directly with the poor who have squatted illegally on private or public land. By working with the NPOs and not with the squatters, the government avoids creating the impression that it is encouraging illegality. Similarly, the government must appear neutral toward its citizens. That is why in a multiethnic country if any particular ethnic group needs special assistance with housing, the government may choose to provide that assistance through an NPO to avoid the criticism that it is biased in favor of that particular ethnic group (James 1987).

There may be other reasons for government-NPO partnership. NPOs, particularly the smaller ones, may find it useful to work with the government in projects where they would identify the prospective beneficiaries. Many NPOs expand their membership in this way, by requiring that the project beneficiaries also become members of the NPO if their names are to be proposed to the government. Increased membership of NPOs is important for two reasons. First, it makes NPOs attractive to foreign donors who, being concerned about broad-based impact, usually choose NPOs with a large membership. Second, by requiring a membership initiation fee, the NPOs can muster crucial resources at the early stages of their growth (Sanyal 1993, 1994).

NPOs also may cooperate with the government to establish an official track record, which is important to dispel any suspicion on the part of the government that foreign assistance was channeled through the NPOs to undermine the government, and to expand their operations. NPOs could also extend their scope by pooling resources with other NPOs. But, as I mentioned earlier, NPOs are not known to cooperate with each other; rather, they prefer to work with the government, even though they may face some constraints.

On the government side, an interesting reason for cooperation with NPOs may have to do with upper-level bureaucrats who use such cooperative projects

as a way of disciplining their juniors.[1] In developing countries where govern-
ment-administered projects—for example, for housing provision or employment generation—fail to be implemented well, the upper-level bureaucrats may
want to hold accountable the lower-level bureaucrats who are responsible for
project implementation. This can be achieved by financing a similar project
administered solely by an NPO. If the NPO-run project performs better—say
by providing housing to a larger number of people or by providing small business loans to a larger percentage of the target population than was achieved in
the government-run projects—then the upper-level bureaucrats can use these
examples of higher performance by NPOs to demand that the lower-level
bureaucrats improve their performance.

On a similar note, governments in many developing countries may want
to work with NPOs with the ulterior motive to control or co-opt them (Uphoff
1987; Society for Participatory Research in Asia 1989). Since much has been
written about this issue, I will not dwell on it except to raise a question that, I
believe, is central to our understanding of NPO-government relationship. Which
factors are likely to influence the government's motivation to either co-opt or
control NPOs? Conversely, under what circumstances are governments likely to
cooperate with NPOs without wanting to co-opt or control them? We may
articulate these questions in an even more general way by inquiring which factors are likely to most influence the motivations of governments and NPOs with
regard to possible partnership between them? Unfortunately, even after two
decades of research on NPOs we do not have a good answer to these questions.
Because rarely did we situate the NPO-government relationship issue within a
political context. That is not to say, however, that NPO proponents never argued
about their political implications. Most studies of NPOs either imply or argue
directly that NPOs are a democratizing force that allows poor people to hold
their government accountable (Sethi and Kothari 1984; Korten 1990).[2]

What these studies lack, however, is the analytical power to explain the
varied role NPOs have played around the world, opposing government in some
countries, cooperating with it in other countries, and even ignoring it in some
instances. To explain these variations, the political context of NPO-government
relationships needs to be taken into account in a more serious way than simply
subscribing them a democratic role.

The Politics of the NPO-Government Relationship[3]

To understand the politics of NPO-government relationship in any specific
context, one needs to be aware of the institutional characteristics of the political
regime in power in that place. This could present a massive intellectual task if it
were necessary to understand all the intricate details of a political regime. But,

for our purposes, the inquiry may be confined to three key variables. I will argue, they can provide an adequate sense of the political regime in power.

The first variable is the nature of the political system—meaning, Is it a democratic system with more than one political party to contest elections at regular intervals? If so, one could predict that the government would be likely to work with NPOs in responding to housing and employment needs. In a multiparty system, it is in the interest of the party in power to have NPOs, rather than opposition parties, respond to these needs.

That is a very simple portrayal of what is otherwise a much more complex reality. Part of the complexity is created by factors, such as the political affiliation and sympathies of the NPO leaders, which constitute the second critical variable to understand. This variable is rarely discussed in the literature on NPOs. In part, this is because NPOs are usually portrayed as politically neutral institutions that are above the corrupt political process, in which they have no intention of participating (Kothari 1987; Bhatt 1989). The reality is that NPOs do not emerge within a political vacuum. In fact, they are often the outcome of a political process that may limit peoples' participation in that process through traditional means such as by creating a new political party to weaken the one in power.

The internal management and political coherence of the political party in power is the third variable that influences the nature of the relationship between the government and NPOs. As I elaborate later through an example from India, the internal management of the party in power—particularly, the level of centralization or decentralization of decision-making within the party and how that affects the ability of the members at the grassroots level to respond to the needs of the poor—is a key factor that may influence the ruling party's attitude toward NPOs. In countries where the ruling party is overtly centralized, which is typical when a party has been in power for long, the party leaders may lose touch with their grassroots-based cadres. This can deter the party from effectively mobilizing the poor at the grassroots level, leaving room for NPOs to fill the void. If NPO leaders are not affiliated with the opposition political parties, the government may, under this circumstance, opt to join hands with NPOs in responding to the housing and employment needs of the poor.

Another possible outcome that may result from this situation depends on the political coherence of the ruling regime. In many developing countries the ruling party, particularly if it has been in power for a long time, is composed of multiple groups, which may differ in their ideological orientation, but are all interested in being part of the ruling regime. Political leaders who are unsure about their support base within the party may seek to create an alternative institutional base outside it, in case the internal struggles within the party become pronounced. The creation of NPOs by political leaders themselves is often the outcome of such a situation. Needless to say, political leaders would never openly acknowledge their vital role in creating an NPO. Rather, they are likely to offer "their blessings" to the NPO, emphasizing at the same time the virtues of NPO autonomy from the political process.

Three examples from India and Bangladesh substantiate my arguments. I do not claim that either Bangladesh or India is a representative case for all developing countries. What happened in each of these two countries can hardly be used as a guide for predicting NPO-government relationship elsewhere. Still, these example are useful for raising questions about the relationship between the political context and the nature of NPO-government partnership.

Political Regime and NPOs: The Case of Bangladesh[4]

In Bangladesh the NPOs emerged initially after the civil war in 1971 that led to the creation of the country. The civil war, and the famine that followed in 1974–75, required a level of relief work that the newly formed government could not undertake. As a result, NPOs, which were relatively few in number, were encouraged by the government to engage in relief work, particularly in remote areas.

After the assassination of Mujibar Rahaman, the first president of the country, and when the army general Zia-ur-Rahman came to power through a violent coup, there was a sharp increase in the number of NPOs. Many of them expanded their activities from relief work to employment generation and similar activities, with governmental assistance. This increase in NPO activities could be attributed to the withdrawal of the cadres of the Awami League, the political party of the assassinated president, from grassroots activities. Since the new president had no intention of encouraging the Awani League's cadres to continue working at the grassroots level and did not have his own political party with its own cadres (because he was an army general prior to the coup), he openly encouraged the creation of "apolitical NPOs" that could work with the government at the grassroots level.

Political Coherence of Ruling Party and NPOs: The Cases of Gujarat and West Bengal in India

What is striking about the difference between Gujarat and West Bengal, two states in India, is the extent of NPO activities in these states. In Gujarat there are at least a hundred different NPOs involved in housing provision, employment generation, and many other activities. In contrast, in West Bengal there are at most five or so well-established NPOs carrying on similar activities.

The conventional explanation for this difference in NPO activities between the two states is that Gujarat has a long history of NPO activities, which received a further boost from Gandhi, a Gujrati, who was a strong supporter of voluntary activities. But this explanation is inadequate for two reasons. First, West Bengal, too, has a long tradition of voluntary activities; in fact, the level of voluntary activities in West Bengal was higher than in Gujarat at the turn of the century (Alliband 1983). Second, this does not explain the sharp increase in NPO activities in Gujarat in the 1970s, and the sharp decline in NPO activities in West Bengal during the same period (Frenda 1983).

The clue to this puzzle, I propose, is in the nature of the political party in power in the two states (Kohli 1990). West Bengal has had a Communist-led government since 1977. The Communist Party of India (CPM), which runs the government, is an extremely well-organized party with a vast network of committed cadres receiving clear and consistent instructions from the party bosses at the capital and carrying them out diligently at the grassroots level. This does not leave much scope for activities by NPOs, which are generally distrusted by the CPM. In contrast, Gujarat has been ruled by the Congress Party, which is fraught with internal battles among competing leaders. The party had been reconstituted several times without any strong leadership. As a result, the politicians were understandably nervous about the stability of the party and their own positions within it. No one really knows how long a party in its current form can remain in power or what organizational changes may occur next. This anxiety has compelled many politicians, both conservative and liberal, to seek alternative institutional bases in the event that that may lose their power within the party.

The NPO form has provided this alternative institutional structure, because it does not appear to be a splinter political institution and, hence, is not threatening, at least on the surface. It also allows politicians to muster resources without paying taxes. And, most importantly, through the development activities in which they are engaged, NPOs of this nature allow politicians to respond to the needs of their constituencies without having to battle over resource allocation within an ideologically fractured party.

Political Connections of NPO Leaders

In Bangladesh, the second president, Zia-ur-Rahman, referred to above, was also killed, in a second bloody coup, which brought General H. M Ershad to power. Zia had encouraged the growth of NPOs, as I mentioned earlier, and by the time General Ershad became the country's third president, there were more than 700 NPOs operating within Bangladesh. But President Ershad did not like the NPOs, and his first response to their growing number was to instruct the ministry of finance to scrutinize the flow of donor support to them. There were at least two reasons for this move. First, President Ershad had banned all political parties. He feared that some of the NPOs were serving as surrogates for political parties and were being assisted by countries that did not approve of his regime and wanted to undermine it by supporting NPOs who could discredit his government by performing better in providing assistance to the poor.

Ershad also perceived that the NPO-managed projects, which were heavily funded from external sources, reduced the amount of external assistance for the government. This would probably not have been considered a problem if President Ershad had viewed the NPO leaders as sympathetic to his regime. But precisely because Ershad had banned all formal political activities against his regime, he suspected that the NPO leaders, who came from urban middle-class to upper middle-class families and never accepted the legitimacy of his government, were trying to erode the power of his appeal to his countrymen.

President Ershad's response to this political problem was to "decentralize" the government's administrative machinery by creating a new local-level administrative structure that would be responsible for resource allocation at the grassroots level (Huque 1986; Khan 1987). Although he described this effort as one motivated by his concern for democracy, its primary goal was to undermine the power of NPOs by creating a new group of stakeholders at the local level. He was unsuccessful in implementing the decentralization policy because he was strongly opposed by the bureaucrats within his own government who saw in that policy a threat to their power. President Ershad could not override the opposition of the bureaucrats because he lacked a broad base of political support, which is not surprising for an army general who came to power through a coup.

Epilogue

My main objective in this article was to introduce a political dimension to our understanding of NPO-government relationship. I have pursued this objective in four steps. First, I provided an intellectual history of how NPOs became popular as development agents in the 1970s and how they implemented numerous bottom-up projects, ignoring both the economics and politics at "the top." Then, I analyzed the shortcomings of NPOs and the bottom-up projects. I described why development planners came to acknowledge that NPOs and governments should cooperate to combine development efforts from "the top" and "the bottom." I then argued that the prevailing view of NPO-government cooperation is based on the notion of comparative advantage, which explains why the two institutions *should* cooperate but fails to explain how they actually do cooperate or do not cooperate in any specific context. We can only overcome this deficiency in our explanatory power, I proposed, by better understanding the varying motivations of the governments as well as of the NPOs, motivations which are deeply influenced by the specific nature of local politics—in particular, the relationship between the political party in power and NPOs.

What are the theoretical and practical implications of incorporating this political dimension in our understanding of NPO-government relationship? For one, it can better explain the circumstances under which NPOs are likely to contribute to the democratization of the development process. At present, advocates of NPOs virtually take it for granted that NPOs are a democratizing force. But this is mere wishful thinking. Without taking into account the political factors, hardly anything of significance can be said about the political impact of NPOs.

Second, proponents of NPO-government collaboration may benefit from an enhanced understanding of the political factors. It would help them to decipher the institutional motives on both sides, and thus identify better the windows of opportunity for cooperative action.

Third, a good understanding of the political factors will help us better address other debates about larger issues, such as the relationship between political democracy and economic development. Although much has already been written about this relationship, we remain uncertain about the precise nature of causality between the two domains. A grounded understanding of the political factors in any context will go a long way in specifying the nature of this causal relationship and thereby temper the current euphoria about the "end of history."

Notes

1. This idea is based on my field work in India in March 1989 when I interviewed a number of government bureaucrats on their attitudes toward NPOs.

2. The only two studies I am aware of which attempt to discuss explicitly the political role of NPOs are Frohling (1985) and Loveman (1991).

3. This section of the paper is based on my field work in Bangladesh and India.

4. For a detailed discussion of the points raised in this section, see Sanyal (1991) and Westergaard (1992).

References

Alliband, Terry. 1983. *Catalysts of Development: Voluntary Agencies in India.* West Hartford: Kunarian Press.

Bhatt, E. 1989. "Toward empowerment." *World Development.* 17(7) 1059–66.

Bromley, Ray. 1985. "Small may be beautiful, but it takes more than beauty to ensure success." In *Planning for Small Enterprises in Third World Cities.* R. Bromley, ed. Oxford: Pergamon Press.

Cernea, Michael M. 1988. *Non-Governmental organizations and local development.* World Bank Discussion Paper number 40. Washington, D.C.: World Bank.

Cohen, Michael. 1983. "The challenge of replicability: Toward a new paradigm for urban shelter in developing countries." World Bank Reprint Series: number 287. Washington, D.C.: World Bank.

Drabek, Anne G., ed. 1987. "Development alternatives: The challenge of NGOs." Special issue *World Development* 15.

Fernandes, W., ed. 1981. *Voluntary action and government control.* New Delhi: India Social Science Institute.

Frantz, T. R. 1987. "The Role of NPOs in the strengthening of civil society." *World Development* 15. 121–29.

Franda, Marcus F. 1983. *Voluntary associations and local development: The Janata phase.* New Delhi: Young Asia Publishers.

Fruhling, Hugo. 1985. "Non-Profit organizations as opposition to authoritarian rule: The case of human rights organizations and private research centers in Chile." PONPO Working Paper number 96. Yale: Institution for Social Policy Studies.

Gorman, Robert F., ed. 1984. *Private voluntary organization as agents of development.* Boulder, Colorado: Westview Press.

Hart, Keith. 1973. "Informal income opportunities and urban employment in Ghana." *The Journal of Modern African* Studies. II (1) 61–89.

Huque, Ashrath. 1986. "Reflections on local government reforms in developing countries: The experience of Bangladesh." *Planning and Development* 13(2).

James, Estelle. 1987. "The non-profit sector in comparative perspective." In *The nonprofit sector: A research handbook.* Walter Powell, ed. New Haven: York University Press.

Khan, Mohiuddin 1987. "Politics of administrative reform and reorganization in Bangladesh." *Public Administration and Development* 7(4).

Keare, Douglass H., and Scott Parris. 1982. *Evaluations of shelter programs for urban poor.* World Bank Staff Working Paper number 547. Washington, D.C.: World Bank.

Kohli, Atue. 1990. *Democracy and discontent: India's growing crisis of governability.* Cambridge: Cambridge University Press.

Korten, David C. 1990. *Getting to the 21st century: Voluntary action and the global agenda.* West Hartford: Kumarian Press.

Korten, David C., and Rudi Klauss, eds. 1984. *People centered development.* West Hartford: Kurmarian Press.

Kothari, Rajni. 1987. "Party and state in our times: The rise of non-party political formations." *Alternatives* IX. 595–618.

Lipsky, Michael, and Steven R. Smith. 1988. "Providing social services through nonprofit organizations." Mimeo. Cambridge, Massachusetts: MIT.

Loveman, Brian 1991. "NGOs and the transition to democracy in Chile." *Grassroots Development* 572. 8–19.

May, Richard 1989. "The emerging role of non-governmental organizations in shelter and urban development." In *The urbanization revolution: Planning a new agenda for human settlements.* New York: Plenum Press.

Mayo, Steven, Steven Malpezzi, and David J. Gross. 1988. "Shelter strategies for the urban poor in developing countries." *Research Observer* 1 (2)183–203.

McGee, Terence G. 1976. "The persistence of the proto-proletariat: Occupational structures and planning for the future of third world cities." *Progress in Geography* 9. 1–38.

Peattie, Lisa R. 1980. "Anthropological perspectives on the concepts of dualism, the informal sector, and marginality in developing urban economics." *International Regional Science Review* 5 (1)1–31.

Perlman, Janice. 1978. *The myth of marginality: Urban poverty and politics in Rio de Janeiro.* Berkeley: University of California Press.

Ralston, Lenore, et. al. 1983. *Voluntary efforts in decentralized management.* Berkeley, Calif.: Institute of International Studies.

Rodwin, Lloyd, and Bishwapriya Sanyal. 1987. "Shelter, settlement and development: An overview." In *Shelter, Settlement and Development.* Lloyd Rodwin, ed. Boston: Allen and Unwin.

Sanyal, Bishwapriya. 1987. "Problems of cost-recovery in development projects: Experience of the Lusaka upgrading and site/service projects." *Urban Studies* 24.

———. 1990. "Does development trickle up?" *Trialog* 23/24. 6–9.

———. 1991. "Antagonistic cooperation: A case study of non-governmental organizations, government and donors' relationships in income-generating projects in Bangladesh." *World Development* 19 (10)1367–79.

———. 1993. "Conservative origins of progressive social movements." Talk delivered at the Population Center at Harvard University. May.

———. 1994. *Cooperative autonomy: the dialect of state-NGO relationship in developing countries.* Geneva. International Institute for Labour Studies.

Sethi, H., and S. Kothari. eds. 1984. *The non-party political process: Uncertain alternatives.* New Delhi: United Nations Research Institute for Social Policy/Lokayan.

Society for Participatory Research in Asia (PRIA). 1989. *NPO-Government relations: A breath of life or kiss of death.* New Delhi: PRIA.

Stearns, Katherine, and Maria Otero. 1990. *The critical connection: Government, private institutions and the informal sector in Latin America.* Monograph Series number 5. Washington, D.C.: Acción International.

Tendler, Judith. 1982. *Turning private voluntary organizations into development agencies: Questions for evaluation.* USAID Program Evaluation Discussion Paper number 12. Washington, D.C.: USAID.

———. 1989. "Whatever happened to poverty alleviation?" *World Development* 17(7). 1033–44.

Turner, John F. C. 1976. *Housing by people: Towards autonomy in building environments.* London: Marion Boyars.

Uphoff, Norman. 1987. "Relations between governmental and non-governmental organizations and the promotion of autonomous development." Paper presented at the Conference for Autonomous Development, Oegstgust, the Netherlands.

USAID, 1985. "Report on the workshop on private voluntary organizations and small-scale enterprise development." AID Program Evaluation discussion paper no. 22.

Westergaard, Kirsten. 1992. "NGOs, empowerment and the State in Bangladesh." Center for Development Research working paper number 92–2. Copenhagen: CDR.

Part II

Research

Chapter 5

Philanthropy and the Housing Crisis:
Dilemmas of Private Charity and Public Policy
in the United States

Peter Dreier

Philanthropy has played an important role in the history of housing policy in the United States and has contributed to the development of nonprofit housing. This chapter reviews the role of philanthropy in housing during two periods—the era of initial industrialization and urban expansion, and the current era. The challenges facing philanthropy and the strategems used for improving housing are remarkably similar in these two eras. Peter Dreier examines the shortcomings of philanthropic support for nonprofit housing when fundamental political and economic issues are ignored. He concludes with recommendations for a new agenda for philanthropic support of nonprofit housing.

Introduction

This chapter examines how American philanthropy has sought to address the nation's housing crisis, especially among the poor. Since the mid-1800s, wealthy philanthropists and private charitable foundations have tried in various ways to tackle America's low-income housing problems. Since the early 1980s, private philanthropy (primarily through corporate and community foundations) has significantly increased its role in housing. What lessons can we draw from these efforts in terms of solving America's housing problems?

Americans have always been ambivalent about private philanthropy by wealthy individuals, families, and businesses—especially when their charity is directed at helping the poor. Do their "good works" reflect a humanitarian commitment to social justice and a more egalitarian society? Do they represent the upper class's "helping hand" paternalism—a form of noblesse oblige? Do they reflect the moneyed class's attempt to pacify the poor, who might otherwise foment social unrest? Do they serve as a way to lend credibility to volunteer private charity as a better way than an activist government to solve social problems? (Johnson 1988; Magat 1989; Odendahl 1990).

As with other aspects of upper-class charity, philanthropy's involvement in housing raises profound questions about how society meets basic needs. Is housing a basic right, which should be guaranteed by society? Or should housing be treated as a private good allocated by the marketplace? Should philanthropy promote government action or directly help those who are not well served by the private sector?

This chapter compares private philanthropy's response to the housing crisis in two important eras of economic transformation—the period between the Civil War and World War 1 (the progressive era), when the United States was undergoing large-scale urbanization and industrialization, and the period from the 1980s through today, when the United States became integrated into a global economy and confronted the shock of deindustrialization, widening economic disparities, and deepening urban decay. Following that historical review, the chapter focuses briefly on the current housing crisis and the dilemmas that private foundations and nonprofit organizations face in trying to develop a coherent strategy to address the problem. It closes with a proposal for a partnership between private foundations and housing organizations that can address the need to change both public opinion and public policy toward housing.

In both the progressive era and the current period, the efforts of private philanthropy to address the housing crisis took three directions, reflecting differences in ideology and worldview regarding the role of private wealth, of government, and of the causes of poverty itself.

First, private philanthropy sought to change the behavior of the poor and to ameliorate the most visible symptoms of poverty and housing problems. During the progressive era, this meant the creation of poor houses, settlement houses, and the beginning of the social work profession. During the 1980s, many foundations provided grants to social agencies, religious organizations, and other groups to provide emergency services (shelters, soup kitchens, health care) as well as counseling and rehabilitative services to homeless people.

Second, private philanthropy sought to improve housing conditions for the poor by sponsoring model housing projects. In the progressive era, this took the form of "model tenements." In the more recent period, foundations have helped sustain and expand the capacity of community-based housing development organizations. Foundation support has enabled a variety of local nonprofit groups to rehabilitate, construct and manage low-income housing.

Third, private philanthropy has sought to reform public policy to give the government a stronger role in regulating housing conditions and providing subsidies to house the poor. The progressive era reformers focused their activities on establishing government standards for safety and health in slum housing. In the recent era, some foundations provided grants to groups involved in various forms of advocacy and grassroots community and tenant organizing to change housing *policy* at the local, state, and national levels.[1]

Progressive-Era Philanthropy and Slum Housing

Beginning in the mid-1800s, rising immigration, growing cities, and increasing labor exploitation led to urban slums. The poor typically lived into unsafe, unsanitary, poorly constructed, and overcrowded tenement housing. Philanthropists worked with middle-class reformers to investigate and expose the suffering of slum dwellers. They formed private committees and task forces to conduct firsthand studies. They wrote magazine articles, reports, and books (such as Jacob Riis's *How the Other Half Lives* in 1890) to inform the public about the squalid conditions of slum life. But they did more than study the slums; they acted. Parallel to their counterparts in the 1980s, these early philanthropists sought to address this problem in three ways: improving the behavior and values of the poor living in the teeming slums, building model tenements, and pushing for government regulation of slum housing.

Their motivations were complex. For many, religious belief led to a genuine concern for the suffering of the poor. They were sincerely horrified by the conditions they saw. Some viewed cleaning up the slums as necessary to stop crime and diseases from spreading to the more affluent sections of the city. Others saw the slums as breeding grounds for riots and civil disorder (Marcuse 1986). Indeed, it was the draft riots of July 1863 that led the Council of Hygiene of the Citizens Association, an upper class organization, to launch a campaign to improve housing and sanitary standards in New York City (Lubove 1962:12).

Alfred T. White of New York reflected the many-sided spirit of upper class philanthropy. In *The Progressives and the Slums*, Lubove described White as "a wealthy man in search of a philanthropy" who "discovered in housing reform an outlet for his benevolent impulses." White warned that the tenement slums were "the nurseries of the epidemics which spread with certain destructiveness into the fairest homes" (Lubove 1962: 34–35).

Care-Giving: The Origins of Modern Social Work

As Wright (1981:128) notes in *Building the Dream,* "Housing reformers saw themselves as a moral police force, using environmental change to enforce propriety." As early as 1843, wealthy merchants and businessmen formed the New York Association for Improving the Condition of the Poor (AICP) to clean up the slums and the "disease, vice, and crime which seemed to characterize their inhabitants" (Lubove 1962:4). The AICP saw itself as a citywide umbrella group to coordinate the multiplicity of private charities that worked in specific neighborhoods or with specific groups (such as indigent Episcopalian widows). The charitable impulse was mixed with upper-class paternalism, which viewed poverty as rooted in the defective character, laziness, or ignorance of the poor themselves. Their objective was "the elevation of the moral and physical condition of the indigent" (Vellier, cited in Lubove 1962:4).

These upper-class views shaped the emergence of the settlement house movement later in the century. Wealthy philanthropists funded settlement houses (social service agencies), which taught immigrants English and job skills, and ran theater and art classes and recreation programs—all to uplift and Americanize them. These early reformers—volunteer women, nurses, and social workers—often visited people in their slum apartments and offered suggestions for improving personal hygiene, cooking meals and other housekeeping, raising their children, and even how to dress. This activities were part of what was called "friendly visiting," the "domestic science" movement, or "scientific charity" (Ehrenreich 1985; Katz 1986).

Model Tenements

Most housing reformers at the time rejected the idea, then popular in western Europe, that local government should build and manage housing for the poor. They believed, according to Lubove, that "it was 'bad principle and worse policy' for municipalities to spend public money competing with private enterprise in housing the masses" (Lubove 1962:104).

To demonstrate that the private sector could help address housing problems without resorting to government-run "socialist" housing, a variety of settlement houses, wealthy philanthropists, and private investors sponsored "model tenements." Unlike company towns and company-owned housing, these were not directly linked to the profit-maximizing interests of a particular employer. Unlike slum housing owned by speculators, they were not operated to squeeze every penny of profit out of their investment. Instead, these were limited dividend organizations, seeking a modest profit. This movement was thus known as "philanthropy and five percent" or "investment philanthropy" (Birch and Gardner 1981; Lubove 1962:104). They viewed their activities as a business, not charity. They charged market rents, but they took pride in the higher quality of the model housing. Lubove explained that "model tenements, sound investments rather than speculative adventures, might reap diminished profits but investors would be rewarded by the pleasure of having served the poor" (Lubove 1962: 8).

Only a handful of model tenements were based on philanthropy alone—that is, on a nonprofit basis. Even by 1919, housing reformer Edith Wood knew of only two such projects: Charlesbank Homes in Boston (built in 1911) and Mullanphy Apartments in St. Louis (Friedman 1968:76). However, from the mid-1800s through the 1920s, limited dividend societies produced model tenement projects in cities across the country. The New York AICP formed a subsidiary company in 1854 to build a model tenement—a "Workmen's Home"—that contained 87 apartments, two stores, and a large hall. Rents ranged from $5.50 to $8.50 per month (Lubove 1962:9). In 1871, Dr. H.P. Bowditch helped organize the Boston Cooperative Building Company, which the following year erected five tenement projects. Another philanthropic organization, the Improved Dwellings Association, built a model tenement in Manhattan in 1882. By buying up an entire block that would otherwise have had 32 separate buildings, the association was able to build a large single building with 218 apartments. The size of each apartment was about the same as some slum tenements, but the design of the model tenement was a vast improvement in terms of air and sunlight (Wright 1981:124).

The model tenements improved the living conditions in other ways. In most slum buildings, tenants used sinks in the halls. Because the water pressure came from the street, the water couldn't reach the top floors; tenants on the top floors had to use outdoor hydrants. In the model tenements, large tanks on the roof provided enough water pressure for sinks, washtubs, and toilets on every floor (Wright 1981:124). Some of the model tenements had large courtyards, which served several functions. They discouraged children from playing in the streets (which reformers viewed as dangerous breeding grounds for crime and delinquency), provided places for adults to socialize (often while drying their clothes), and allowed more light to reach the apartments. Some of the later model tenements added playgrounds on the roofs, kindergartens, and communal laundries in the basement to encourage a common social life among residents (Wright 1981:125).

At the same time, some housing reformers sought to design model tenements to give families greater privacy and a sense of individual attachment to their apartments. Some had front doorbells, private entrances for each unit, and bay windows to approximate the idea of a single-family home. The great architect Frank Lloyd Wright designed a two-story model tenement, Francisco Terrace in Chicago, for philanthropist Edward Waller in 1895. Each entryway on the courtyard side had its own hood. Some philanthropists went even further and built model housing developments on the city's outskirts and in suburbs. In Boston, wealthy philanthropist Robert Treat Paine formed the Workingmen's Building Association, a limited dividend corporation that built 116 small cottages for the "substantial workingman" in the 1890s (Wright 1981:127). The largest limited-dividend corporation, the New York City and Suburban Homes Company, whose investors included some of the city's wealthiest people, built model housing for more than 11,000 people, including a Junior League Hotel for women and two developments for blacks. One of its projects, Homewood, was located in Brooklyn, which was then a suburb. According to Wright:

> A typical cottage in this 53-acre tract consisted of a diminutive two-story brick-and-timber structure with a porch and gabled roof to "add quaintness." The company insisted on a firmly authoritarian policy: each resident was required to take out life insurance for the cost of his home. Multiple-family dwellings, saloons, and factories were prohibited in the neighborhood, as were flat-roofed buildings.

The Tuskegee, a model tenement built in 1901 by City and Suburban Homes, was one of several projects targeted for black families, who faced incredible discrimination in the housing market. The success of the Tuskegee led former Surgeon-General George Sternberg to organize the Sanitary Housing Company, which built a hundred two-flat dwellings for black families in Washington, D.C., over the next ten years. In 1911, Jacob Schmidlapp built Washington Terrace, small row houses for 326 black families in Cincinnati.

These philanthropic projects had inherent limitations. Although the quality of these model housing projects was, for the most part, much better than the slum housing that surrounded them, the philanthropists' desire to create model housing ran up against the realities of housing economics. As Catherine Bauer, one of the nation's leading early housing reformers, pointed out, the philanthropists sought to "provide good dwellings, on an 'economic' basis, at a price which everyone could pay, and without disturbing or even questioning any part of the current social-economic system" (quoted in Friedman 1968:87). But good quality housing simply cost more to build and manage than the poor could afford, even with the builders getting a small profit or no profit at all. For example, in Chicago philanthropist Julius Rosenwald built Michigan Boulevard Garden Apartments for African-Americans and the trustees of the Field family fortune constructed Marshall Field Gardens for modest-income white families. Despite "minimal profit expectations" and "low-interest capital," both developments had to charge tenants an average of over $62 a month when Chicago's media rents were $55 (Radford 1996:23–24). Ironically, many of the model apartment buildings sooner or later turned into slums.

Even so, the model tenement crusade had a long-lasting influence. As Birch and Gardner (1981:406) note, "their projects had a profound effect on the design and philosophy of American housing. They germinated ideas relating to architecture, management and tenant selection which later shaped the course of the twentieth century housing movement." In addition, the model tenement efforts brought many women into progressive era reform. Women were involved both as investors and as social workers and managers within the buildings sponsored by investor philanthropists.

Public Policy Reform: Regulating the Slums

Despite these well-intended efforts, the overall number of model tenement units was a drop in the bucket compared with the housing needs of the poor. Few wealthy capitalists were attracted to the limited dividend approach. Most of the urban poor continued to live in squalid, overcrowded slums, built and owned primarily by small entrepreneurs who made a significant profit—from 6 to 18 percent on their investment (Lubove 1962:39). In 1910 Lawrence Vellier pointed out that during the previous forty years in Manhattan alone, investor philanthropists had created twenty-five groups of model tenements, housing only 3,588 families or 17,940 persons. At the same time, speculative builders had constructed 27,100 tenements, holding 253,510 families, or over one million people (Lubove 1962:175).

Most housing reformers, therefore, pushed for stricter government *regulation* of privately owned housing to improve the living conditions of the poor—a part of the broader progressive era movement to regulate private enterprise (Ehrenreich 1985; Katz 1986). Some reformers, like Veiller, who was the most effective of the early housing reformers, organized private committees and municipal task forces to expose the problem and pressure local governments to adopt building, health, fire, and other safety codes. They pushed local and state governments to set up agencies to inspect buildings and enforce the codes. They dueled with lobbyists for builders and landlords. They formed watchdog groups, composed of wealthy and influential people, to making sure that these government departments were doing their job. In response to this pressure, in 1893 Congress asked Carroll D. Wright, commissioner of the U.S. Bureau of Labor, to do a statistical study of slum conditions in Chicago, Baltimore, and New York.

From the 1860s through the 1920s, cities and states across the country incrementally improved minimum housing code standards. The major achievement of these early housing reformers was the New York Tenement Law of 1901, written by Vellier, that "set strict standards for ventilation, fireproofing, overcrowding, private sanitary facilities, basement apartments, and courtyard dimensions" (Wright 1981:129). In fact, Vellier's work sparked a national housing reform movement. As head of the Tenement House Commission of the Charity Organization Society of New York, Vellier worked closely with many wealthy and influential people. One of his closest allies was Robert W. DeForest, a New York aristocrat and philanthropist who at various times served as president of the Charity Organization Society, founder of the New York School of Social Work, president of the Russell Sage Foundation, chairman of the state's Tenement House Commission, and (with Vellier as his deputy) first commissioner of New York City's Tenement House Department. Vellier used this network to spread his ideas across the country. Throughout the progressive era, groups had formed in cities outside New York to reform municipal housing law. But Vellier helped pull them together into a national force. He did surveys and wrote articles about slum housing conditions in other cities. He taught reformers in these cities how to set up watchdog groups and enact housing reform laws.

Thanks in part to this work, many other cities and states followed New York's lead in adopting stronger housing codes. In 1910, with a grant from the Russell Sage Foundation, Vellier formed the National Housing Association, which held annual meetings, published pamphlets for popular consumption, and sponsored a quarterly journal, *Housing Betterment*. He became its executive director and convinced DeForest to serve as president (Lubove 1962:144). These reforms made a significant improvement in slum housing conditions and helped to reduce the number of fires and the threat of epidemics of contagious diseases, such as tuberculosis. To this day, the enforcement of housing codes and the strengthening of existing standards are a key battleground in the struggle for decent housing.

Housing Reform from the Depression to the 1970s

Even during the progressive era, however, some housing reformers recognized the shortcomings of the care-giving approach, the model tenement approach, and the housing regulation approach. Many model tenements turned into slums because working class people could not pay sufficient rent to guarantee even a modest profit to the investor philanthropists.[2] Similarly, stricter housing code standards, while improving the physical condition of buildings, led builders and landlords to set rents beyond what many workers could afford. Some kind of government subsidy was required to fill the gap. As reformer Edith Wood observed, housing regulation "may forbid the bad house, but it does not provide the good one" (cited in Radford 1996:31).

Until the depression, housing reformers—planners, architects, economists, social workers, and others—who advocated federal government involvement were lonely voices in the political wilderness. The depression helped make the reformers' point that the private market, even assisted by private philanthropy and charity, could not solve the economic and housing problems of the poor. Some of the earlier progressive era housing reformers like Edith Wood, joined by a younger generation of activists like Catherine Bauer, pushed for a strong government-led response to housing problems. Along with the labor union movement, they lobbied for a public housing program, union-sponsored cooperative housing, and new communities guided by cooperative principles. The private real estate industry opposed these initiatives, viewing them as the first steps toward "creeping socialism," but they supported federal policies to promote homeownership and homebuilding, to stabilize the banking industry, and to give private developers incentives to house the poor. The New Deal and later Great Society housing programs were thus compromises between these political forces (Lubove 1962; Wright 1981; Marcuse 1986; Hays 1995; Oberlander and Newbrun 1995; Radford 1996).

The period from the depression through the 1970s represents the next phase of American housing history, one in which the federal government played an increasing role and private philanthropy played a less visible role. It did so primarily by promoting private bank lending to developers and homeowners, as well as by providing subsidies to local public housing authorities and private developers for low-income and moderate-income housing. In one way or another, all housing policy through the 1970s was a variation of these themes.

The tenement reform laws had set the precedent that *local* government would set standards and regulate housing safety. Beginning in the 1930s, the public housing program and banking reforms established the *federal* government's role in expanding homeownership and providing subsidies to the poor (Radford 1996). All housing policy since then has been a variation of these themes. Federal policies stabilized the banking industry, giving lenders greater incentives to make long-term loans to home buyers. During World War II, the federal government's focus was on regulating rental housing as part of the wartime emergency. After World War II, Federal Housing Administration and Veterans Administration mortgage insurance, along with federal highway programs, promoted increasing homeownership and suburbanization, especially among white middle-class families. The Fair Housing Act of 1968 initiated the federal government's role in monitoring and attempting to reduce racial discrimination in housing.

Some federally subsidized housing developments during this period were undertaken by a new generation of limited dividend corporations, but—unlike their predecessors—these relied on government subsidies and tax breaks. There was no pretense of a philanthropic impulse. Two early examples, built in the 1940s by the Metropolitan Life Insurance for moderate-income families, are Peter Cooper Village and Stuyvesant Town in New York City. In response to the civil rights movement and urban unrest, the 1960s witnessed a new round of federally subsidized rental housing. Some labor unions sponsored nonprofit cooperative housing projects, utilizing their pension funds as well as federal housing subsidies.

During this period, national housing policy was based on the belief that the federal government could help solve the nation's housing problems. Conservatives, liberals, and radicals debated how much the government should spend and how much it should regulate lenders, landlords, and real estate agents. But they agreed on the basic premise that Washington had a key role to play. For example, Senator Robert Taft (R–Ohio), a leading conservative, was co-sponsor of the 1949 Housing Act, which pledged to guarantee every American decent housing. Every president between FDR and Jimmy Carter, Democrats and Republicans alike, increased federal housing assistance.

During this period of government activism, private philanthropy played a less conspicuous role in housing issues until the 1960s, when it served as a catalyst for the federal war on poverty. The Ford Foundation was the first large philanthropy to focus its attention and resources on poverty and slum conditions in the northern ghettoes. Its first initiative was the Gray Areas Project, which devoted $12 million a year in the early 1960s to improve job training and education in several northern black slums. The largest Gray Areas Project grant went to Mobilization for Youth (MFY), an antipoverty organization on the lower east side of New York City. MFY not only offered training and educational services, it also hired organizers to mobilize low-income residents to take political action—for example, to organize rent strikes against slum landlords. Conservative critics charged that the Ford Foundation was financing radicalism (Lemann 1991; Ford Foundation 1989).

The support of the Ford Foundation gave MFY enough credibility to apply for, and receive, funds from the federal government, which was then, under President Kennedy, launching a cautious antipoverty program, initially with the mandate to reduce juvenile delinquency in the slums. Much of Kennedy's (and, more generously funded, President Johnson's) war on poverty was based on the Ford-funded Mobilization for Youth model of "community action." But, as Lemann notes, MFY faced a dilemma: "Confrontational tactics could imperil its existence, because it was dependent on the largesse of the power structure it intended to confront" (Lemann 1991:123).

The War on Poverty had adopted the Gray Areas Project view that poverty was a symptom of social and physical environments, not the personal failings of the poor themselves. Based on this view, the solution was to improve the physical environment by improving the slums (especially slum housing) and by mobilizing the poor to gain political power and to control ghetto institutions, such as schools, businesses, and social agencies.

The controversy around the Gray Areas Project made the Ford Foundation somewhat cautious. Although it has continued to support a variety of social movement organizations involved in voter registration, civil rights, and other concerns, its primary urban focus for the past thirty years has been attacking the physical deterioration of America's ghettoes by supporting nonprofit, community-based development organizations.

In 1964, Ford granted $575,000 to Urban America (later called the Nonprofit Housing Center). In 1967 Ford made its first direct grant to a community development corporation—the Bedford-Stuyvesant Restoration Corporation in the Brooklyn borough of New York. Around the same time, Ford provided grants to community development corporations (CDCs) in the Watts section of Los Angeles and the Woodlawn area of Chicago. In 1970 Ford expanded its CDC program, including grants to Hispanic organizations in San Antonio and Oakland. By the end of the 1970s, Ford's largesse was spread to CDCs in urban and rural areas, and in black, white, Native American, and Hispanic neighbor-hoods. Ford's success led the federal government—reacting also to the urban riots, civil disobedience, and climate of political protest—to initiate a pilot pro-gram to support CDCs, Title VII of the Community Services Act of 1972.

In 1972 Ford also began providing grants to two other housing initiatives in America's troubled cities. The Neighborhood Housing Services (NHS) program brought neighborhood leaders together with local government officials and banks to address the problem of redlining and housing decay. Based on a model of cooperation rather than confrontation, local NHS chapters sought to get banks to make loans to low-income and working-class homeowners to make repairs (thus stemming neighborhood decline) and to get local governments enforce housing code violations by landlords. The NHS program grew signifi-cantly, especially after 1980, when the federal government chartered the Neigh-borhood Reinvestment Corporation to provide direct support to NHS groups.

The other Ford initiative that year was the creation of Tenant Management Corporations (TMCs) in public housing. The idea was to put residents in charge of managing their own housing projects. Ford officials hoped that this would improve the day-to-day operation of public housing and prevent further blight. The TMC program combined an emphasis on physical redevelopment and tenant self-help mobilization. The Ford grants did not include funds for physical repairs, but the foundation believed that by giving tenants a stronger voice in management, the TMCs would pressure local housing authorities and, in turn, the federal government, to devote more funds to upgrade public hous-ing projects. Ford gave the first grant to the Tenant Affairs Board in St. Louis, the site of the most infamous public housing project in the country, Pruitt-Igoe. Between 1972 and 1979, Ford gave $1.7 million to TMCs around the country. Encouraged by Ford's experience, HUD set up a demonstration program to fund TMCs in six cities, run by the Manpower Demonstration Research Cor-poration. These experiments in tenant management had mixed success and the demonstration program was not continued beyond its initial funding. In the 1980s, however, the Reagan and Bush administrations, prompted by Congress-man (later HUD Secretary) Jack Kemp, embraced the idea of tenant manage-ment and, going further, tenant ownership, of public housing.

Philanthropic Responses to Homelessness

During the 1980s, the transformation to a postindustrial economy and the erosion of public benefits drove down U.S. wages and incomes. For the first time in the postwar period, the majority of American workers—includ-ing many white-collar and professional employees—saw their incomes decline (Mishel and Bernstein 1993). Poverty rates increased and poverty became more geographically concentrated.[3] The number of low-cost apartments dwindled, much of it lost to the urban renewal bulldozer, condominium conversion, and gentrification.[4] Rent burdens worsened, especially for the poor.[5] Millions of Americans lived doubled up or tripled up in overcrowded apartments. Millions more paid more than they could reasonably afford for substandard housing—one emergency (rent increase, hospital stay, layoff) away from becoming homeless.

While private market forces were reducing low-rent apartments, the federal government was slashing housing assistance to the poor, reversing a trend begun in the New Deal. Soon after Ronald Reagan entered the White House in 1981 he set up a task force to examine federal housing policy. Dominated by bankers and developers, the task force concluded that Washington was too involved with housing regulations and subsidies, and called for a new approach based on "free and deregulated markets." During the next twelve years the Reagan and Bush administrations sought, with partial success, to follow this "privatization" blueprint. The Reagan administration reduced the annual HUD budget from $30 billion to $9 billion. By the late 1980s, only 29 percent of the 13.8 million low-income renter households eligible for federal assistance received any housing subsidy—the lowest level of any industrial nation in the world. This left the rest of poor households at the mercy of the private housing market, facing swelling waiting lists for even the most deteriorated subsidized housing projects (Casey 1992; Lazere et al. 1991; Interagency Council on Homelessness 1994; Joint Center for Housing Studies 1994; U.S. HUD 1994).

The homeless were the most tragic victims of these trends. By moderate accounts, including an Urban Institute report, by the late 1980s, the ranks of the homeless swelled to 600,000 on any given night and 1.2 million over the course of a year. Shelters reported that demand for their services increased by about 20 percent a year during the 1980s (Appelbaum et al. 1991; Blau 1992; Burt 1992; U.S. Conference of Mayors 1993; Link et al. 1994; Newman 1995).[6]

Although exact figures are unavailable, it is clear that many foundations were stirred to address this increasingly visible problem. By 1987 a survey of 130 large corporations found that homelessness ranked sixth in philanthropic giving (Blau 1992:95). During the 1990s, foundation giving for "housing and shelter" has remained steady at between 1.2 percent and 1.4 percent of all grant-making. In 1990 foundations allocated $58 million in this category, 1.3 percent of all dollars; in 1995, the absolute figure had increased to $77 million, or 1.2 percent of the total (the Foundation Center 1996a and 1996b).[7] Like the upper-class philanthropists and reformers of the progressive era, the modern-day foundations responded to this social crisis in three basic ways: caring-giving, model housing development, and public policy reform.

Care-Giving: Shelters and Soup Kitchens

The vast majority of foundations that sought to address housing problems focused on efforts to provide immediate relief to and to help "rehabilitate" homeless people. Foundations provided grants to social agencies to start or expand shelters for individuals and families, soup kitchens, drug and alcohol treatment programs, health programs, and counseling services for mentally ill persons. The number of shelters for homeless people—sponsored by religious groups, social service agencies, community organizations, and other institutions—grew dramatically.

The largest initiative within this approach was the Health Care for the Homeless program funded jointly by Robert Wood Johnson Foundation of New Jersey and the Pew Memorial Trust of Philadelphia. The two funders provided $25 million over five years to nineteen cities to establish comprehensive and coordinated health care programs for homeless people. The two foundations viewed their program as "seed money," hoping that after the five-year grant was completed, local governments and funders would continue the programs.

Some foundations preferred to support various forms of specialized housing that address the problems of homeless people with special needs. These include transitional housing and rooming houses. The nonprofit sponsors of these projects often included a variety of job training, literacy, parenting, drug and alcohol treatment, and other programs, designed to help homeless individuals become more self-confident and independent. CDCs were often not equipped or interested in undertaking these projects, so a different breed of nonprofit group emerged, specializing in these housing–plus–services programs. Groups created thousands of such projects around the country. With funding from several local foundations, the Pine Street Inn, Boston's oldest and largest shelter, started a subsidiary called the Sullivan Lodging Trust to create a series of small rooming houses that could provide support services as well as low-rent housing. Denver's Piton Foundation provided grant support to create a transitional housing program for homeless women and children, many of them victims of domestic violence.

Some critics complained that the nation was creating a new "shelter industry" that had a stake in the continuation of homelessness. Critics also complained that by focusing the response primarily on emergency services and treatment, funders were stigmatizing the homeless, attributing their suffering to personal pathology, and downplaying the role of public policy and market forces in the growth of poverty and destitution.

Model Housing: Expanding the Nonprofit Sector

Like their philanthropic predecessors, the foundations' second approach to the housing and homelessness crisis of the 1980s was to encourage the development of affordable low-income housing rather than emergency shelter and individualized treatment. The sharp decline in federal assistance for low-income housing and the decrease in the nation's inventory of low-rent apartments during the 1980s led many foundations to focus on increasing the overall supply of affordable housing.

The major vehicle for this approach was foundations' growing support for Community Development Corporations, pioneered by the Ford Foundation in the 1960s. Most CDCs favor the construction and repair of apartments and cooperatives, not emergency shelter or specialized housing. In most other industrial nations, the "third sector" plays a key role in the provision of housing and human services (Schill 1994; Salamon 1995). In the U.S., this sector has been relatively small and isolated, but during the 1980s it began to become more professionalized, sophisticated, and mainstream (Mayer 1990; Peirce and Steinbach 1990; Vidal 1992, 1995; Dreier and Hulchanski 1993; Goetz 1993; Sullivan 1993; Walker 1993; Bratt, Keyes, Schwartz, and Vidal 1994; Rubin 1994; Schill 1994; Urban Institute 1994; Committee for Economic Development 1995; Harrison et al. 1995; Steinbach 1995).

In the 1980s, the Ford Foundation helped catalyze a renewed interest by private philanthropy in CDCs. Its most enduring housing initiative was its creation of the Local Initiatives Support Corporation (LISC) in 1979. LISC became the major catalyst for the dramatic expansion of CDCs throughout the United States. A year later, the Enterprise Foundation was founded by developer James Rouse to undertake similar projects. Both LISC and Enterprise serve two major purposes. They have used their establishment networks to get major corporations, banks, local governments, and local community foundations to provide operating support, loans, and equity to CDCs and their housing developments. They also provide technical assistance to CDCs to help improve their development, management, and fund-raising skills.

One of the primary revenue sources for funding CDC-sponsored housing is the federal Low-Income Housing Tax Credit (LIHTC), created by Congress in 1986, to encourage private investment in low-income rental housing by giving corporations tax breaks for investing in these projects. In some ways, it is comparable to the "investment philanthropy" of the progressive era. Organizations such as LISC and Enterprise Foundation not only serve as conduits between the corporate investors and CDCs, they also help these corporations obtain considerable good will and positive publicity. Corporations—especially banks that need to demonstrate their commitment to low-income areas under the federal Community Reinvestment Act—use the LIHTC as evidence of their community involvement. In fact, investors earn a healthy return on their investment, often 15 to 20 percent; it is hardly philanthropy.

The success of LISC and Enterprise, in particular, led other national and local foundations to invest in CDCs as a vehicle to rebuild inner-city ghettoes and troubled rural communities.[8] Overall, America's foundations have dramatically increased their support for community-based development, mostly for housing and, to a lesser extent, commercial projects. In 1987, 196 foundations and corporations (usually through corporate foundations) made grants totaling almost $68 million to support nonprofit development. By 1991 the numbers had grown to 512 funders and $179 million. In the latter year, 53 of the nation's 100 largest foundations provided grant support for community-based development. Between 1987 and 1991 many small and large foundations dramatically increased (or initiated) their support for community development. The list of grantors reads like a Who's Who of American business and philanthropy.[9]

The growth of foundation support for these projects led to the formation in 1986 of the Council for Community-based Development, a national umbrella group of major funders. Its primary goal was to expand private sector funding of CDCs and other community-based development activities.[10] Several of the largest funders formed a Neighborhood Funders Group (NFG), which sponsors conferences to discuss their common concerns.

The foundations' growing investment in CDCs helped change the attitude of local United Way organizations. In most cities, the United Way is the major charity, raising funds primarily by soliciting donations from employees at their workplaces. United Way boards are dominated by top executives from local businesses. As a result, United Way allocations have tended to be very mainstream and unlikely to fund organizations that "rock the boat."[11]

Protests by community groups in the late 1970s and 1980s helped change some of United Way practices. More community representatives were added to local United Way boards and more community-oriented and activist-oriented groups (from battered women's shelters, to tenants' rights organizations, to community groups fighting redlining or housing discrimination) were funded. During the 1980s, some United Ways started funding shelters for the homeless and CDCs. The pioneer in this direction was Boston's United Way, which joined with LISC to create the Neighborhood Development Support Collaborative to provide CDCs (which often survive on hand-to-mouth budgets and from project to project) with multiyear operating grants. By 1992 a survey conducted by United Way of America found that over 70 local United Ways were supporting community-based development. Inspired by the Boston program, and encouraged by a Ford Foundation grant, the United Way of America launched its own national Housing Initiative in 1988.[12]

Despite this impressive shift in emphasis, the large and increasing dollar figures associated with foundations' support for community development can be misleading. In fact, most foundations allocate a tiny part of their grants in this area. In 1987, for example, grants for this purpose represented only 2.4 percent of all foundation giving. More traditional philanthropic goals—such as higher education, medical research, art, music, theater, and dance—received considerably more foundation support. Most of these grants are targeted to institutions that cater to more affluent Americans, such as symphony orchestras, art museums, and private colleges. The Ford Foundation's $26.5 million represented 10 percent of its overall grants in 1991. The Kellogg Foundation's $5.5 million represented 2 percent of its giving, while the Rockefeller Foundation's $1.43 million represented 1 percent of its total allocation. Some foundations focus much of their attention on community development. For example, the McKnight Foundation's $24.6 million in this area represented 53 percent of its entire giving. The Northwest Area Foundation's $5.5 million was 47 percent of all its grants. In 1993, the Fannie Mae Foundation committed 52 percent of its $8.3 million grant allocations in this area.

Public Policy Reform: Advocacy and Grassroots Organizing

Starting in the 1980s, a small number of foundations sought to address the root causes of homelessness. They focused their grant-giving on changing public policy to address the deepening problems of poverty, the shortage of housing, and urban neighborhood decay. Like their counterparts earlier in the century, they funded the growing number of groups that sought to advocate for and organize the homeless and the poor. These included umbrella coalitions of church groups, shelter and service providers, and housing activists as well as self-help groups among the homeless themselves.[13] These advocacy and self-help groups, along with big-city mayors, shelter providers and others, became a major voice for increasing public sector funding for housing subsidies, shelters, counseling and treatment programs, and health care services.

A growing number of foundations began to recognize that solving the root causes of America's housing crisis, rather than simply addressing its symptoms, requires significant changes in government policy and major reform of market forces that create a wide gap between incomes and housing prices. This was the key finding of a Boston Foundation survey conducted in 1992 of 312 foundations involved in grant-making on housing and homelessness projects. The study found that the majority (53 percent) of these philanthropic organizations said that grant-making to promote changes in public policy, rather than to provide social services, education, and job training (32 percent), or to provide rehabilitation and treatment for drug and alcohol abuse (16 percent), best reflected their overall grant-making strategy. None of the funders surveyed said that the best approach was for private charity to provide emergency services such as food and shelter.

The survey's original sample of 750 foundations was skewed toward philanthropies already concerned with housing and homelessness problems.[14] So perhaps it is not surprising that, according to the report, "most funders surveyed believe that advocacy and public policy initiatives ultimately have the greatest impact on overall prevention of homelessness."

But the survey found that, even among these concerned foundations, a serious gap existed between their beliefs and their practice. More than half (52 percent) supported direct services to the homeless and 48 percent supported specialized housing. Thirty-seven percent supported housing development (primarily sponsored by CDCs and other nonprofit organizations) although these grants tend to be larger. Only 33 percent supported organizing and advocacy, some of which primarily involves research (McCambridge 1992). In other words, these foundations actually made few grants to groups to mobilize people or advocate for major changes in public policy.

If even these concerned foundations rarely support organizations engaged in advocacy and organizing, it should not be surprising that foundations in general are reluctant to do so. In 1989 only 16 percent of all foundation grants for housing were specifically designated for what the survey called "organizing or advocacy" activities. By 1991 the proportion targeted for these activities had declined to 7 percent of all grants (Council on Community-Based Development 1989 and 1991).

A few major foundations, such as the Boston Foundation, Surdna Foundation, and the Wieboldt Foundation, devoted a considerable portion of their overall funding to advocacy and organizing on housing and related issues. The Ford Foundation allocated a relatively small part of its community-based housing funds for organizing and advocacy, but because it is so large, even this small proportion was quite sizable. For example, in 1991, Ford joined several other major national funders to provide the National Low Income Housing Coalition with a three-year, $3 million grant to help influence public policy, primarily by building state housing coalitions in twelve states to monitor the allocation of federal housing funds.[15]

If there was a silver lining during the 1980s housing crisis, it was the emergence of locally based efforts to address housing needs. These forces gained momentum in part as a result of the growing visibility of homelessness, but sought to address wider housing problems. This fledgling grassroots housing movement was composed of tenant groups, homeless advocacy organizations, fair housing and fair lending groups, church-based institutions, community-based nonprofit developers, neighborhood associations, and some senior citizen groups, women's organizations, and civil rights groups. These groups, many of them supported by private foundations and philanthropies, spent much of the 1980s decade working—primarily on the local and state levels—to plug some of the gaps left by the federal government's withdrawal from housing programs (Nenno 1991; Nenno and Colyer 1988; National Low Income Housing Coalition 1995; Goetz 1993). These groups were part of a remarkable resurgence of citizen activism in urban neighborhoods involving tens of thousands of neighborhood organizations engaged in a wide range of community improvement efforts (Boyte 1980, 1989; Berry, Portney, and Thompson 1993).

These community-based housing groups pressured local governments to protect tenants against unfair evictions. They lobbied for stricter enforcement of health and safety codes, and for "linked deposit" and "linked development" policies. They published reports to dramatize the plight of the homeless, the widening gap between incomes and housing prices, and the continuing practice of bank redlining. They persuaded banks to open branches in minority neighborhoods and increase available mortgage loans for low-income consumers. They pressured and worked with city and state housing agencies to expand available funds for affordable housing and to target more assistance to nonprofit community development groups to fix up abandoned buildings and construct new homes for the poor.

In some cities, the mosaic of housing organizations forged coalitions to work together around a common agenda. In a few cities—Boston, Chicago, San Francisco, Pittsburgh, and elsewhere—they played important roles in helping elect progressive pro-housing candidates to public office (Clavel 1986; Clavel and Wiewel 1991; Metzger 1992; Berry, Portney, and Thompson 1993; DeLeon 1992; Dreier 1993b; Davis 1994; Krumholz and Clavel 1994). In a growing number of cities, grassroots community-based housing organizations have formed partnerships and alliances with municipal governments and business groups. They developed a wide range of innovative local programs and strategies to cope with the impact of federal housing cutbacks and changes in local housing markets. Foundations played a key role in catalyzing these partnerships (Suchman 1990; Keyes, Schwartz, Vidal, and Bratt 1996).

In several states, advocacy organizations representing the homeless, tenants, seniors, and others forged statewide housing coalitions to push for progressive housing policy. Under pressure from housing activists, many state and local governments began identifying new resources for housing assistance and initiated new housing programs that involved new construction, rehabilitation, neighborhood revitalization, housing mobility, and other concerns (Nenno and Colyer 1988; Brooks 1989; Peirce and Steinbach 1990; Suchman 1990; Nenno 1991; Goetz 1993; Davis 1994; National Low Income Housing Coalition 1995).

During the 1980s, the number of local housing groups mushroomed, and they scored many local victories. But their work was primarily defensive—brushfire battles to keep things from getting worse. Their overall impact—in terms of preventing displacement and improving the day-to-day housing conditions for America's poor and working families and elderly citizens—was relatively small. The reason is not hard to fathom. As the decade progressed, the growing fiscal crises of cities and states made it increasingly difficult to squeeze housing resources out of mayors and city councils, county supervisors, governors, and state legislatures. Most states began cutting their housing budgets. It was increasingly clear that only at the federal level did enough resources exist to seriously address the housing crisis.[16]

At the national level, housing advocates not only confronted opposition from the White House, but they also encountered an increasingly hostile ideological climate that opposed the very idea of government activism. Nevertheless, they scored some victories. They successfully pushed to enact the Stewart B. McKinney Homeless Assistance Act in 1987. Each year the act was expanded to incorporate new programs—rent subsidies for lodging houses, funds to continue and expand local Health Care for the Homeless projects, transitional housing with supportive services, adult literacy, job training, and others. They helped enact and then preserve the Low Income Housing Tax Credit, a program to promote investment in low-income rental housing. Most of the projects created under this program have been sponsored by nonprofit community-based organizations. Housing advocacy groups also helped pass legislation to protect the existing inventory of federally subsidized housing developments. They had been threatened by the potential withdrawal of subsidies as their low-income "use restrictions" expired in the 1980s. Perhaps the most impressive federal victory was the strengthening of the Community Reinvestment Act, a result both of local activism around the issue of redlining *and* increasing coordination of efforts.[17] The entire community reinvestment climate has changed dramatically since the mid-1980s.[18]

Philanthropy played a key role in these small but important victories. Several major foundations, including Ford and Surdna, made a major investment in community organizations and networks engaged in antiredlining work. Foundation-supported intermediary groups, such as LISC, Enterprise, and the National Housing Trust, helped coordinate national efforts, targeted at Congress and the media, to protect the Low Income Housing Tax Credit and to preserve HUD-assisted housing developments. Local and national foundations provided grants to advocacy groups working on homelessness issues. The Washington-based Villers Foundation (now called Families USA) played a critical role when it agreed to provide a one-time $100,000 grant for a national demonstration to focus national attention on homelessness, the Housing Now! march in October 1989.

These patterns of philanthropic support for housing advocacy and organizing reflect the patterns in the larger foundation world. Funding for grassroots activism—what Jenkins (1989 and 1996) calls "social movement philanthropy"—is a small but important niche in the nation's philanthropic community.[19]

Nielsen (1985:423) noted that major foundations are devoted to "social continuity, not change." Not surprisingly, few fund social movement organizations. Among those that do, one can identify three kinds of social movement funders. First, there are relatively small foundations that specialize in social movement philanthropy. These are typically family foundations (where the original donors still remain active) and "alternative" foundations (a network of social change-oriented foundations established by wealthy donors but who assign control to community funding boards).[20] Second are religious-based funders, some of which devote a substantial proportion of their grant-making to social activist groups. The most prominent among these is the Catholic Church's Campaign for Human Development.[21] Third, large mainstream foundations, including corporate foundations and community foundations, typically provide a relatively small proportion of their grants to social movement organizations.

Social movement philanthropy began in the early 1950s with three family foundations—the Field Foundation, the Emil Schwartzhaupt Foundation, and the Wiebolt Foundation—that focused their grant-making on civil rights (both protest and litigation-oriented groups) and community organizing. By the late 1950s, nine more funders joined the ranks, adding grassroots voter registration, a component of the civil rights movement, to their agendas.[22] The 1960s saw the entry of large mainstream foundations (such as Ford, Carnegie, Rockefeller, Sloan, and Lilly) into the social movement field. In addition to support for civil rights and community organizing, they expanded their grant-making to areas such as women's rights, the environment and consumer protection, peace, and urban poverty. In 1970, 65 foundations provided 311 grants and $11 million for social movement activities, a figure that was over thirty-two times the movement funding in 1960, adjusting for inflation (Jenkins and Halcli 1996). The number of social movement funders grew in the 1970s, but the inflation-adjusted level of funding declined.

Jenkins (1989: 294) found that between 1953 and 1980, "out of more than 22,000 active grant-giving foundations, only 131 funded a social movement project."[23] During that period, foundation giving to social movements accounted for only 0.24 percent of total foundation giving. The peak year during that period was 1977, when social movement philanthropy accounted for 0.69 percent of all grantmaking, or $24.1 million.

Both the number of grantmakers and the overall grant dollars expanded in the 1980s. In 1990, 146 foundations invested over $88 million in social movement projects. This represented 1.1 percent of total foundation giving. These facts led Jenkins and Halcli (1996) to conclude that social movement philanthropy had become "a tiny but institutionalized factor in American society."[24]

Philanthropy and the Housing Movement: A Partnership Agenda

What lessons can we learn from the experience of philanthropy's efforts to address housing problems? This review underscores the limits of both the care-giving work and the model housing approaches. The first approach focuses on individual needs, but does not recognize the social causes of poverty and urban distress. The second approach provides support for innovative housing development, but does not recognize the realities of housing economics, especially for the poor.

As reformers like Edith Wood and Catherine Bauer recognized several generations ago, there is a limit to what philanthropists can realistically accomplish without renewed involvement and greater resources from the public sector—particularly the federal government. It is critical to address the shortage of public resources targeted for housing. That can occur only through advocacy and organizing. Progressive housing policy has made the most headway when housing activism is part of a movement for social change. But it is precisely these efforts that most major foundations have been reluctant to support. If the philanthropic community is to play an effective role in addressing the housing crisis, this reluctance has to change.

America's housing crisis is fundamentally about affordability—the gap between housing costs and household incomes. It requires money to fill the gap. For example, one study in the late 1980s calculated that it would cost $106 million a year to provide every low- and moderate-income renter household in Boston with enough subsidy to bring the rent down to 30 percent of household income, an amount far beyond the combined level of federal, state, and local subsidies for housing in the city (Stevens, Dreier, and Brown 1989). State and local regulatory mechanisms, such as zoning, can play some role in reducing production costs by streamlining development costs and increasing densities, but these actions are relatively marginal to the overall problem (Downs 1991). Cities and states simply lack the resources to fill much of this gap. America's cities now face a shrinking tax base and fiscal traumas (Ladd and Yinger 1989; Bahl 1994).

The victories won by housing advocacy and organizing groups during the past decade are small, almost pyrrhic, in light of the enormity of the nation's housing crisis. Today's philanthropists concerned about the decay of our cities and the shortage of affordable housing confront a dilemma similar to their counterparts around the turn of the century. The nation's housing crisis has deepened as the federal government has withdrawn from the affordable housing field, and as many local and state governments have reached the limits of their fiscal capacities to fund low-income housing. In this environment, foundations are being asked to fill a bigger and bigger vacuum.

Foundations have succeeded in helping to expand the capacity of community-based housing developers, whose numbers and sophistication have grown dramatically during the 1980s and early 1990s. But these groups cannot produce even close to an adequate supply of housing for the poor, primarily because of the lack of subsidies that fill the gap between what it costs to develop housing and what the poor can afford to pay. Even the most generous estimates indicate that the nation's CDC sector has produced only 30,000 to 40,000 housing units a year during the past decade, a far cry from the need (Steinbach 1995). This is not due primarily to the lack of capacity (although that is a problem in some areas), but to the lack of funds to subsidize more projects.[25] The public resources

needed for these groups to expand housing—to "make the numbers work"—
are nowhere close to the need.

As Lew Finfer, a long-time organizer and founder of the philanthropy-
supported Massachusetts Affordable Housing Alliance, observed:

> In two years, a nonprofit developer might build 200 units of housing, while
> around him 500 units are lost through abandonment or higher rents. If devel-
> opment is not tied to advocacy and community organizing, it's incomplete.
> Unless that's part of the strategy, we'll continue to lose ground. (Quoted in
> Greene 1989)

How should the philanthropic sector invest its valuable resources most cost-
effectively to address the nation's housing problems? It is critical for the foundation world to help reverse the declining support for federal housing assistance.
This doesn't mean supporting an agenda that emphasizes "more of the same"—
that is, simply expanding current federal housing programs, many of which are
wasteful and inefficient. It means helping to rebuild the political constituency for
federal housing support around a new policy agenda that can marshal broad support. The key to solving our nation's housing crisis is to expand and strengthen
the constituency for a progressive national housing policy that can link the needs
of the poor and the concerns of the middle class. Doing so requires strengthening the organizations that can mobilize their constituencies and, equally important, coordinating these organizational efforts into a coherent strategy that can
make an impact on public opinion and public policy (Dreier 1997).

To do this effectively, foundations must recognize the current political realities surrounding national housing policy and to honestly assess the current state
of the housing advocacy movement.

The hard truth is that the nation's housing crisis is still a marginal issue in
American politics. For example, when journalists for major national newspapers
and news magazines write about key domestic problems—or where the major
candidates stand on the major issues—the list always includes the economy,
crime, the environment, welfare, and education. With a few exceptions (such as
DeParle 1996), however, they rarely include the plight of our cities in general
or housing in particular.

When housing policy *does* get on the political screen, it revolves around
HUD, which these days hardly anyone can be found to defend. "Politically,
HUD is about as popular as smallpox," reported the *Washington Post* (Gugliotta
1995). This is due, in part, to widely-held stereotypes about public housing.[26] In
a speech before the National Association of Realtors in April, Republican presidential candidate Robert Dole labeled public housing "one of the last bastion's
of socialism in the world" and said that local housing authorities have become
"landlords of misery." A few weeks later, Rep. Rick Lazio (R-N.Y.), chair of

the house subcommittee on housing, attacked "the hulks of failure that characterize high-rise public housing." A variety of conservative pundits and Republican politicians opposed the new "Moving to Opportunity" program—a small pilot program to help the ghetto poor find apartments in better neighborhoods—as "social engineering" (Dreier and Moberg, 1996). House Speaker Newt Gingrich told the *Washington Post*, "You could abolish HUD tomorrow morning and improve life in most of America" (Cooper 1994). Senator Lauch Faircloth of North Carolina, chair of the HUD oversight subcommittee, filed legislation to eliminate the agency, asserting, "I think we need to put this department to rest" (Housing Affairs Letter 1995).

Moreover, the political constituency for housing policy is weaker and more fragmented now than it has been in decades (Dreier 1997). Indeed, Gingrich was candid about the reasons for HUD's vulnerability. Its "weak political constituency," he told the *Washington Post* in December 1994, "makes it a prime candidate for cuts." Housing policy is viewed as a narrow "special interest" concern—big city-mayors, developers, and do-gooder groups—rather than as part of the broad social contract. It is viewed primarily as a "social welfare" issue rather than as a key component of the nation's economic well-being.

Many housing activists hoped that the Clinton administration would not only stem, but reverse, the tide. But Clinton was elected in 1992 without a majority mandate. He received only 43 percent of the overall vote. Equally important, his own party, while capturing a majority of the seats in Congress, was deeply divided, with many members closely linked to big business interests who oppose progressive taxation, Keynesian pump-priming, and social spending. Congress defeated two of the Clinton administration's early priorities—a major public investment program and health care reform—both of which would have had a significant impact on the problems of the poor and the cities. In housing policy, Clinton's first two years saw an increase in HUD's budget, revisions in some long-standing policies on public housing and housing mobility, a pilot "empowerment zone" program in several cities, and stronger anti-redlining enforcement.

After the November 1994 elections, the Republican majority in Congress appeared to be ready to complete the Reagan revolution in housing policy. In December 1994, in response to congressional threats to eliminate HUD altogether, President Clinton and HUD Secretary Henry Cisneros unveiled a plan to "reinvent" HUD, emphasizing streamlining and consolidating HUD's crazy-quilt programs and handing the funds over to states and cities. It also called for a dramatic cutback of HUD's mission by virtually eliminating federal funding for existing subsidized housing developments with about three million low-income apartments (Vanhorenbeck 1995). By the end of 1996, the Clinton administration and Congress had reached a stalemate. They reduced HUD's budget from $26 billion to $19 billion. This is 28 percent of the HUD budget in 1980 in constant dollars (Dolbeare 1996).[27] They also gave more authority to states and cities, and agreed to "privatize" some of HUD's functions.

Housing was barely an issue during the 1996 presidential election campaign. The Republican platform and presidential candidate Bob Dole called for the elimination of HUD. The outcome of the November 1996 election—with a Republican majority in Congress and many Democrats indifferent to housing concerns—does not bode well for federal housing policy. In the current political climate, HUD is likely to continue to face serious opposition. Moreover, in tandem with welfare reform, a bipartisan consensus is emerging to "devolve" federal housing funds to states and local governments, justified by the mantra that they "know best" how to craft programs and spend money to meet the diversity of local housing needs. State and local governments are being asked to do "more with less."[28]

This wasn't always the case. After World War II, federal housing policy had a broad political constituency: young families who wanted to buy homes, developers who wanted to build them, brokers and lenders who wanted to help them buy, and labor unions whose members wanted to buy homes and construct them. So long as federal policy helped the blue-collar working class achieve the middle-class American dream of home ownership, it was politically acceptable for Washington to build public housing for the poor as a temporary way-station on the road to upward mobility (Wright 1981; Hays 1995).

In the current political climate, it is critical for housing advocacy and organizing groups to mount effective campaigns to change public opinion and public policy—a long haul, not a quick fix. But the housing movement is in organizational disarray—and foundations have unwittingly exacerbated the situation by their practices. How can foundations identify effective housing organizations, networks, and issues so that can leverage their grant-making most productively?

An analysis of the housing movement reveals enormous commitment and talent, but an incredible degree of fragmentation. It is a mosaic of local, state, and national groups dedicated to improving housing conditions for poor and working-class people, but with little overall coherence and direction, and little sense of themselves as a "movement."

The lessons of the past two decades of local housing activism are sobering. Activists can put pressure on banks to stop redlining, force landlords to fix up slum buildings and stop rent gouging, and pressure local governments to target housing funds to nonprofit development organizations. But despite the existence of thousands of local grassroots community organizations, hundreds of statewide housing advocacy groups, and about a dozen national coalitions and networks engaged in housing issues, the whole of the housing movement is smaller than the sum of its parts. In large part this is because all these local efforts are fragmented, isolated from each other, and unable to build on each other.

Moreover, the various segments of the housing constituency often work at crosspurposes, lobbying for their own specific piece of the HUD pie, weakening the overall impact of their efforts, and undermining the likelihood of building broad support for federal housing programs.[29] With some exceptions, local community groups and even national organizations and networks that are essentially engaged in the same thing basically ignore each other's work rather than finding ways to work together strategically (Dreier 1996).

Most local and even state housing groups are only loosely tied together. As such, it is difficult to design a national agenda and a national strategy that can build from year to year. It is difficult to develop local and national leaders, to mobilize people around direct action, legislation or electoral campaigns, or to form lasting alliances.

No one expects the housing movement to overhaul national housing debate or policy overnight. On its own, a single-issue housing movement cannot be expected to make more than a small dent in national policy. But even within these limited expectations, the housing movement is relatively isolated. Moreover, as a movement, it has no strategy to move itself out of this isolated box.

The emergence and expansion of these specific advocacy groups in the 1980s was understandable. Each group, on its own, did work that needed to be done. Each group had its own organizing agenda. Each group had its own office, stationery, newsletter, and annual meeting. Each group had its own mailing list and fund-raising list. Each group held fund-raising events and applied to the same foundations for support. Each group hired staff and trained leaders to speak and organize on behalf of its constituents. Each group fought for federal, state, and local legislation to serve the needs of its constituency.

But activists and advocates, and their allies in the foundation world, can no longer afford the luxury of this fragmentation of effort—the "let a thousand flowers bloom" approach—that characterized the 1980s and early 1990s. In the current climate of fiscal crisis and government austerity, grassroots groups must work even harder—and in greater cooperation—to guarantee that the concerns of the needy are not lost in the political cacophony. In Congress and in state legislatures, for example, some legislators believe that the different low-income advocacy groups are working at crosspurposes, or that their priorities are mutually exclusive. Journalists often share this perception as well. The housing movement is weakened to the extent to which it is fragmented.

A choice is called for here: activist groups can either fight each other for the crumbs that remain as social program budgets are dismantled—*or they can decide to join forces and develop a common ground approach that will be more effective in addressing the needs of low-income and working-class people.

Like the housing movement, the foundation world is fragmented. There is no overall housing and community development strategy within the philanthropic world—even among those funders that support organizing and advocacy.[30] There are several problematic foundation practices that contribute to the fragmentation of grassroots organizing and advocacy groups.

First, foundations all have different guidelines, application forms, and funding cycles. Thus, grassroots and advocacy organizations are constantly rewriting and revising proposals to different foundations to do essentially the same thing. Second, most foundations like to provide "seed" funding to a group for a year, two, or three, and then withdraw, hoping that in that time the group has learned how to raise funds from its own members or other sources. This, of course, is an unrealistic expectation for organizations based in low-income neighborhoods, but it remains the guiding principle of many foundations. Third, most foundations want to get some credit for being innovative. Thus, they carve out a programmatic niche to demonstrate their distinctiveness. In the business world, this is called "product differentiation"—companies need to show why their brand of car or toothpaste is different and better than the products of their competitors. But foundations are not profit-maximizing corporations and this approach to grant-making can be burdensome to grassroots and advocacy organizations, who have to figure out what foundations are looking for and tell them what they want to hear without significantly changing their advocacy or organizing agenda. As a result of these foundation practices, grantee organizations spend an inordinate amount of their time "hustling" grants from a wide variety of foundations. This diverts their attention from their primary task of mobilizing and advocacy for the disenfranchised.

In other words, foundations concerned about housing and grassroots/ advocacy organizations have a common stake in getting their acts together. What is needed is a multiyear national effort to coordinate grassroots organizing, provide technical assistance to local and state housing activist groups, improve media coverage of housing issues, and expand public awareness of housing policy so that they can better educate their elected officials and expand the public resources available for housing programs.

A coordinated national campaign for affordable housing—linked to local and state advocacy—can succeed in reshaping national housing policy if foundations recognize that the key to a successful campaign is strategic advocacy. For housing advocacy to be more effective, the crazy-quilt of local, state, and national groups must become more coherent, more strategic, and more sophisticated.

America's foundations should begin to direct an increasing part of their resources toward supporting the development of the national organizational infrastructure and strategically planned campaign of public education that will galvanize both grassroots community and national leaders to devise an effective housing policy. This effort could make the American public, the media, and elected officials aware of, and willing to change, the inadequacies of national housing policy and resources.[31] The most effective way to target resources toward this goal is to focus grant-making on *intermediary organizations—national*

networks and organizing training centers. They should play a key role in any philanthropic commitment of housing advocacy.

There are two kinds of national networks. Some—including organiza-
tions like the National Coalition for the Homeless, the National Low-Income
Housing Coalition, the National Community Reinvestment Coalition, the
Center for Community Change, and the National Congress for Community
Economic Development—focus almost entirely on housing issues. Others—
such as ACORN, the Industrial Areas Foundation, Citizen Action, and
National People's Action—are multi-issue networks that focus on housing as
one of a number of priority issues.

The first group occasionally activates its loose affiliates of local housing
activists (tenants groups, homeless shelters, community and church organizations, nonprofit developers) to protect or expand federal housing programs for
the poor. They tend, however, to be engaged more in advocacy than in mobilization. The organizations in the second group are somewhat tighter national
federations with the capacity to mobilize their member groups around both
local and national issues simultaneously. ACORN, the Industrial Areas Foundation, and Citizen Action, in particular, have a strong "movement-building"
agenda and have some capacity to carry out a coherent strategy. These organizations and networks have different strengths and weaknesses—grassroots organizing, leadership development, research, legal advocacy, lobbying, media
relations, political, and strategy. Their strengths could compliment each other if
they worked cooperatively. Efforts to get these national networks and organizations to work together have been problematic.

In addition to these national organizing networks and organizations, more
than twenty organizing training centers have successful track records of teach-
ing community organizations the skills needed to develop indigenous leaders,
build strong community organizations, and win victories that improve social
and economic conditions in their neighborhoods. Many local groups and
thousands of leaders and staff members have participated in these training programs during the past decade.[32] Some training programs (like those linked to
IAF and ACORN) are affiliated with national community organizing networks, while others provide training and support to any group that wants it.
For example, the Midwest Academy in Chicago provides training and technical assistance to statewide and neighborhood organizations linked to the Citizen Action network, but it also provides these services to hundreds of other
community organizations, including many housing groups. Some centers provide technical assistance to groups across the country, while some focus on particular regions. These training centers have developed well-honed techniques,
books, manuals, videos, and other materials to train grassroots leaders and create vibrant community organizations. (See Delgado 1994; Wolter 1991 and
1993; and Dreier 1996.)

One of the most important functions of these networks and training centers is linking local and state-level organizations to national issues, so that local groups can work on issues whose solutions require them to move outside their neighborhood, city, or state, such as efforts to address redlining at both local and national levels.

There are lessons for advocacy and organizing to be learned from the recent experience of the CDC sector. As noted earlier, a key ingredient in the numerical growth and improved capacity of the community development sector has been the creation and expansion of national, regional, and local nonprofit intermediary institutions.[33] These organizations provide technical assistance to help existing organizations improve their skills and to help new organizations learn the basics of community development. They help channel private, philanthropic, and government funding to community-based development groups, to help them undertake projects successfully. Thanks in part to the work of these intermediary institutions, community-based development organizations have become increasingly sophisticated in terms of finance, construction, management, and other key functions. This has been accomplished not simply by targeting technical assistance and funds to individual groups, but by enabling groups to learn from one another, build on one another's successes, and form partnerships and coalitions.

Like their counterparts among intermediaries and training programs in the community development sector, these organizing networks and training centers have the capacity to expand significantly the scope and effectiveness of the nation's grassroots organizations engaged in housing. They have the staff, experience, track record, staying power, and vision to help community groups put in place the components they need for broader success: leadership development, organizational capacity building, and forging alliances. Compared with their community development counterparts, however, community organizing networks and training centers operate on shoestring budgets. They comprise an incredible untapped resource. They, and groups that could take advantage of their expertise, lack the funds to move much beyond their current level of activity. These networks and training centers could play a more important role in catalyzing successful housing advocacy and organizing at the local level as well as helping local housing groups form alliances with their counterparts in other neighborhoods, cities, and regions.

The housing agenda has always made the most headway when the concerns of the poor and the middle class were joined. In the progressive era, that meant improving health standards in tenements for immigrant workers in the teeming slums as well as building apartments houses for the middle class. In the depression and the postwar years, it meant building subsidized housing for the working class and shoring up homeownership for the middle class. But the political vehicles to fashion this coalition need to be rebuilt if the issue is to move from the margins to the mainstream of the nation's agenda.

The key to success is to broaden the political constituency for housing and to develop a coherent organizational strategy for putting the housing issue on the nation's agenda. A strategy of this type could include the three common goals that are emerging as priorities among national, state, and local housing advocacy groups.

First, mobilize and educate large numbers of poor and moderate-income Americans around housing issues. This requires building strong local and state-level grassroots advocacy organizations and coalitions. It involves leadership development and staff training. It involves helping groups develop a common legislative agenda around which to focus organizing efforts.[34]

Second, help grassroots citizens groups educate their public officials, journalists, and opinion-leaders—at the national as well as local level—about the inadequacy of current housing policy and the need for new approaches and additional resources. This involves providing support for a national media campaign to improve media coverage of housing issues and housing organizations (Dreier and Dubro 1991). It also involves providing support for research and public policy analysis linked to housing advocacy work.[35]

Third, help link together national organizing networks and advocacy groups around a common strategy. This involves providing incentives for national groups to join forces, to mobilize their constituents around a common agenda, to agree on targets of opportunity for influencing elections and legislation, and to forge alliances with various groups (unions, churches, good government organizations, businesses, environmental and women's groups) for which housing is not a central focus but which nevertheless significantly affects their constituency.

With the housing problems of vast numbers of poor and working-class Americans rapidly increasing, the national mood is changing and housing is becoming a more visible issue. The building blocks for a strong national housing policy are in place, but grassroots and national housing groups need to develop a common agenda and a broader constituency if they are to translate their successes at the local level into meaningful national policy changes.

America's foundations can help make this happen. No single foundation can make much of a difference by itself, the way it could in the past. But foundations can pool resources to work together. By strategically expanding their resources for housing advocacy and organizing—as well as by supporting a grassroots-based national infrastructure for a more progressive federal housing policy—the philanthropic community can make a dramatic impact on our current housing crisis.

Notes

1. In current usage, *advocacy groups* primarily do research on social problems and issue reports promoting changes in public policy. Examples include the Low Income

Housing Information Service's reports on the shortage of low-income housing in major cities, the National Housing Institute's study linking campaign contributions from the real estate industry to Congress and congress members' voting records, and the Woodstock Institute's analysis of bank mortgage lending in Chicago. *Organizing groups* mobilize people to fight for themselves to challenge slum landlords, redlining by banks, discrimination by realtors and landlords, and government officials and bureaucrats who fail to enforce housing standards or allocate insufficient funds to low-income areas.

2. Similarly, a number of progressive unions that sponsored cooperative housing developments for their members in the 1920s discovered that, without subsidies, the housing was too expensive for low-wage workers (Radford 1996).

3. The overall poverty rate was 11.6% in 1980, 12.8% in 1989, and 14.2% in 1991. In 1992, 14.5% of all Americans—and 22% of all children—lived below the official poverty line. The number of poor Americans—almost 36.9 million—represented the most poor people since 1964. Poverty became more geographically concentrated. From 1970 to 1990, the number of census tracts with 20% or more poverty in the 100 largest cities increased from 3,430 to 5,596 (Kasarda 1993). In addition to an increase in the overall number of poor Americans, the poor were poorer than a decade earlier, and they were poorer for a longer period of time. During the 1980s and early 1990s, the poor also got a smaller share of the nation's income. In 1979 the poorest 20% of the population had 5.1% of the country's pretax income; by 1991, their share fell to 3.8% of the total. For statistics on falling wages and incomes, and widening economic disparities, see Mishel and Bernstein 1993.

4. In 1970, there were 6.8 million rental units with housing costs of $250 or less a month (in 1989 dollars). By 1989, there were only 5.5 million rental units in this range (in 1989 dollars). During that same period, however, the number of families in poverty, including the number of low-income renters, increased significantly. Single-room occupancy (SRO) hotels and rooming houses were once home to many economically marginal renters. The number of SRO and rooming house units dropped from 640,000 in 1960, to 204,000 in 1980, to about 137,000 in 1990.

5. In 1970, the average income of renters was 64.9% of the average income of homeowners; by 1992, it was 47.9%. During those years, the average rent burden (rent as a percent of income) increased from 23.0% to 31.2%, the highest during the period. The biggest jump occurred during the 1980s, as real incomes fell and rents rose. In 1990 nearly one-fifth (17.8%) of all American renter households devoted more than half their income to meeting housing costs. This problem is nationwide. At least one-third of all renters in every single state could not afford market-level rents and had paid more than 30% of their incomes for housing. Measured in 1989 dollars, the median monthly gross rents paid by poor households living in unsubsidized housing jumped from $258 in 1974 to $359 in 1991. (Median gross rent consumed 43.5% of the poverty-level income—$9,885—for a family of three.) More than half of all poor renters (56%) spent at least 50% of their income on rent and utilities in 1989. More than four-of-five poor renter households (81%) spent at least 30% of their income on rent and utilities.

6. During the 1980s, the composition of the homeless population changed, from the initial stereotype of an alcoholic or mentally ill middle-aged man or "bag lady," many

of them victims of the "deinstitutionalization" policies of the 1970s, to include more families, even many with young children. A U.S. Conference of Mayors survey found that almost one quarter of the homeless were employed but simply could not earn enough to afford permanent housing. About one-third of homeless single men were veterans.

7. The Foundation Center identifies grants for "housing and shelter" as a subcategory under "human services." Two other subcategories—"community improvement and development" and "civil rights and social action" under the "public/society benefit" category—also probably include grants for housing-related efforts, but these are not clearly identified. As a result, however, the 1.3 percent figure is certainly an underestimate.

8. Most foundations restrict their grant-making to a particular region or metropolitan area. As Stoecker (1991) observes, some cities have stronger "philanthropic cultures" than others. The wealthy in older northeastern and midwestern cities such as Boston (with a long tradition of Brahmin do-gooderism) and Minneapolis (with a strong egalitarian ethos) tend to be more generous than their counterparts in the south and west. Local foundations in areas with strong economies often have more resources, but in healthy cities dominated by "new wealth" (particularly in the south and west), philanthropy tends to be weaker.

9. During the 1980s and early 1990s, the Ford Foundation was still the largest funder ($26.5 million in 1991) of community based development, followed by the Mc-Knight, Lilly, MacArthur, Kellogg, Northwest Area, Mott, Penn, Heinz, Irvine, Pew Charitable Trusts, Boston, St. Paul Companies, Surdna, Gund, Fannie Mae, Joyce, Hewlett, U.S. West, and Rockefeller Foundations (Council on Community-Based Development 1989, 1991, 1993).

10. This organization folded in the early 1990s.

11. For example, a 1983 study of Boston's United Way found that 38 of the 59-member board of directors represented major Boston corporations. The bulk of the Boston United Way's dollars went to traditional charities like the Red Cross, YMCA and YWCA, the Boys and Girls Clubs, the Boys and Girls Scouts, and the Salvation Army (Boston Urban Study Group 1984).

12. Its first project was to provide $100,000 challenge grants to United Ways in five cities (Chicago, Houston, York, Pa., Rochester, and Pontiac, Mich.), to encourage local United Ways, businesses and foundations to add funding. Since then, the UWA and local United Ways have expanded their support for CDCs.

13. As suggested in this chapter, there is a distinction between community organizing, community development, and community-based service provision. Most organizations engage in only one of these activities, but some seek to branch out to engage in two or even three of these activities. Efforts to balance these components are not without tension. Community groups that focus primarily on service delivery or community development often lose the energy and momentum required to do effective community organizing. Service delivery and community development are more effective when they are part of a community organizing strategy, especially when the tasks are clearly delineated within the organization (Eisen 1992; Traynor, 1993; Miller 1992; Lenz 1988;

Stone 1996). For example, in a number of cities, ACORN has drawn on its success in challenging bank redlining to become involved in housing counseling for potential homeowners. In Lowell, Massachusetts, the Coalition for a Better Acre began as an affiliate of Massachusetts Fair Share, a citizen action group. After several years of successful organizing around neighborhood issues, the group formed its own community development corporation (CDC) to repair and build affordable housing. East Brooklyn Churches, a coalition of New York City religious congregations that is part of the Industrial Areas Foundation (IAF) network, spent a decade working on neighborhood issues before establishing its own housing development program (Nehemiah Homes), which has become one of the largest nonprofit development projects in the country.

14. The original survey was distributed to all members of the Neighborhood Funders Group, all community foundations, and all foundations categorized as funding homelessness and housing-related projects (according to the *Foundation Directory*) and all those foundations present at a workshop on "The Homeless: Will They Always Be With Us?" at the 1991 National Council on Foundations conference (McCambridge 1992).

15. These foundations included the MacArthur, Fannie Mae, Mott, Hewlett, Irvine, Surdna, the New York Community Trust, Ohio's Gund Foundation and New Jersey's Prudential Foundation, MCJ Foundation and the Fund for New Jersey. Each of these foundations has a track record of providing significant grants for advocacy and organizing activities, even though they constitute a small part of their overall grant-making in the area of housing and neighborhood improvement.

16. Observers of urban neighborhood problems recognize that sources of urban decay and housing problems reside primarily outside neighborhood boundaries. Symptoms of urban decay—poverty, unemployment, homelessness, violent crime, racial segregation, and high infant mortality rates—have their roots in large-scale economic forces and federal government policy. The forces and policies include economic restructuring toward a low-wage service economy; corporate disinvestment (encouraged by federal tax laws); bidding wars among cities and states to attract businesses that undermine local fiscal health; redlining by banks and insurance companies; federal housing, transportation, tax, and defense spending policies that have subsidized the migration of people and businesses to the suburbs (exacerbating urban fiscal traumas); and federal cutbacks of various financial assistance, housing, social service, economic development, and other programs. These large-scale forces can undermine the economic and social fabric of urban neighborhoods. (See Dreier 1993; Massey and Denton 1993; Wilson 1987 and 1996; Fishman 1990.)

17. In response to grassroots pressure from the emerging neighborhood movement, Congress (with the support of the Carter administration after 1976) sponsored a number of initiatives to promote community self-help efforts against redlining. These included two key pieces of legislation—the Home Mortgage Disclosure Act (HMDA) of 1975 and the Community Reinvestment Act (CRA) of 1977. In combination, HMDA and CRA provided an effective tool for local groups to push banks to invest in low-income and minority neighborhoods. HMDA provided the data needed to systematically analyze the banks' lending patterns (for housing, but not commercial loans). HMDA gave many community groups and university-based scholars—and some local governments, daily newspapers, and other agencies—the data to investigate geographic and racial bias in

lending. From 1977 through the late 1980s, federal regulators were asleep at the switch in terms of monitoring and enforcing the CRA. As a result, community reinvestment activities primarily involved "bottom-up enforcement"—local campaigns between a community organization or coalition and a local bank. Only in the late 1980s did these local activities coalesce into a national presence. Thanks to the work of ACORN, the Center for Community Change, and National People's Action—three national community organizing networks—these local efforts became building blocks for a truly national effort that has produced dramatic results in the past few years alone. Locally-crafted CRA agreements alone have catalyzed over $60 billion in bank lending and services over the years. But even more important, many banks are now much more proactive in working with community organizations in successful neighborhood rebuilding partnerships. (See Dreier 1991; Squires 1992; and Fishbein 1992.)

18. Banks are now much more proactive in working with community organizations to identify credit needs and create partnerships to meet them. Regulators are much more proactive in evaluating lenders' CRA performance and using regulatory carrots and sticks to insure compliance. Fulfilling its campaign pledge, the Clinton administration has made the issue of redlining and community reinvestment by banks and insurance companies—and support for community-based development—a centerpiece of its urban policy agenda. What were the key ingredients for success? Local groups working on the same issue were able to communicate and learn from each other because of the existence of several national organizing networks and training centers. National groups such as ACORN, NPA, and CCC helped expand the capacity of local community groups to use the CRA and HMDA to rebuild and revitalize neighborhoods. They did so by providing groups with training and by linking them together to make the federal government—legislators and regulators alike—more responsive to neighborhood credit needs. Also, local groups had access to training and leadership development to empower them to stabilize their organizations in terms of membership and fund-raising; form coalitions with a variety of groups (including church-based organizations, civil rights groups, nonprofit developers, and social service agencies) that often crossed boundaries of race, income, and neighborhood; learn how to develop strategies for working on several issues simultaneously and for building on small victories; develop a strategy to negotiate with lenders and government; and deal with the mass media.

19. Social movement philanthropy involves grants to organizations that engage in grassroots organizing, advocacy, and training.

20. During the 1970s and 1980s, a small number of wealthy radicals, often heirs to America's major corporate fortunes, set up foundations dedicated to progressive social change. The Bread and Roses Fund began in Philadelphia in 1971 and the Vanguard Foundation began in San Francisco in 1972. There are now about 20 foundations of this kind. The founders of these small radical foundations created a network (the Funding Exchange) to share ideas and published a book in 1977 reflecting their philosophy, entitled *Robin Hood Was Right* (The Funding Exchange, 1977). (See Mogil and Slepian 1992; Roelofs 1989; Odendahl 1990; Rabinowitz 1990; Shaw 1995.) One of the earliest, the Haymarket Foundation in Boston, was started in 1974 by George Pillsbury, heir to the Pillsbury baking and food conglomerate. Pillsbury took the unusual step of setting up a

board of community activists to run the foundation, establish funding criteria, and allocate the funds. Although Haymarket was started with Pillbury's money, it—like the others in the network—continues to raise funds from other affluent progressive individuals, thus serving as a conduit for their philanthropy (Ostrander 1995). These social activist foundations target their grant-making to local grassroots organizing efforts—environmental and women's groups, prisoners' rights organizations, consumer and community activist groups, and organizations involved in peace and antiwar struggles. Most of these progressive foundations give some portion of their grants to housing-related activists—tenants rights organization, community groups fighting redlining and other forms of housing discrimination, and coalitions of groups seeking more government funding for low-income housing (Rabinowitz 1990; Odendahl 1990; Mogil and Slepian 1992). One small progressive funder, the Discount Foundation, has focused *all* its grant-making (about $200,000-$300,000 a year) on housing organizing and advocacy groups. In its survey of foundations, the Council on Community-based Development identified Discount as the only funder that concentrates 100% of its grantmaking in this area (Council on Community-Based Development, 1993). Overall, these small foundations represent a tiny portion of all philanthropic giving, but by their grant-making successes and through their work in national foundation networks (such as the Council on Foundations, the Funding Exchange, the Neighborhood Funders Group, and the National Network of Grantmakers), they have helped to push much larger foundations to support social activist causes and organizations. At the urging of housing activists and some of the more radical funders, for example, several of the NFG retreats focused discussion on community organizing and public policy advocacy as well as on bricks-and-mortar development. In most major cities, community activists have set up their own alternative community funds to challenge and compete with the United Ways' monopoly on soliciting funds from employees in their workplaces. Critical of the United Ways' bias toward mainstream social service organizations, these groups sought to give employees in large and small organizations a choice to donate, through payroll deductions, to grassroots organizations involved in social action on environmental causes, women's rights, housing, child care, and other causes. Through the 1970s and 1980s, these groups made progress in getting reluctant employers to open their doors to these alternative funds. City governments, universities, and newspapers are often the first employers to permit alternative funds to compete with the United Way for their employees' contributions, followed by more mainstream private companies. Today, these include some of America's largest corporations—including ATT, Aetna, Hewlett Packard, Nike, Polaroid, Prudential, Safeway, Wells Fargo, and Weyerhaeuser. The National Committee for Responsive Philanthropy, based in Washington, D.C., serves as the umbrella organization for the growing network of alternative funds. When Boston Mayor Ray Flynn took office in 1984, he gave Community Works the opportunity to raise funds from city employees on an equal footing with the United Way. That precedent made it easier for Community Works—which raises money for the Massachusetts Tenants Organization, the Massachusetts Affordable Housing Coalition, and other grassroots organizations—to gain acceptance in other large workplaces. Its fund-raising from payroll deductions increased from $11,450 in 1982 to $314,237 in 1991. Among the 33 other local social justice funds, the Cooperating Fund Drive of Minneapolis-St. Paul raised $719,519 from payroll deductions in 1991; the Fund for Community Progress in Providence raised $222,580; the

Community Services Fund in Lincoln, Nebraska, netted $72,024; Community Shares of Knoxville received $109,577; and Greater Cleveland Community Shares $238,708. Some alternative funds support groups dealing with specific issues, such as women's rights, the environment, or African-American concerns. (National Committee for Responsive Philanthropy 1992.)

21. By far the largest religious-oriented funder of social activism is the Campaign for Human Development (CHD), founded in 1970 by the U.S. Catholic Conference (the nation's bishops) in the wake of Vatican II and in the aftermath of the urban uprisings of the 1960s. CHD raises its funds from one-Sunday-a-year collections in local parishes across the country. It allocates these funds to progressive social change groups in every part of the nation. CHD gives a large part of its grant-making to housing activist groups. During the 1980s, CHD allocated between $5.5 million and $7.5 million a year. In 1987, a typical year, CHD grants for local housing organizing projects accounted for $652,000 of its $6.5 million in grants. Among the recipients were ACORN chapters involved in organizing public housing tenants and mobilizing residents against bank redlining; South Carolina Fair Share for organizing public housing residents; the National Training and Information Center, to train local community groups to fight redlining; Greater Bridgeport Interfaith Action, a multi-issue, citywide coalition of religious groups, that includes developing tenant leaders in public and private housing; the Callahan Neighborhood Association in Orlando, Florida, to fight displacement of poor people resulting from the city's use of federal CDBG funds to "revitalize" neighborhoods; and the Coachella Valley Housing Coalition in California to organize low-income Hispanic farmworkers to organize a cooperative mobile home project. (See Rabinowitz 1990; and McCarthy and Castelli 1994.) Other church-based philanthropies share CHD's philosophy of movement-building. The Veatch Foundation, sponsored by a Unitarian Universalist church in Long Island, supports grassroots activism across the country. In Boston, the Episcopal City Mission, a philanthropy launched by the affluent Trinity Church to improve inner-city neighborhoods, has been an important resource since the 1970s, providing small grants to local tenant groups and housing activist organizations.

22. During the 1950s, a few wealthy liberals (such as newspaper publisher and department store heir Marshall Field) and their foundations had given money to organizer Saul Alinsky to develop grassroots neighborhood organizations in Chicago. In 1953 the Schwartzhaupt Foundation, and soon thereafter the Rosenwald and Field foundations, began supporting the Highlander Folk School (now the Highlander Center) in Tennessee, a controversial training center for trade union, civil rights, and community organizers. In the 1960s, a number of liberal foundations (such as the Taconic, Norman, Field, and New York foundations) funded a variety of civil rights organizations to undertake voter registration and desegregation campaigns in the south, to organize the March on Washington in 1963, and to push for school integration, open (nondiscriminatory) housing, and welfare rights in the north.

23. Among the 131 foundations that supported social movement activism, only 39 contributed more than one-third of their annual giving to activist projects. These philanthropies donated to a wide variety of activist groups dealing with environmentalism, feminism, racism, consumer protection, children, prisoners, peace, and civil liberties.

Groups addressing the problems of racial minorities received 40.7% of all grant dollars. The category called "economic justice"—which includes advocacy and organizing around the concerns of poor and working class people—accounted for almost one-fifth (19.07%) of total grant dollars. Jenkins' study did not identify housing activism—such as tenants rights groups, fair housing organizations, community organizations fighting redlining—as a separate category. These groups would fall under several categories: economic justice, racial justice, and consumer rights.

24. The late 1970s and 1980s saw the emergence of major "new right" funders that promoted conservative causes, including think tanks, publications, nonprofit law firms, and advocacy organizations. This network of right-wing funders played an important role in changing the ideological and political climate, beginning in the 1980s. They were considerably more coordinated and aggressive than their more liberal counterparts. One of their primary efforts was a campaign to "defund the left"—to get both government and foundations to terminate support for liberal and progressive organizations. In light of the data cited here, their characterization of major foundations as predominantly liberal is obviously misleading. But they succeeded in using the mainstream media and their own networks to promote this image and their agenda. They did this by funding reports identifying corporations and mainstream foundations, as well as government agencies, that provided grants to liberal and progressive organizations, including federally-funded legal services agencies for the poor. (The conservative Capital Research Center is a source for many of these reports.) During the Reagan and Bush administrations, they used the Internal Revenue Service monitoring to promote this agenda by harassing and intimidating both funders and grantees. During the 1990s, especially after the ascendancy of Speaker of the House Newt Gingrich, conservative members of Congress sponsored legislation to cut off federal grants to liberal grassroots organizations that engage in lobbying and political activism. The community organization ACORN was one of Gingrich's key targets. One example of this effort is the "new right" effort to discredit rent control as a public policy. During the mid-1980s, conservative think tanks and publications promoted the notion that local rent regulations led to an increase in homelessness. This idea was not only picked by the mainstream media but used by conservative members of Congress and HUD Secretary Jack Kemp to back legislation to withhold federal HUD funds to localities with rent control. (For a discussion of this campaign, see Appelbaum, Gilderbloom, and Dreier 1991).

25. The CDC sector is composed mainly of relatively small organizations which limits their ability to achieve economies-of-scale in terms of development, staffing, management, and overall community impact. Of the 1,160 groups responding to the NCCED survey, only 421 had produced one hundred or more housing units. This represented a significant increase from the 244 groups with that production level only two years earlier, but it still reveals that most CDCs are still small-scale operations. By the end of the 1980s, a small number of CDCs produced most of the housing units sponsored by nonprofit community organizations. For example, a survey of 744 CDCs found that only 1.7% of the groups produced an average of 200 or more housing units a year between 1988 and 1990, but these groups accounted for 25.3% of total CDC production during those years. At the other end, 48.7% of the CDCs produced ten or fewer

units a year during that three-year period, accounting for only 7.9% of the CDC sponsored units (Walker 1993:376). Examining these numbers, the Urban Institute discovered that some of the newer CDCs were among the most productive, suggesting that "under the right conditions, CDCs can develop capacity fairly rapidly" (Walker: 376). CDCs with larger staffs typically produce more housing, but most CDCs are small-scale operations. Nationwide, they employ a median staff of seven people (Walker 1993). One nationwide study found the median CDC budget to be $700,000, but the groups in this sample tended to be larger than the typical group (Vidal 1992). In 1988-90, only 39% of the CDCs had 10 or more staff, but these groups produced 52.6% of all CDC-sponsored units. The small size of most CDCs is exacerbated by the complexities of their task, especially under adverse funding conditions. The patchwork of funding sources makes the development of affordable housing extremely complex. To create a 25-unit housing development, for example, a CDC may need to obtain subsidies and grants from ten different sources—corporations, foundations, governments. The various funding programs have different—in fact, often conflicting—deadlines, timetables, and guidelines. As a result, CDC staff persons often spend more time devoted to "grant-grubbing" than to the development and management of housing. The legal and financial complexities also require CDCs to engage the services of many lawyers and consultants, adding to the cost and time for getting housing projects underway.

26. The biggest secret about public housing is that most of it is well-managed and the majority of units are in small and mid-size developments. But many older projects in the big cities are physically isolated, high-rise ghettos, underfunded and poorly maintained. About 86,000 public housing units are "severely distressed," many of them vacant, because of the lack of funds for ongoing maintenance and repairs. Once targeted to the working poor, public housing has increasingly become home to the extremely poor. Today, the median household income in public housing is only $5,850—19% of the national median income. Only about 40% of its nonelderly households have a wage earner. There are about 900,000 families on the waiting lists for the nation's public housing apartments. This is true even though many local housing authories have closed off their waiting lists because it takes several years (or more) to get into an apartment—evidence that public housing is, in the eyes of many clients, a preferred option to the private rental market (National Commission on Severely Distressed Public Housing 1992; Vale 1993; Lazere 1995).

27. In fact, HUD constitutes only a small part of the federal government's housing policies. In 1995 the United States devoted $113 billion a year to housing subsidies, less than one-quarter of it through HUD. The Departments of Agriculture and Health and Human Services provide housing subsidies as well, but none contribute as much as our phantom housing agency, the Internal Revenue Service, through deductions for home mortgage interest and property taxes, as well as tax breaks to investors in rental housing and mortgage revenue bonds. Much of it is spent wastefully and inefficiently. (See Dreier 1997.)

28. During the summer of 1996, Clinton and the GOP Congress passed a welfare revision bill that gave states greater flexibility but less money. One consequence will be to reduce the funds available to low-income families to pay rent.

29. HUD has dozens of different pockets of money to help public housing agencies and an almost equal number of distinct programs for private owners of HUD subsidized developments. HUD also has two programs allocated by formulas to municipal governments, the Community Development Block Grant and HOME. There are separate programs to house the elderly, Native Americans, rural populations, people with AIDS, and homeless people. HUD created a variety of programs to address the various subpopulations of the homeless. Separate programs were created to help homeless families, homeless veterans, homeless people with AIDS, and the elderly homeless, and to create single room occupancy apartments (rooming houses), transitional housing for women and children, and shelters as well as health care clinics for homeless persons. There are distinct programs for new housing construction, for moderate rehabilitation, and for major rehabilitation. HUD has two housing allowance programs, vouchers, and certificates, that have different standards, and various specialized programs, like Moving to Opportunity, to target these allowances for specific purposes. HUD is also in the fair housing business, monitoring (often through contracts with community-based groups) discrimination by landlords, lenders, and local governments. Most HUD funds go directly to cities and towns, but some circumvent local governments and go to community groups and owners of HUD assisted projects. Through the FHA, HUD also insures mortgages for individual homebuyers and developers of subsidized low income housing.

30. There is nothing in the organizing/advocacy world even comparable to the National Community Development Initiative, a consortium of 13 foundations, working through LISC and the Enterprise Foundation, that began in 1991 and was designed to expand the capacity of CDCs.

31. In Massachusetts, for example, these groups played a key role in pushing the state to significantly expand its housing efforts during the boom years of the 1980s. During that period, Massachusetts was frequently seen as an innovator in housing policy. But the state's current economic downturn, its fiscal crisis, and the failure of most elected officials to address these problems have led to a sweeping attack on housing and other programs. Mirroring the Reagan-era agenda in Washington, the state's housing budget under Republican governor William Weld was slashed in 1991. In response, housing advocate groups formed the HOME Coalition (with key funding from the Boston Foundation) to develop a common agenda and a common organizing strategy to protect state housing resources and to build a stronger grassroots movement to fight for housing reform in the future.

32. The two oldest training centers are the Industrial Areas Foundation and the Highlander Center. Others now include the Midwest Academy, Center for Third World Organizing, National Training and Information Center, Institute for Social Justice, National Housing Institute, Gamaliel Foundation, the Organizing and Leadership Training Center in Boston, Organize Training Center in San Francisco, Grassroots Leadership, Pacific Institute for Community Organizations in Oakland, the Community Training and Assistance Center in Boston, the Regional Council of Neighborhood Organizations in Philadelphia, and United Connecticut Action for Neighborhoods. The Center for Community Change is both an organizing network and a training center.

33. These include organizations such as the Local Initiatives Support Corporation (LISC), Enterprise Foundation, Neighborhood Reinvestment Corporation, Telesis Corporation, Development Training Institute, Community Builders, Community Economics, Institute for Community Economics, and McAuley Institute.

34. For a proposal to fashion a new progressive housing policy, see Dreier 1997.

35. A good example of this is the growing number of academics who analyze HMDA data on behalf of local and national organizing and advocacy groups. This is a highly technical and specialized area of expertise, but these academics have worked closely with activist groups not only to provide essential information around mortgage lending trends, but also to teach staffpersons how to assemble and utilize the information.

References

Appelbaum, Richard, Peter Dreier, and John Gilderbloom. 1991. "Scapegoating rent control: Masking the causes of homelessness." *Journal of the American Planning Association* 57 (2)153–64.

Atlas, John, and Peter Dreier. 1992. "From projects to communities: How to redeem public housing." *The American Prospect* (summer) 74–85.

Bahl, Roy. 1994. "Metropolitan Fiscal Disparities." *Cityscape* 1 (1) 293–303.

Berry, Jeffrey M., Kent E. Portney, and Ken Thomson. 1993. *The Rebirth of Urban Democracy*. Washington, D.C.: Brookings Institution.

Birch, E.L. and D.S. Gardner. 1981. "The Seven Percent Solution: A Review of Philanthropic Housing, 1870–1910." *Journal of Urban History* 7.403–38.

Blau, Joel. 1992. *The visible poor: Homelessness in the United States*. New York: Oxford University Press.

Boston Urban Study Group. 1984. *Who rules Boston? A citizen's guide*. Somerville: Center for the Study of Public Policy.

Boyte, Harry. 1980. *The backyard revolution: Understanding the new citizen movement*. Philadelphia: Temple University Press.

———. 1989. *Commonwealth: A return to citizen politics*. New York: Free Press.

Branch, Taylor. 1988. *Parting the waters*. New York: Simon and Schuster.

Bratt, Rachel, Langley Keyes, Alex Schwartz, and Avis Vidal. 1994. *Confronting the management challenge: Affordable housing in the nonprofit sector*. New York: Community Development Research Center, New School for Social Research.

Brooks, Mary. 1989. *A survey of housing trust funds*. Washington, D.C: Center for Community Change.

Burt, Martha. 1992. *Over the edge: The growth of homelessness in the 1980s.* New York: Russell Sage Foundation.

Casey, Connie. 1992. *Characteristics of HUD-assisted renters and their units in 1989.* Washington, D.C.: U.S. Department of Housing and Urban Development, Office of Policy Development and Research.

Clavel, Peter, and Wim Wiewel, eds. 1991. *Harold Washington and the neighborhoods: Progressive city government in Chicago.* New Brunswick, N.J.: Rutgers University Press.

Clavel, Pierre. 1986. *The Progressive City.* New Brunswick, N.J.: Rutgers University Press.

Committee for Economic Development. 1995. *Rebuilding inner-city communities: A new approach to the nation's urban crisis.* New York: Committee for Economic Development, Research and Policy Committee.

Cooper, Kenneth J. 1994. "Gingrich pledges a major package of spending cuts early next year." *Washington Post* December 13. A1.

Council on Community-Based Development. 1989. *Expanding horizons: Foundation support of community-based development.* New York: Council on Community-Based Development.

———. 1991. *Expanding horizons II: A research report on corporate and foundation grant support of community-based development.* New York: Council on Community-Based Development.

———. 1993. *Expanding horizons III: A research report on corporate and foundation grant support of community-based development.* New York: Council on Community-Based Development.

Davis, John, ed. 1994. *The affordable city.* Philadelphia: Temple University Press.

DeLeon, Richard. 1992. *Left coast city.* Lawrence: University of Kansas Press.

Delgado, Gary. 1986. *Organizing the movement: The roots and growth of ACORN.* Philadelphia: Temple University Press.

——— 1994. *Beyond the politics of place: New directions in community organizing in the 1990s.* Oakland, Calif.: Applied Research Center.

———. Guadalupe Guajardo, Nancy Nye, and Richard Schramm. 1995. *Cultivating the grassroots: An assessment of intermediary support program of the Charles Stewart Mott foundation.* Oakland, Calif.: Applied Research Center.

DeParle, Jason. 1996. "Slamming the door." *New York Times Magazine* October 20.

Dolbeare, Cushing. 1996. *Housing at a snail's pace.* Washington, D.C.: National Low Income Housing Coalition.

Downs, Anthony. 1991. "The advisory commission on regulatory barriers to affordable housing: Its behavior and accomplishments." *Housing Policy Debate* 2 (4)1095–137.

Dreier, Peter. 1984. "The tenants movement in the United States." *International Journal of Urban and Regional Research* 8 (2)255–79.

———. 1991. "Redlining cities: How banks color community development." *Challenge: The Magazine of Economic Affairs* 34 (6)15–23.

———. 1993a. "America's urban crisis: Symptoms, causes, solutions." *North Carolina Law Review* 71 (5)1351–402.

———. 1993b. "Ray Flynn's legacy: American cities and the progressive agenda." *National Civic Review* fall.

———. 1993c. "America's urban crisis: Symptoms, causes, solutions." *North Carolina Law Review* June.

———. 1993d. *Community empowerment: The experience of community-based problem-solving and recommendations for federal policy.* A report to the U.S. Department of Housing and Urban Development, December.

———. 1996. "Community empowerment strategies: The limits and potential of community organizing in urban neighborhoods." *Cityscape: A Journal of Policy Development and Research* 2 (2)121–59.

———. 1997. "The new politics of housing: How to rebuild the constituency for a progressive federal housing policy." *Journal of the American Planning Association* 63 (1)5–27.

———, and John Atlas. 1989. "Grassroots strategies for the housing crisis: A national agenda for the 1990s." *Social Policy 19* (3)25–38.

———, and Richard Appelbaum. 1991. "Homelessness: The American nightmare." *Challenge: The Magazine of Economic Affairs* 34 (2)46–52.

———, and J. David Hulchanski. 1993. "The role of nonprofit housing in Canada and the United States." *Housing Policy Debate* 4 (1)43–80.

———, and Alec Dubro. 1991. "Housing: The invisible crisis." *Washington Journalism Review* May.

———, Dennis Keating. 1991. "The limits of localism: Progressive municipal housing policies in Boston." *Urban Affairs Quarterly* 26 (2)191–216.

———, and David Moberg. 1996. "Moving from the 'hood': The mixed success of integrating suburbia." *The American Prospect* winter 75–79.

———, David Schwartz, and Ann Greiner. 1988. "What every business can do about housing." *Harvard Business Review* 66 (5)52–61.

Ehrenreich, John H. 1985. *The altruistic imagination: A history of social work and social policy in the United States.* Ithaca: Cornell University Press.

Eisen, Arlene. 1992. *A report on foundations' support for comprehensive neighborhood-based community empowerment initiatives.* San Francisco: East Bay Funders, the Ford Foundation, New York Community Trust, Piton Foundation, and Riley Foundation.

Fishbein, Allen J. 1992. "The ongoing experiment with 'regulation from below': Expanded reporting requirements for HMDA and CRA." *Housing Policy Debate* 3 (2) 601–36.

Fisher, Robert. 1984. *Let the people decide: Neighborhood organizing in America.* Boston: Twayne Publishers.

Fishman, Robert. 1990. "America's new city: Megalopolis unbound." *Wilson Quarterly* winter.

Ford Foundation. 1989. *Affordable housing: The years ahead.* New York: Ford Foundation. *The Foundation Center.* Ford Foundation. 1996a. *Foundation Giving.* New York: Foundation Center.

The Foundation Center. 1996b. *Grants Index.* New York: Foundation Center.

Friedman, Lawrence M. 1968. *Government and slum housing: A century of frustration.* Chicago: Rand McNally.

The Funding Exchange. 1977. *Robin Hood was right: A guide to giving your money for social change.* San Francisco: Vanguard Public Foundation.

Goetz, Edward G. 1993. *Shelter burden: Local politics and progressive housing policy.* Philadelphia: Temple University Press.

Greene, Stephen G. 1989. "Housing crisis draws foundations' interest, but activists say it's not enough." *Chronicle of Philanthropy* May 2.

Gugliotta, Guy. 1995. "HUD mans its lifeboats," *Washington Post National Weekly Edition* February 13–19.

Hall, Peter Dobkin. 1992. *Inventing the nonprofit sector.* Baltimore: Johns Hopkins University Press.

Harrison, Bennett, Marcus Weiss, and Jon Grant. 1995. *Building bridges: Community development corporations and the world of employment training.* New York: Ford Foundation.

Hays, R. Allen. 1995. *The federal government and urban housing.* Second edition. Albany: SUNY Press.

Hodgkinson, Virginia A., Richard W. Lyman and Associates, eds. 1989. *The future of the nonprofit sector.* San Francisco: Jossey-Bass.

Horwitt, Sanford D. 1989. *Let them call me rebel: Saul Alinsky, his life and legacy.* New York: Alfred A. Knopf.

Housing Affairs Letter. 1995. "Adm'n wins first round of HUD fight." January 30.

Interagency Council on Homelessness. 1994. *Priority: Home.* Washington, D.C.: Interagency Council on Homelessness.

Jenkins, J. Craig. 1989. "Social movement philanthropy and American democracy," in Richard Magat, ed., *Philanthropic giving: Studies in varieties and goals.* New York: Oxford University Press.

————, and Abigail Halcli. 1996. "Grassrooting the system? The development and impact of social movement philanthropy. 1953–1990." Paper presented at the conference on Philanthropic Foundations in History, New York University.

Johnson, Robert Matthews. 1988. *The first charity: How philanthropy can contribute to democracy in America.* Cabin John, Md.: Seven Locks Press.

Joint Center for Housing Studies. 1994. *The state of the nation's housing: 1994.* Cambridge, Mass.: Joint Center for Housing Studies, Harvard University.

Kasarda, John. 1993. "Inner city concentrated poverty and neighborhood distress," *Housing Policy Debate* 4 (3)253–302.

Katz, Michael B. 1986. *In the shadow of the poorhouse: A social history of welfare in America.* New York: Basic Books.

Keyes, Langley, Alex Schwartz, Avis Vidal, and Rachel Bratt. 1996. "Networks and non-profits: Opportunities and challenges in a era of federal devolution." *Housing Policy Debate* 7 (2)201–29.

Krumholz, Norman, and Pierre Clavel. 1994. *Reinventing cities: Equity planners tell their stories.* Philadelphia: Temple University Press.

Ladd, Helen, and John Yinger. 1989. *America's ailing cities: Fiscal health and the design of urban policy.* Baltimore: Johns Hopkins University Press.

Lazere, Edward B. 1995. *In short supply: The growing affordable housing gap.* Washington, D.C.: Center on Budget and Policy Priorities.

————, Cushing Dolbeare, Paul Leonard, and Barry Zigas. 1991. *A place to call home: The low-income housing crisis continues.* Washington, D.C.: Center on Budget and Policy Priorities and Low Income Housing Information Service.

Lemann, Nicholas. 1991. *The promised land: The great black migration and how it changed america.* New York: Alfred A. Knopf.

Lenz, Thomas. 1988. "Neighborhood development: Issues and models." *Social Policy* spring.

Levine, Mark L., and Alan Brickman. 1992. *Assessment of the united way of America housing initiatives program.* Brookline, Mass.: Levine Associates.

Link, Bruce, Ezra Susser, Ann Stueve, Jo Phelan, Robert Moore, and Elmer Struening. 1994. "Lifetime and five-year prevalence of homelessness in the United States." *American Journal of Public Health* 84 (12)1907–12.

Lubove, Roy. 1962. *The progressives and the slums: Tenement house reform in New York city, 1890–1917.* Pittsburgh: University of Pittsburgh Press.

Magat, Richard, ed. 1989. *Philanthropic giving: Studies in varieties and goals.* New York: Oxford University Press.

Mallach, Alan. 1984. *Inclusionary housing programs.* New Brunswick, N.J.: Center for Urban Policy Research.

Marcuse, Peter. 1986. "Housing policy and the myth of the benevolent state," in Rachel Bratt, Chester Hartman, and Ann Meyerson, eds. *Critical perspectives on housing.* Philadelphia: Temple University Press.

Massey, Douglas S. and Nancy M. Denton. 1993. *American apartheid: Segregation and the making of the underclass.* Cambridge: Harvard University Press.

Mayer, Neil. 1990. "The role of nonprofits in renewed federal housing efforts," in Denise DiPasquale and Langley Keyes, eds. *Building Foundations.* Philadelphia: University of Pennsylvania Press.

McCambridge, Ruth. 1992. *Giving to end homelessness: A study of the national philanthropic response to homelessness.* Boston: Boston Foundation Fund for the Homeless.

McCarthy, John D., and Jim Castelli. 1994. *Working for justice: The campaign for human development and poor empowerment groups.* Washington, D.C.: Life Cycle Institute, Catholic University of America.

Metzger, John. 1992. "The community reinvestment act and neighborhood revitalization in Pittsburgh," in Gregory Squires, ed. *From redlining to reinvestment.* Philadelphia: Temple University Press.

Miller, Mike. 1992. "Citizens groups: Whom do they represent?" *Social Policy* spring.

Mishel, Lawrence, and Jared Bernstein. 1993. *The state of working America.* Armonk, New York: M.E. Sharpe.

Mogil, Christopher, and Anne Slepian. 1992. *We gave away a fortune: Stories of people who have devoted themselves and their wealth to peace, justice and a healthy environment.* Philadelphia: New Society Publishers.

Morris, Aldon. 1984. *The origins of the civil rights movement.* New York: Free Press.

National Committee for Responsive Philanthropy. 1988. *The great charity drive expansion.* Washington, D.C.: National Committee for Responsive Philanthropy.

————. 1992. *Charity in the Workplace. 1992.* Washington, D.C.: National Committee for Responsive Philanthropy.

National Congress for Community Economic Development. 1987. *Community-based development: Investing in renewal: The report of the task force on community-based development.* Washington, D.C.: National Congress for Community Economic Development.

National Low Income Housing Coalition. 1995. *Slicing the pie: A report on state and local housing strategies.* Washington, D.C.

Nenno, Mary K. 1991. "State and local governments: New initiatives in low-income housing preservation." *Housing Policy Debate* 2 (2)467–97.

————, and George Colyer. 1988. *New money and new methods: A catalog of state and local initiatives in housing and community development.* Washington, D.C.: National Association of Housing and Redevelopment Officials.

Newman, Sandra. 1995. "The implications of current welfare reform proposals for the housing assistance system." *Fordham Urban Law Journal* 22.1231–47.

———, and Ann Schnare. 1994. "Back to the future: Housing assistance policy for the next century." Paper prepared for the Center for Housing Policy. Washington, D.C.: Center for Housing Policy.

Nielsen, Waldemar. 1985. *The golden donors: A new anatomy of the great foundations*. New York: Dutton.

O'Connell, Brian, and Ann Brown O'Connell. 1989. *Volunteers in action*. New York: Foundation Center.

Odendahl, Teresa. 1990. *Charity begins at home: Generosity and self-interest among the philanthropic elite*. New York: Basic Books.

O'Donnell, Sandra, Yvonne Jeffries, Frank Sanchez, and Pat Selmi. 1995. *Evaluation of the fund's community organizing grant program*. Chicago: Woods Fund of Chicago.

O'Neill, Michael. 1989. *The third America: The emergence of the nonprofit sector in the United States*. San Francisco, Jossey-Bass.

Peirce, Neal R., and Carol F. Steinbach. 1990. *Enterprising communities: Community-based development in America*. Washington, D.C.: Council for Community-Based Development.

Peterman, William. 1993. "Resident management and other approaches to tenant control of public housing," in R. Allen Hays, ed. *Ownership, control and the future of housing policy*. Westport, Conn.: Greenwood Press.

Putnam, Robert. 1995. "Tuning in, tuning out: The strange disappearance of social capital in America." *PS: Political Science and Politics* 28.4.

Rabinowitz, Alan. 1990. *Social change and philanthropy in America*. New York: Quorum Books.

Radford, Gail. 1996. *Modern housing for America: Policy struggles in the new deal era*. Chicago: University of Chicago Press.

Riis, Jacob A. 1890 [1957]. *How the other half lives*. New York: Hill & Wang.

Roelofs, Joan. 1987. "Foundations and social change organizations." *The Insurgent Sociologist* 14 (3)31–72.

Rogers, Mary Beth. 1990. *Cold anger: A story of faith and power in politics*. Denton: University of North Texas Press.

Rubin, Herbert. 1994. "There aren't going to be any bakeries here if there is no money to afford jellyrolls: The organic theory of community based development." *Social Problems* 41 (3)401–24.

Salamon, Lester M. 1995. *Partners in public service: Government-nonprofit relations in the modern welfare state*. Baltimore: Johns Hopkins University Press.

Schill, Michael H. 1994. "The role of the nonprofit sector in low-income housing production: A comparative perspective." *Urban Affairs Quarterly* 30 (1)74–101.

Shaw, Aileen M. 1995. *Fostering change: The challenge to progressive philanthropy. A history of the national network of grantmakers 1980–1995.* San Diego: National Network of Grantmakers.

Squires, Gregory, ed. 1992. *From redlining to reinvestment: Community responses to urban disinvestment.* Philadelphia: Temple University Press.

Steinbach, Carol. 1995. *Tying it all together: The comprehensive achievements of community-based development organizations.* Washington, D.C.: National Congress for Community Economic Development.

Stevens, Rebecca, Peter Dreier, and Jeff Brown. 1989. *From a military to a housing buildup: The impact in Boston of a six percent shift in the federal budget from the military to housing.* Boston: Boston Redevelopment Authority.

Stoecker, Randy. 1991. *Foundation funding for community-based development in the system of cities.* Toledo: Urban Affairs Center, University of Toledo.

Stone, Rebecca, ed. 1996. *Core issues in comprehensive community-building initiatives.* Chicago: Chapin Hall Center for Children at the University of Chicago.

Suchman, Diane R. 1990. *Public/Private housing partnerships.* Washington, D.C.: Urban Land Institute.

Sullivan, Mercer. 1993. *More than housing: How community development corporations go about changing lives and neighborhoods.* New York: Community Development Research Center, New School for Social Research.

Traynor, Bill. 1993. "Community development and community organizing," *Shelterforce* March/April.

U.S. Conference of Mayors. 1993. *A status report on hunger and homelessness in American cities: 1993.* Washington, D.C.

U.S. Department of Housing and Urban Development. 1994. *Worst case needs for housing assistance in the United States in 1990 and 1991.* Washington, D.C.: Office of Policy Development and Research.

United Way of America. 1992. *Housing initiatives program: 1992 survey.* Alexandria, Va.: United Way of America.

Urban Institute. 1994. *Status and prospects of the nonprofit sector: Report to the U.S. department of housing and urban development.* Washington, D.C: U.S. Department of Housing and Urban Development.

Vanhorenbeck, Susan. 1995. *A new HUD? The administration's proposal.* Washington, D.C.: Congressional Research Service, Library of Congress.

Vidal, Avis C. 1992. *Rebuilding communities: A national study of urban community development corporations.* New York: Community Development Research Center, New School for Social Research.

————. 1995. "Reintegrating disadvantaged communities into the fabric of urban life: The role of community development." *Housing Policy Debate* 6 (1)169–230.

Walker, Christopher. 1993. "Nonprofit housing development: Status, trends, and prospects." *Housing Policy Debate* 4 (3)369–414.

Wilson, William J. 1987. *The truly disadvantaged.* Chicago: University of Chicago Press.

————. 1996. *When work disappears.* Cambridge: Harvard University Press.

Wolter, Patti. 1991. "Consumer's guide to organizer training." *The Neighborhood Works* October/November.

———— 1993. "Tools of the Trade: A Resource Guide for Organizing Communities." *City Limits* August/September.

Wright, Gwendolyn. 1981. *Building the dream: A social history of housing in America.* Cambridge: MIT Press.

Chapter 6

Nonprofit Developers and Managers:
The Evolution of their Role in U.S. Housing Policy

Rachel G. Bratt

This chapter examines the historical development of housing policy in the United States relative to the nonprofit housing sector. The perception of a steady progression in U.S. housing policy toward nonprofit housing is challenged. Similar to Sanyal's emphasis on political context in chapter 4, Bratt shows housing programs have been designed in response to powerful political constituencies and that nonprofit housing has been "a sub-plot." Rather than the development of housing policy centered on nonprofit provision, Bratt argues that current initiatives are consistent with a policy history of sporadic and piecemeal attention to the nation's housing problems. There are increased expectations of the nonprofit sector but these expectations are accompanied by decreased resources and continued avoidance of comprehensive housing policies.

Introduction

There are at least two ways to describe the history of nonprofit housing groups in the United States. The first tells a linear story, starting with nineteenth-century reformers and bringing us to the nonprofit developers of the 1990s. The way the story generally is told, there is a continuous movement, a progression from one type of initiative to the next. It is a plausible story that has been told by several writers on the subject, including myself (Bratt 1989; Rasey et al. 1991). In further reviewing the literature, however, it is apparent that this, by now reasonably well accepted version of the history of nonprofit housing groups is flawed.

The drawback with the prevailing historical perspective is reminiscent of the central argument in Peter Marcuse's "Housing Policy and the Myth of the Benevolent State" (1986). In that article, Marcuse refutes the notion that we have, or ever had, a housing policy. He argues that the stages of federal involvement with housing, while often told in a sequential fashion, do not really constitute a flowing, continuous story at all. The housing programs that were created were the result of a series of political, economic, and social needs. They were not primarily a response to the need for housing, or due to the federal government's benevolent concern about the needs of the poor.

This chapter makes a first attempt at presenting a new, revised view of the history and growth of nonprofit housing organizations (NHOs) in the United States that follows Marcuse's analysis. The central argument is that at each period during which NHOs have arisen, the decision by government to use NHOs is the outcome of a series of political, economic, and social needs. The NHOs, themselves, are not the key actors in the story and federal initiatives have generally not been concerned with how to make these organizations and the nonprofit sector work more efficiently. NHOs, it is argued, are a subplot. In this new, reconstructed view, the history of NHOs in the U.S. is more a story about this country's overall negative view of the public housing program and about the confusion over the appropriate role of the private for-profit sector in affordable housing production, than it is a story about the nonprofit housing sector.

If our federal initiatives had been clearly targeted at advancing the capacity of NHOs to produce and manage affordable housing, we would expect to find a series of policies that clearly indicate progression, or learning, from one to the next; are unequivocally aimed at developing the NHOs; and are well coordinated. This would include adequate funding: to cover the organizational operations of the NHOs; to launch their developments; and to subsidize the tenants and assist with maintenance costs once the housing is built. It would also include a comprehensive support system, in terms of technical assistance and opportunities for the NHOs to network both among themselves and with other public and private actors who play a role in affordable housing development.

This article posits that we have never had such a series of initiatives, or what can be called a "nonprofit-centric housing policy." The programs that have been tried, which generally include one or more of the above components, have formed a discontinuous series of initiatives, which have not generally built on the experiences of their predecessors. To the extent that NHOs have recently captured national attention, and that we can be seduced into thinking that we are making serious moves toward a nonprofit-centric set of policies, we will be sorely disappointed and the fledgling movement is bound to suffer.

In recent years there have been many reports and studies that have demonstrated that NHOs present perhaps the best model for providing affordable housing and have argued for greater public support (Mayer 1984; Bratt 1989; Clay 1990; Goetz 1992; Vidal 1992). Nevertheless, we still have nowhere near the real commitment that would be needed to create a comprehensive support system for NHOs. Indeed, our present situation, in which the NHOs may be receiving "half (or not even half) a loaf of bread" may be worse than if they were receiving "no bread at all." If the present initiatives that involve NHOs are found wanting or, avoiding euphemisms, are failures, we may see an early demise of the contemporary nonprofit housing movement. Many may conclude that the programs don't work when, in fact, they were never given a real chance at success.

This new, and hopefully, more accurate depiction of how NHOs have evolved should clarify the extent to which their current problems are a direct result of political contstraints or to programs that have grown piecemeal and that have responded to one or more "urgent needs," and not necessarily to the needs and priorities of the NHOs.

Reform Movement

The story about NHOs usually starts with the efforts of the reformers in the nineteenth century. Responding to a general concern about the welfare of immigrants living in dense slum-type dwellings, the reformers were committed to improving housing conditions. Spurred by the dreary images publicized by Jacob Riis, in his famous photographic essay, *How the Other Half Lives,* the reformers were committed to improving the devastating housing conditions. However, as Lawrence Friedman has noted, an important concern of the reform movement involved the "social costs" that slums produced, in addition to the impacts on the individuals who resided there, or "welfare costs" (Friedman 1968:30).

Despite some real altruism on the part of the reformers, there were actually very few projects that were purely philanthropic. According to one of the key activists of the period, Edith Wood, as of 1919 there were only two no-profit housing developments in existence and, she further noted, "pure philanthropy cannot be described as the American method of solving the housing problem" (quoted in Friedman: 77). In place of purely charitable activities, housing reformers promoted the idea of limited-profit or limited-dividend model tenements for the poor. Although it was hoped that the opportunity to earn a modest profit would lure businessmen into producing low-rent housing, another leading reformer, Catherine Bauer, noted that the economics of even the limited dividend plan were not workable. The model builders wanted "to provide good dwellings, on an 'economic' basis, at a price which everyone could pay, and without disturbing or even questioning any part of the current social-economic system," it was an "impossible job" (quoted in Friedman 1968:87).

Lawrence Friedman's summation of the reform movement was grim. "The *movement* itself failed; it did not solve the slum problem, and, like the tenement house laws, did not succeed in keeping the love and admiration of housing experts" (Friedman 1968:82). This hardly can be considered a building block for the next generation of nonprofit housing producers. Although these groups are often cited as the precursors to the contemporary nonprofit housing movement, a more careful reading of the past seems to indicate that there was an abrupt cessation of the early nonprofit movement and little or nothing of that experience found its way into more recent initiatives.

Section 202 Program

Nonprofit housing organizations did not emerge again until about a half-century later, in 1959. Although a linear view of history places them right after the reform movement, these NHOs emerged for different reasons and had a completely different mandate. The Section 202 program, enacted as part of the Housing Act of 1959, was to provide "independent living" for elderly and handicapped individuals. A preceding program, administered by the Federal Housing Administration (FHA), did not include any subsidy, and the resulting rents were considered "too high for most elderly couples and individuals" (quoted in Bratt: 1989, 88). The Section 202 program was aimed at people whose incomes made them ineligible for conventional public housing, but too low to afford an unsubsidized unit in the private rental market, with or without FHA insurance.

The Section 202 program represented the first time that Congress gave responsibility to NHOs to implement a housing program aimed at the general public. The prevailing major housing subsidy program, the public housing program, was administered through local public housing authorities, and an unsubsidized mortgage insurance program, which utilized private homebuilders and financial institutions, was administered by the FHA.

The Section 202 program provided a direct, below-market-interest rate loan to nonprofit developers to build low-rent housing for the elderly and handicapped. It was modeled after the College Housing Program, created in 1950, which also provided direct below-market-interest rate loans to colleges or universities. As I have written elsewhere, since the Section 202 program represented a major departure from the public housing program, one might have expected substantial debate in Congress concerning the advisability of nonprofit organizations sponsoring low-income housing. Yet the only groups opposed to the program's being limited to NHOs were, as could be expected, the home building and real estate lobby (the same groups that had opposed the conventional public housing program). More typical was the following "motherhood-and-apple-pie" view, expressed by a congressman from Colorado: The nonprofit is an organization "whose interest is the well-being of the members and the persons whom it serves. . . . There is no desire to profiteer, there is no desire to cheat. There is a desire only to give the maximum service for the money available" (Bratt 1989:184).

One plausible reason why Congress limited participation in the Section 202 program to NHOs is the following: "Since the Section 202 program was modeled after the College Housing Program, and since colleges are nonprofit institutions, restricting the Section 202 program to NHOs may have been an unquestioned assumption" (Bratt 1989:184).

Sponsors of Section 202 housing generally were well-established religious, occupational, and fraternal groups who were able to raise funds from their members. Although the NHOs enjoyed a good reputation, as did the overall Section 202 program, this particular form of sponsorship was only partly responsible for the positive assessment of the program.[1]

In terms of our present attempt to understand the history of the NHOs, these nonprofit sponsors were different from the limited dividend sponsors of the reform period. They were truly nonprofit organizations and they were primarily civic associations, rather than altruistic businessmen. In tracing the history of the Section 202 program, neither references to the reform movement, nor to the lessons learned, were part of the discussion surrounding the creation of the newer program. Again, NHOs were chosen as the vehicles to produce housing because of the circumstances of the times and as an outgrowth of what likely was a nonprofit housing program by chance, rather than by design, but not as the next chapter in an evolving saga about nonprofit housing organizations.

The third period during which NHOs became prominent on the housing landscape was the 1960s. There were three distinct sets of programs that contributed to the proliferation of NHOs during this period. This, in itself, provides further corroboration of the thesis of this chapter: the history of nonprofit housing initiatives does not form a coherent, continuous progression. Instead, it reveals programs that were created to meet differing goals and to respond to a variety of situations. If, on the other hand, an overriding goal of the 1960s had been to create a system of affordable housing development through NHOs, it would have been absurd to do it in three distinct ways, using three sets of programs, as discussed below.

The First Federal Public–Private Subsidized Housing Programs— Sections 221(d)(3) and 236

By the 1960s, public housing was becoming the target of substantial criticism. The relentless opposition by the National Association of Home Builders and the National Association of Real Estate Boards further eroded congressional support for the public housing program. President Johnson's 1968 Committee on Urban Housing issued a report that clearly articulated the shift in federal housing policy toward the private sector and, implicitly, away from the public housing program:

> The nation has been slow to realize that private industry in many cases is an efficient vehicle for achieving social goals . . . some programs still make too little use

of the talents of private entrepreneurs. . . . One of the basic lessons of the history of Federal housing programs seems to be that the programs which work best— such as the FHA mortgage insurance programs—are those that channel the forces of existing economic institutions into productive areas. This approach has proved to be better than wholly ignoring existing institutions and starting afresh outside the prevailing market system. Reliance on market forces should be increased in the future. (Report of the President's Committee on Urban Housing 1968:54).

The Section 221(d)(3) and 236 programs, enacted in 1961 and 1968 respectively, were, in part, a direct response to the growing opposition to the public housing program. Known as the "below-market-interest-rate programs," these two initiatives provided the first major opportunities to the private sector to become involved with subsidized rental housing production.[2] Among the eligible sponsors for this housing were NHOs, although they were not nearly as prominent as the for-profit developers. By June 1970 only about 28 percent of all units built under these two programs had been sponsored by NHOs (Keyes 1971). Unlike the generally positive experiences of the NHOs in the Section 202 program, the NHOs utilizing these two later programs encountered far more difficulties, including: inadequate resources, lack of experience, and an unsympathetic HUD. Additional problems and constraints were caused by the NHO desire to incorporate social goals and tackle particularly difficult situations, such as launching developments in depressed inner-city areas (Bratt 1989). The outcome was that nonprofit-owned developments failed at two to four times the rate experienced by their for-profit counterparts (Friedland and MacRae 1979; GAO 1978).

Although it would be convenient to view the NHOs operating under these programs as a direct outgrowth of the NHOs in the Section 202 program, there was probably little link between the two. The NHOs in the 1960s programs were allowed to participate because of an overall shift in federal policy away from the public provision of subsidized housing and toward the private sector. While private for-profit developers were the dominant sponsors of these programs, it is likely that the NHOs under the 202 program did help to pave the way for NHOs to be included in the 221(d)(3) and 236 programs. But the experiences of the two sets of nonprofit developers were radically different, with those developing the nonelderly housing encountering serious obstacles. If, however, the lessons of the 202 program had been heeded, and if the nonprofit experience had been a continuous one, it is possible that many of the problems confronting these groups would not have surfaced.

War on Poverty Era

The second set of nonprofit housing programs operating in the 1960s grew out of a different series of concerns from those that gave rise to the below-market-interest rate programs. During the War on Poverty, the Office of Economic

Opportunity and the Model Cities Program supported the creation of community action agencies and housing development corporations, respectively. Although these entities were supposed to provide opportunities for maximum feasible participation of the poor and contribute to resident empowerment, they were "top down" initiatives—programs mandated by a central authority, rather than spontaneously formed by neighborhood groups. These efforts, however well intentioned, never grew into a significant movement and, according to a major evaluation of the housing development corporations undertaken during that period: "They are saddled with goals and objectives that are far beyond their resources to achieve" (quoted in Keyes 1971:169).

Again, the important point in terms of this analysis is that these NHOs, which were operating at exactly the same time as the NHOs utilizing the Section 221(d)(3) and 236 programs, emerged out of a separate set of concerns. While some housing development corporations participated in the below-market-interest rate programs, it was an essentially unplanned happening, rather than a targeted and well thought out arrangement.

Special Impact Program and Title VII

The third and probably most significant set of programs to emerge during the 1960s were the community development corporations (CDCs)[3] funded through the 1966 Special Impact Amendment to the Economic Opportunity Act. In 1974, additional funding was provided through Title VII of the Community Services Act. With a mission that reached far beyond the housing goals of the preceding NHOs, these organizations were aimed at promoting a broad economic development agenda. From 1966 to 1981, more than $500 million in federal funds were allocated to 63 CDCs through these two programs (National Center for Economic Alternatives 1981:25, 27; see also Abt Associates 1973). The outcomes and levels of success among these organizations have varied dramatically. A few are still operating on multimillion dollar budgets and have produced hundreds of housing units, jobs, and business ventures. However, seven of the sixty-three CDCs were never able to proceed beyond the planning stages. In between, there has been a wide range of productivity and experience (National Center for Economic Alternatives 1981:49).

Journalists Neil Peirce and Carol Steinbach claim that the Title VII CDCs embodied an important idea: "rather than federal aid alone, rather than simply opening the doors to political participation of the poor, it was time to create new economic bases in troubled communities" (1987:20). Although this concept was relatively new, it had already been embraced by the Ford Foundation. Its Grey Areas program provided funding directly to local community groups engaged in various aspects of economic development and was the forerunner to the War on Poverty's Community Action Program.

Peirce and Steinbach attribute the birth of the "modern CDC movement" to "the February day in 1966 when Senator Robert F. Kennedy toured the dilapidated streets of Bed-Stuy and planted the seeds for what would become the Bedford-Stuyvesant Restoration Corporation and the beginnings of federal involvement with CDCs. Kennedy was despondent over urban riots, just begun with Watts in 1965" (1987:20). Thus, according to this account, this group of CDCs emerged from a unique set of events: a response to the urban riots and to a political commitment to do something positive about deteriorated urban areas.

The driving force behind these CDCs is reminiscent of the motivations of the early reformers. However, the nonprofit vehicle chosen bore little resemblance to the quasi-business, quasi-philanthropic associations of that period. In comparison with the other contemporary nonprofit initiatives, these NHOs had little, if anything, to do with the disappointment with the conventional public housing program (as with the NHOs in the Section 221(d)(3) and 236 programs). And, although they shared many of the same philosophical underpinnings as the War on Poverty era housing development corporations, there seemed to be no self-conscious attempt to link the two burgeoning movements.

From Advocacy to Development: 1970s

During the 1970s scores of housing and advocacy groups, which had organized to protest bank redlining, arson, and urban renewal or to support rent control campaigns, eventually coalesced behind a housing development agenda. The frustration with the limited goals of the tenants' movement led one Boston community organizer to conclude: "The programmatic proposals of the tenants' movement have been almost entirely defensive ones. Instead, campaigns for defensive measures like rent control must be accompanied by positive proposals for saving and increasing the supply of affordable housing" (McAfee 1986:418).

The key vehicle that groups have pursued to enhance the supply of affordable housing has been NHOs. According to Avis Vidal's 1987–88 survey of 130 CDCs across the country, "In a majority of cases (53 percent) CDC formation was an outgrowth of other ongoing community-based activities. These included community organizing efforts around opposition to urban renewal plans, Community Reinvestment Act challenges, tenant organizing or counseling, and the provision of social service programs for poor or elderly households" (Vidal 1992:37–38).

Another group of NHOs that developed during the 1970s did so as a direct result of federal initiatives. First, the Neighborhood Housing Services (NHS) program, originally created in Pittsburgh in 1968, became a model that was vigorously promoted during the 1970s, first by the Federal Home Loan Bank Board and HUD and, after the enactment of 1978 federal legislation, by a new free-standing federal agency, the Neighborhood Reinvestment Corporation. Although the original goal of most NHS groups has been to provide a revolving loan fund to promote housing rehabilitation, some NHSs have moved into housing development, and generally are considered a type of CDC (see, for example, Vidal 1992:175). As of FY 1992, there were 158 NHSs in existence (U.S. General Accounting Office 1992:9).

A second federal initiative of the 1970s was the Neighborhood Self-Help Development program. This model program, enacted in 1978, provided a total of $15 million in direct federal grants of up to $100,000 to community development groups in 1979 and 1980. The NSHD program was the direct outcome of President Jimmy Carter's Urban Policy Report, which called for the creation of partnerships among local government, the private sector and residents, and underscored the importance of the neighborhood in city building and rebuilding efforts. The report stated:

> Many neighborhood groups around the country have begun successful, innovative community planning and neighborhood revitalization activities. This trend should be encouraged by the Federal government. Neighborhood residents and groups are the ones affected most directly by revitalization efforts. They are the closest to some of the problems and often best able to judge what solutions will be most effective. No urban policy can succeed if it ignores the views of neighborhood people and groups and if it does not secure their continuous involvement in varied neighborhood improvement efforts. (HUD-*The President's National Urban Policy Report* 1978: 121).[4]

Research on the NSHD program, conducted by the Urban Institute in the early 1980s, revealed that the program had compiled a good record (Mayer 1984). Nevertheless, early during President Reagan's first term, the NSHD program was removed from the federal agenda.

Also noteworthy during the 1970s was the absence of any specific role for nonprofit groups in the major community development legislation of the decade—the Community Development Block Grant program. Although NHOs were eligible to, and have received CDBG funds, they were neither targeted as recipients of the funding, nor were any specific programs created to assist in their development. (Nevertheless, according to Vidal [1992:3], 78 percent of the surveyed CDCs received federal funds, most commonly from the CDBG program.)

Despite the weak federal support for NHOs during the 1970s, including the phaseout of a major source of federal funding that had been utilized by the NHOs—the Section 8 New Construction and Substantial Rehabilitation programs—the number of these groups grew significantly during the decade. According to Vidal's survey, 53 percent of the CDCs in the sample were created between 1973 and 1980 (1992:35).

In summary, many community action and advocacy groups from the 1960s embraced housing development during the 1970s and a small-scale, successful federal program, NSHD, was launched. Also, through the assistance of the Neighborhood Reinvestment Corporation, NHS programs proliferated. But these groups appear to have related very little, if at all, to one another. Coordination between the contemporary efforts and earlier ones, such as Title VII, were absent. By the end of the 1970s, what emerged was a complex series of programs, each created for its own unique purposes, attempting to satisfy or respond to some specific needs, but in no way resembling a coherent nonprofit housing system. Yet it is probably fair to say that the contemporary nonprofit housing movement was launched during the early 1970s, despite the federal retrenchment that has continued to the present time.

Federal Retrenchment and Nonprofit Growth in the 1980s

Perhaps it was this sense of chaos that stimulated the creation of two major new national intermediaries to assist NHOs. The Local Initiatives Support Corporation (LISC) was formed in 1980 and the Enterprise Foundation in 1981. The mission of both is to channel private financial resources and technical assistance to community-based development groups. Together, these organizations have raised millions of dollars that have been loaned or given to NHOs, resulting in the production of thousands of units of affordable housing and the creation of jobs and business opportunities.

During the 1980s a unique type of NHO became increasingly prevalent. Groups were created all across the country committed to developing shelters and other types of facilities for the homeless. These NHOs also do not appear to fit into a continuous link with their NHO predecessors. Instead, they are, by and large, service providers and often were developed as spinoffs to preexisting community organizations and churches aimed at assisting the poor. The McKinney Act, enacted in 1987, provided direct federal support to assist organizations to develop homeless shelters and subsidized various types of emergency programs targeted at this population.

Although federal support for other types of nonprofit housing was virtually nonexistent during the early 1980s, the Housing and Urban-Rural Recovery Act of 1983 created a new, small-scale Neighborhood Development Demonstration Program (NDD) aimed at increasing the capacity of organizations to raise funds from local private donors and to become more self-sufficient. Between 1984 and 1989 $7 million was appropriated. The final evaluation of the program's operation during this period revealed that two-thirds of the community-based organizations receiving funding met or exceeded the amounts they planned to raise from their neighborhoods. Further, the program had some success in assisting groups to become self-sufficient by developing new, lasting sources of funding (Urban Institute 1992:v–vi). But the strategy chosen reflected the prevailing views of the Reagan and Bush administrations.

Clearly, the NDD program's shift in federal funding (compared to the NSHD program), its requirement for matching funds, and its focus on fund-raising capacity are all consistent with the kind of public-private partnership advocated by the Reagan administration—limited on the public side and sub-stantial on the private side. Despite the program's small scale, it did provide some much needed resources and helped keep alive the promise of community-based housing in a financially constrained period (Bratt 1989:171).

For fiscal years 1990–1992 an additional $6 million was appropriated for the NDD. But in view of the overall reduced commitment to housing during the Reagan years, many state and local programs were created to help close the gap (Pickman et al. 1986; Stegman and Holden 1987). Many of these initiatives were targeted to NHOs. According to the findings from a survey of cities with populations over 100,000, Edward Goetz found that 95 percent of these cities have CDCs working on affordable housing and that 89 percent provide some form of financial or technical assistance (Goetz 1992:424, 432).

Despite the scarcity of federal funds, one-fifth of the CDCs sampled by Vidal (1992:36) were created between 1981 and 1988. Further evidence of the activity during the 1980s comes from the 1991 survey of 1,160 groups con-ducted by the National Congress for Community Economic Development. Their report states that 39 percent of the CDCs responding to the survey had been operational less than ten years; 16 percent had incorporated between 1986 and 1990 (NCCED 1991:4).

This could lead to a conclusion that would warm the hearts of many con-servatives: the less federal money available for housing, the more state and local governments have moved in to fill the void, and the greater the participation at the community level. Is this evidence that state and local governments can, by themselves, address their own local problems? I would answer, emphatically, no.

State and local governments may have tried during the Reagan-Bush years to help NHOs produce affordable housing and their record of production pro-vides evidence of the tenacity and creativity of these groups, but we have made their job a difficult and convoluted one. The nonprofit development process gen-erally includes dozens of public and private funders, each with different require-ments, and it invariably produces reams of legal documents. The commonly used phrase, "creative financing," is a euphemism for how you make a deal work when there is no single direct and deep source of subsidy. What emerges for most projects is a patchwork quilt of funding sources, somewhat reminiscent of a Rube Goldberg cartoon. The problems that this creates for NHOs include enor-mous amounts of time and money expended to get projects built, and increased management costs due the need to report to multiple funding sources (Bratt et al. 1994). All of these factors ultimately increase the costs of housing.

The 1990s: A Precarious Era

Despite all the difficulties facing nonprofit housing developers, by the end of the 1980s they generally were viewed as credible producers of decent, affordable housing. This message was not lost on Congress, as news of successes at the local level began to be heard in Washington.

NHOs recently have gained visibility in policy debates and have won some important legislative victories. The Financial Institutions Reform, Recovery, and Enforcement Act of 1989 (known as, FIRREA, the savings and loan bailout legislation) provides NHOs the first right to purchase distressed S & L properties from the Resolution Trust Corporation. A similar provision, aimed at the properties owned by failed commercial banks, was included in the Comprehensive Deposit Insurance Reform Act of 1991 (the FDIC bailout legislation). Also significant is the provision under Title VI of the Cranston-Gonzalez National Affordable Housing Act of 1990 that gives NHOs and other "priority purchasers" the first right to make a bona fide offer to purchase a federally subsidized development whose owner has announced an interest in prepaying the mortgage, as a way to permanently solve the "expiring use" problem.

But, pertaining more directly to this chapter, the most important aspect of the 1990 act is Title II, the HOME program, which authorizes a 15 percent setaside for nonprofit producers of affordable housing. In FY 1995 the set-aside was $150 million, based on a total HOME appropriation of $1 billion. Although this set-aside for NHOs provides a real boost to the communitybased development movement, there are compelling reasons why, on balance, the current picture for affordable housing, in general, and federal support for housing produced by NHOs more specifically, is bleak.

First, financial resources, the life-blood of affordable housing, are scarce and diminishing. Since the November 1994 congressional elections, we are witnessing an unprecedented assault on the affordable housing agenda. Although President Clinton ultimately vetoed the bill that would have virtually eliminated HUD, the message sent by the 104th Congress was not lost on the president. The Clinton administration, in what has been characterized as a pre-emptive strike, put forth a massive plan for restructuring and downsizing HUD and its various programs. With the general tenor of the times being anti-big-government and a desire to balance the federal budget and reduce deficits, there seems to be little room for adding resources for affordable housing, let alone to significantly bolster the support system for NHOs.

In addition, with the cessation of the Section 8 New Construction/Substantial Rehabilitation programs and the recent assault on public housing, there has been an end to the era of deep subsidy programs, and the HOME program set-aside funds are far from adequate. Only one year after the HOME program was launched, funding was cut back drastically. But whether the set-aside is

$225 million (as in FY 1992) or $150 million (as in FY 1993 and FY 1995), in either case, the sum is not large. For many localities, the 15 percent set-aside will not result in a great deal of money. The minimum entitlement allocation under HOME for participating jurisdictions is $500,000; 15 percent of this is $75,000. In terms of affordable housing production, it is an understatement to say that this is not a great deal of money. In some jurisdictions, it will be diffi-cult to use this money for development unless additional funds are earmarked for NHOs.

Furthermore, the number of federal programs available for use along with HOME funds, in order to make the housing affordable, is not large. The only possibilities are the Low Income Housing Tax Credit,[5] Section 8 vouchers, and tax-exempt mortgage revenue bonds. We do not have a direct, single source of subsidy money that groups can use to simply produce and maintain affordable housing.

Second, even if we had a more supportive political environment, a num-ber of issues would still present problems for the fledgling nonprofit housing movement. For example, there is still the issue of uneven development of NHOs. Although there are over 2,000 community-based development organi-zations in the U.S. (National Congress for Community Economic Develop-ment 1991), in some locales they are plentiful, while in others they are more scarce. For example, in the Goetz survey of cities with populations over 100,000, cited earlier, officials in seven cities indicated that there were no NHOs in their area; 59 indicated that they had one to four NHOs. In terms of the overall sample, this represented 50 percent of the cities surveyed. Further, both Goetz and Vidal found that NHOs are far more common in the midwest and northeast, than in the south and west (Goetz 1992:424; Vidal 1992:107). It was not until 1992 that Congress acknowledged the lack of capacity problem. The Housing and Community Development Act of 1992 authorized up to 20 percent of a jurisdiction's 15 percent set-aside (but not to exceed $150,000) to be used to help develop the capacity of NHOs,[6] if an insufficient number of capable groups are identified. Despite this effort, we are still a long way from having an adequate number of NHOs in many parts of the country.

Notwithstanding the overall number of NHOs in the U.S., many are rela-tively inexperienced and have minimal track records in housing production. In nearly 60 percent of the cities surveyed in the Goetz study, NHOs had pro-duced less than 50 units in 1989. And, according to the survey by the National Congress for Community Economic Development, nearly two-thirds of the CDCs that were less than ten years old produced fewer units over a three-year period than the overall universe of CDCs in the study (NCCED, 1991).

Finally, Vidal has noted that additional CDC activity in a given locale was most prevalent in those cities that already had the most community-based activ-ity as of the early 1980s. The greatest absolute growth occurred in the largest cities (Vidal 1992:107). In terms of the HOME set-aside, if many locales are unable to use the funds, because of a lack of organizational capacity or because of a dearth of organizations altogether, the community-based housing agenda could suffer a serious setback.

A third problem is that HOME funding is particularly poor in the support that it provides to meet the organizational expenses of NHOs. For FY 1992 only $14 million was available for this purpose, as well as for broader educational efforts and technical assistance aimed at NHOs. In the original HOME program, other monies were explicitly barred from being used for general operating expenses. Again, the Housing and Community Development Act of 1992 attempted to respond to this serious defect. Starting in FY 1993, 5 percent of each jurisdiction's total HOME allocation may be used to meet operating costs of NHOs. This sum is in addition to the 15 percent set-aside. Nevertheless, we can still question whether there will be adequate capacity, even with the newly available funds, to enable NHOs to develop projects.

Fourth, a comprehensive support system for NHOs would have to include financial and technical support for existing NHOs. Yet no HOME funds are earmarked to assist more mature NHOs to manage their existing stocks of affordable housing. In many locales, NHOs have shown that they can build and operate decent, affordable housing over the short term. But there is evidence that groups are having difficulty keeping their projects physically and financially viable (Bratt et al. 1994). In the end, the success of the nonprofit production programs will be measured more by whether the developments built remain viable and affordable over the long term, rather than by whether community-based NHOs can produce needed units over the short term.

HOME presents some good opportunities for NHOs. But the serious limits in funding for operating expenses, combined with uncertainties about the number of groups that will be able to carry out development projects, as well as the overall small-scale of the appropriations, may create serious disappointments. Further, the limitations in the HOME program provide ample evidence that we do not yet have a federal commitment to support NHOs.

Although many states and locales have done a great deal to support nonprofit community-based housing development, these efforts go only part of the way toward building a comprehensive program to support NHOs. Further, this reliance on state and local resources, while providing much of the resources during the Reagan-Bush era, are not secure sources of funds. As many states and locales are facing their own fiscal crises, cutbacks are becoming commonplace. For example, in Massachusetts, a program that provides operating support for CDCs, known as the CEED program, reached a high of over $2.2 million in FY 1989. But only three years later, with a new Republican governor and the official end of the "Massachusetts Miracle," annual funding dropped by two-thirds to $750,000, with the figure falling to $700,000 in FY 1995. Another serious problem for

NHOs in Massachusetts unfolded in late 1992. Dramatic reductions in funding for the state-run rental housing allowance-type program, known as Section 707, put enormous pressure both on low-income households whose subsidies were reduced, as well as on the owners of the housing, including many NHOs, who rely on these subsidies to cover their development's operating expenses.

Based on the above, it is clear that we have not yet made the commitment to fully support NHOs at anything greater than a nominal level. To change this, NHOs and the public, private, and nonprofit organizations that support them will need to be aggressive in articulating the problems they are facing both in managing their stock of housing, as well as in producing affordable units. They need to be clear about the inadequacies of the system in which they have been asked to function and underscore that they are making the best of an extremely tough situation. As Koebel (1992) has noted, "If the nonprofit housing sector becomes identified as a supporter and benefactor of this inefficiency, it runs the risk of being branded as inefficient once again." Further, when problems arise, there will be a strong tendency to blame the NHOs for their inadequacies, rather than to see their problems as the direct outcome of a flawed system. A "blaming the victim" scenario could prove seriously damaging to the struggling nonprofit housing movement.

Strong federal policies, programs, and financing are absolutely critical. While this chapter has argued that we have never had a coherent, progressive set of federal policies aimed at supporting nonprofit programs, this would be a good time to create such a system. A good beginning could involve revisions in the HOME program so that NHOs would be better served. This would, hopefully, bring us closer to reaching that elusive goal of a nonprofit-centric housing system. In making this recommendation, however, it is also critical to underscore that there is a continuing need to support a revitalized public housing program, as well as new forms of public-private partnership programs, in which the lessons from past efforts are incorporated into the new initiatives (see Bratt 1989). There is no single "magic bullet" in the arsenal for attacking housing problems. We must continue to promote a multifaceted housing agenda, so that local and state governments can create programs that best meet their needs. While HOME allows for much of this flexibility, its serious limitations in funding and overall scope will prevent a full-scale effort to meet the housing needs of low-income households.

Of course, these recommendations for increased federal support for affordable housing and direct and deep assistance for NHOs are, as noted earlier, painfully out-of-step with the mood of Congress. Whether the current views of the Republican majority will prevail in the years to come is unknown. But the after-shocks of the 1990s, with both the president and congress keen on downsizing and streamlining HUD, will further delay the time when a series of federal programs to support the work of NHOs in meeting the nation's housing needs will become a reality.

Notes

1. Bratt (1989) details a series of reasons for the overall success of the Section 202 program, only one of which involves the nonprofit sponsors.

2. Known as below-market-interest-rate programs, Section 221(d)(3) provided direct federal loans to private for-profit or nonprofit developers who, in exchange for a mortgage interest rate as low as 3%, agreed to rent their apartments to low and moderate income households. The Section 236 program operated in a similar fashion, except that rather than providing loans directly, the federal government subsidized the interest rate on privately originated loans to as low as 1%.

3. CDCs are essentially the same as the organizations being discussed in this chapter, although the former also often work in nonhousing areas, such as economic development and job training.

4. Despite such highly supportive rhetoric of the community-based approach, there is evidence that the Carter White House was not fully committed to NSHD (Bratt 1989: 170).

5. Prior to FY 1993 HOME funds and the low-income housing tax credit could not be used together.

6. In the 1990 housing legislation, NHOs are called community housing development organizations, or CHDOs. For purposes of this chapter, however, the terms are used synonymously, and NHO is used even if the exact term being referred to by Congress is CHDO.

References

Abt Associates, Inc. 1973. "An evaluation of the special impact program, final report." Vol. 1, Summary. Report prepared for the Office of Economic Opportunity, Contract no. B00–5181. Cambridge, Mass.

Bratt, Rachel G. 1989. *Rebuilding a low-income housing policy.* Philadelphia: Temple University Press.

———, Langley C. Keyes, Alex Schwartz, and Avis C. Vidal. 1994. *Confronting the management challenge: Affordable housing in the nonprofit sector.* New York: Community Development Research Center, New School for Social Research.

Clay, Phillip L. 1990. "Mainstreaming the community builders: The challenge of expanding the capacity of nonprofit housing development organizations." Cambridge, Mass.: Department of Urban Studies and Planning, M.I.T.

Friedland, J. Eric, and C. Duncan MacRae. 1973. "FHA multifamily financial failure: A review of empirical studies." *Journal of American Real Estate and Urban Economics Association* 7 (2) spring 95–122.

Friedman, Lawrence 1968. *Government and slum housing.* Chicago: Rand McNally.

Goetz, Edward G. 1992. "Local government support for nonprofit housing: A survey of U.S. cities." *Urban Affairs Quarterly* 27 (3) March 420–35.

Keyes, Langley C., Jr. 1971. "The role of nonprofit sponsors in the production of housing." In Papers submitted to U.S. House Committee on Banking and Currency, Subcommittee on Housing Panels on Housing Production, Housing Demand, and Developing a Suitable Living Environment." 92nd congress, 1st session, part 1. 159–81.

Koebel, C. Theodore. 1992. "International comparisons of nonprofit housing in the post-welfare state." Unpublished manuscript. Presented at the 1992 AREUEA/USC School of Business Administration, International Conference on Real Estate and Urban Economics. Redondo Beach, California. October 23.

Marcuse, Peter. 1986. "Housing policy and the myth of the benevolent state." In *Critical Perspectives on Housing*. Rachel G. Bratt, Chester Hartman, and Ann Meyerson, eds. Philadelphia: Temple University Press. 248–58.

Mayer, Neil S. 1984. *Neighborhood organizations and community development*. Washington, D.C.: Urban Institute.

McAfee, Kathy 1986. "Socialism and the housing movement: Lessons from Boston." In *Critical Perspectives on Housing*. Rachel G. Bratt, Chester Hartman, and Ann Meyerson, eds. Philadelphia: Temple University Press. 405–27.

National Center for Economic Alternatives, 1981. "Federal assistance to community development corporations: An evaluation of Title VII of the Community Services Act of 1974." Report prepared for the U.S. Community Services Administration, Washington, D.C.

National Congress for Community Economic Development (NCCED). 1991. "Changing the odds." Washington, D.C.

Peirce, Neil R. and Carol F. Steinbach. 1987. *Corrective capitalism: The rise of America's community development corporations*. New York: Ford Foundation.

Pickman, James, Benson F. Roberts, Mindy Leiterman, and Robert N. Mittle. 1986. *Producing lower income housing: Local initiatives*. Washington, D.C.: Bureau of National Affairs.

Rasey, Keith P., W. Dennis Keating, Norman Krumholz, and Philip D. Star. 1991. "Management of neighborhood development: Community development corporations." In *Managing local government*. Newbury Park, Calif.: Sage Publications.

Report of the President's Committee on Urban Housing. 1968. *A decent home*. Washington, D.C.

Riis, Jacob A. 1890 [1957]. *How the other half lives*. New York: Hill & Wang.

Stegman, Michael A., and J. David Holden. 1987. *Nonfederal housing programs*. Washington, D.C.: Urban Land Institute.

U.S. Department of Housing and Urban Development (HUD). 1978. "The president's national urban policy report." Washington, D.C.

U.S. General Accounting Office. 1978. "Section 236 rental housing: An evaluation with lessons for the future." Report to the Congress of the United States by the Comptroller General. PAD 78-13. Washington, D.C.: Government Printing Office.

U.S. General Accounting Office (GAO), 1992. "Community development: Neighborhood reinvestment corporation should improve program management." Report to Congressional Requesters. GAO/RCED–92–174. Washington, D.C.: Government Printing Office.

The Urban Institute. 1992. "Final evaluation of the neighborhood development demonstration program." Final Report. Prepared for U.S. Department of Housing and Urban Development. Contract no. HC–5841.

Vidal, Avis C. 1992. *Rebuilding communities: A national study of urban community development corporations*. New York: Community Development Research Center, New School for Social Research.

Chapter 7

The Development of the Social Rental Sector in Western Europe in Relation to Housing Policy

Peter J. Boelhouwer and Harry M. H. van der Heijden

Many countries in Western Europe have relied heavily on nonprofit provision, particularly since World War II. This chapter examines the development of the social rental sector in seven European countries. Four common stages of housing policy development are identified, characterized in turn by strong government involvement particularly in response to the postwar housing shortage; increasing housing quality; the housing problems of specific target groups and the withdrawal of the government in favor of the private market for the provision of housing to the middle class; and a return to problems of production. Despite the appearance of most of these stages in each country, national housing markets and housing policies are very individualized due to differences in market structures, institutions, ideologies, and traditions.

Introduction

Compared with the USA, in many west European countries the share of the social rental sector in the housing stock is considerable. The growth of this sector was especially strong in the first decades after World War II. In this period there was in many countries strong government intervention, with policy directed toward restructuring of the economy and, as regards housing, making up quantitative arrears in dwellings. In general a major role, supported by extensive subsidies, was assigned to the public or semipublic social rental sector. In many west European countries, the social rental sector provides accommodation to large sections of the population. More recently, however, in most countries the financial support to the social rental sector has decreased, and is increasingly directed toward the lower income groups.

In this chapter we devote attention to the development and the properties of this sector in seven countries: Belgium, Denmark, England, France, the

Netherlands, Germany, and Sweden. The relationship with the government policy followed forms the point of departure of the analyses. For a proper understanding of the development of the social rental sector, the specific properties and the challenges facing the sector in the nineties, it is important that insight is given into the circumstances that have led to the various governments developing an extensive social rental sector in the past. Such insight is also useful for the countries lacking an intermediate sector of this kind (the former eastern bloc countries and the USA) and experiencing problems in providing the lowest income population with suitable housing accommodations.

A distinction is made between two levels of analysis. First we focus on the development of housing policy in general and of the social rental sector in particular. In this section the arguments and the way in which the various governments have decided in the past to intervene in the housing market are discussed. However, a broad-brush comparison does not do justice to the complexity and the diversity that the various social rental sectors have undergone in the seven countries. Therefore we next review the principal properties of the social rental sector per country, to establish whether these correspond to the broad-brush description. The development of the social rented sector and its resultant specific characteristics largely also determine the challenges facing this sector in the nineties. Lastly, we draw general conclusions about the development of the social rental sector and its possible future development.

Housing Policy in Relation to the Development of the Social Rental Sector

The roots of the social rental sector in many western European countries lie at the end of the nineteenth century. Rapid industrialization led to a great drift by the rural population to the overfull cities. Poor private housing construction, a shortage of dwellings, and bitter poverty led to miserable living conditions. To help alleviate this distress, philanthropic societies set up the first social housing construction projects. Incidentally, these actions were also largely inspired by self-interest. Due to the poor state of hygiene in impoverished working-class neighborhoods, epidemics such as cholera and typhus broke out regularly, and social unrest led to threatening proportions among the proletariat. Screening off the working-class neighborhoods proved not to lead to a real solution. Diseases also spread over the more prosperous parts of the city. In most countries this development led to the introduction around 1900 of the first statutory provisions regarding housing construction.

Up to World War I, the development of regulations and housing construction by private associations and employers led in most countries to a very modest social housing construction production of only a small percent of the housing market. The lion's share of housing construction production was by the private sector. However, in many west European countries regulations now established minimum qualitative requirements of these dwellings. This situation changed after the outbreak of World War I. Because of lack of building materials, inflation, rising housing prices, and political instability, governments felt obliged to intervene in the housing market by making subsidies available to private nonprofit institutions known as housing associations. In addition to the original associations inspired by philanthropy and self-interest, new associations set up by the workers' movement also came into being. However, the boom in the production of social rental dwellings was only temporary. By the end of the 1920s production had been taken over again by the private sector. Through this development the social rental sector in western Europe played a modest part in the first half of the twentieth century. Thus in 1945 the proportion of social rental dwellings in the housing stock was relatively limited and varied from less then 5 percent in Belgium and Sweden to more than 10 percent in England and the Netherlands.

After 1945 the golden era dawned for the social rental sector. As several authors (including McGuire 1981, and Adriaansens and Priemus 1986) have already noted, one can distinguish a number of stages in housing policy in these countries since World War II. As a general guide, four stages may be distinguished. The stage a particular country is in depends to a great extent on a number of external factors, the perception of the role and tasks of government in general, and of the housing targets and objectives of the government in particular. With regard to external factors, the level of supply and demand within the housing market and economic conditions play a role of great importance.

Equilibrium in the housing market is determined by a combination of demographic factors and the level of housing construction and demolition. These variables may vary widely between countries. Moreover, economic development also plays a significant role. Both the oil crisis in the 1970s and pressure on public expenditure during the 1980s (partly as a consequence of high oil prices) have had in this respect a significant impact on housing policies in the various countries concerned. On the basis of these factors and of the responses by governments, the following four stages in the development of housing policy can be distinguished (Table 7.1).

Stage I: Addressing Housing Shortages

Most west European countries were confronted with large-scale housing shortages after World War II. Partly on account of these housing shortages, but much more to get the economy disrupted by the war started again, in many countries a government-directed planning of reconstruction activities was opted for.

Table 7.1

Outlines of Housing Policy and its Financing in the Period 1985–1990 and Direct Government Expenditure in 1988 (as a Percentage of Gross Domestic Product) in Seven Western European Countries

(PRIVATE)	Main Outlines of Policy 1985–1989*				Main outlines of Financing of Housing 1985–1989			Direct Government Expenditure on Housing in 1988 (as a Percentage of GDP)		
	I	II	III	IV	Dominant Subsidy	Expenditure on Individual Subsidy	Total Expenditure	Property	Individual	Fiscal Loss
Netherlands	n	n	n[1]		prop.	fluctuation	increase	1.91	0.40	1.23
Belgium		n	n		prop.	increase	decrease	0.23	0.01	0.43
Denmark		n	n	n[1]	indiv.	increase	stable	0.43	0.59	—
France		n	n	n	prop.	increase	decrease	0.45	0.32	0.55
United Kingdom		n	n	n	indiv.	stable	stable	0.36[2]	1.14[2]	1.23[2]
W. Germany		n	n	n[1]	none	increase	decrease	0.19[3]	0.19	0.42
Sweden		n	n		prop.	fluctuation	decrease	1.28	0.73	1.48

Source: Boelhouwer en Van der Heijden 1992:240; Papa 1992:160, 170, 172.

★To describe the development of housing policy from 1945 in outline, a distinction has been made between four stages of development:

I Strong government involvement with the main objective of making up the housing shortage

II Attention to housing quality

III Attention to distribution problems and specific target groups and withdrawal of the government in favor of market influences

IV Recurrence of a quantitative or qualitative housing shortage; government involvement again increases in some countries (France and Germany) to some extent

[1] Very recent shift in policy stress.

[2] Property subsidies as a percentage of gross domestic product (GDP) of England, individual subsidies, and fiscal loss as a percentage of GDP of Great Britain (England, Scotland, and Wales; Northern Ireland is excepted).

[3] Expenditure of the federal government and territories together.

To be able to build large numbers of dwellings within the limited budgetary possibilities, the construction of austere dwellings in relatively large projects was pursued. In many countries the social rented sector was considered to be better able than the private sector to plan, produce, and manage these large numbers of dwellings. Moreover, this sector could be better controlled by the government. Thus, the prevailing opinion that housing construction was primarily the responsibility of the private sector changed and an unusually far-reaching level of involvement by the state in housing was (temporarily) accepted.

This phase forms the heyday of the social rental sector in Europe. Since this period is of crucial importance to the development of the social rental sector, brief attention is devoted to the principal policy considerations in each country.

BELGIUM. After World War II the housing shortage in Belgium was estimated at a minimum of 200,000 dwellings. In making up this housing shortage an important role was assigned to the owner occupied sector (even for low-income groups). In contrast with many other west European countries, the social rented sector has never had a broad function within the housing market in Belgium.

Via a statutory regulation in 1949, the possibilities were increased of providing lower income groups directly with social rented accommodation. Approved building societies were enabled to build a relatively constant number of social rented dwellings every year, coordinated by and financed through the National Housing Society (NMH). The state assumed the costs of the infrastructure, as a result of which the costs (and thus the rents) of these dwellings could be reduced.

From 1962, partly as a result of Belgium's joining the EEC, government endevored to coordinate the uncontrolled economic development in the form of "economic expansion programs." Within this systematic approach a housing construction policy linked to the current economic situation was followed, geared above all to new construction of private (owner-occupied) dwellings (Goossens 1982). As a result of the great increase in the purchasing power of the population in the sixties, combined with lasting favorable employment prospects, many households were able to build a home of their own.

DENMARK. As in many other western European countries, government involvement in housing increased in Denmark after World War II. Unlike other countries, however, war damage was not the principal motive for this. Subsidies were provided on the one hand to underwrite housing construction and to stimulate employment in the construction industry, and on the other to ensure the provision of adequate housing for those with low incomes and other disadvantaged groups in society. In order to realize these aims, after 1945 a number of measures were implemented that were intended to utilize the existing housing stock more efficiently, increase levels of housing construction, and set up a number of housing organizations. Smaller housing associations were encouraged to amalgamate so that they were better organized to undertake the construction of larger complexes. Alongside large-scale housing construction projects, there were also smaller associations involved in small-scale, single-family dwelling projects influenced by the garden city movement in Great Britain. Characteristic of the Danish situation was the fact that considerable attention was paid to the provision of communal facilities (nurseries, restaurants, laundries, and so on). Behind this lay an ideological concern to give more freedom to women and thereby enable them to engage in paid work. Toward the end of the 1940s around 90 percent of all housing was constructed with the assistance of subsidies from the government, with half of all new housing being realized by nonprofit associations (Haywood 1984:183–95).

After the mid-1950s there was a change in government policy when it became clear that subsidies were leading to high levels of public expenditure, resulting in a reconsideration of the tasks of central government. Restrictions enforcing rent controls and the allocation of housing were relaxed. In order to limit the costs of subsidies the government set an annual quota for the nonprofit housing sector of 10,000 dwellings. The result was a fall in the number of new houses built in this sector.

ENGLAND. As was the case in many other European countries, England was faced with a housing crisis after World War II. Compared with the policy followed before the war, great emphasis was laid on the role of the government in housing. The existing subsidy scheme for the building of social rental dwellings by local authorities was improved and included, among other things, inexpensive loans.

The Labor government's 1949 Housing Act extended the role of local authorities to include the provision of housing for the population as a whole and not just the working class. A total of 902,000 homes were built in England and Wales during the period of Labor administration, 1945–51; of these, 78 percent were provided by local authorities (Smith 1984:82).

As soon as it had fulfilled its promise to the electorate, the Conservative government began to put a greater emphasis in its housing policy on the role of the private sector. Local authorities gradually reverted to their traditional role as provider of housing for those who could not afford their own home.

The promotion of home ownership and the private rental sector and reduction of the influence of local authorities were introduced as policy objectives. As a result of the fall in housing production in the social rental sector and the steadily declining importance of the private rental sector, however, the housing shortage remained great, notably for the lower-income groups in cities. In the sixties, extensive subsidized housing construction programs again came about under a Labor government.

FRANCE. Like most countries in western Europe, France was faced with a serious shortage of housing after World War II. Further, the housing shortage was exacerbated by the rising flow of immigrants from southern Europe and Africa and by the postwar baby boom. The level of new housing constructed remained low during the first years after World War II. The private sector concentrated its investment on industrial and commercial infrastructure. The government therefore provided large sums of money and developed a series of initiatives to help stimulate the construction of new housing. Its response may be contrasted with that of, say, West Germany. This broad state involvement in housing led to the following developments. First, a broad public sector, consisting mainly of rental dwellings (financed by public funds), was created. Secondly, a mixed housing sector emerged in which both public and private finance was used in constructing rental and owner-occupied dwellings (Boucher 1988:298).

The social sector (HLM) is still supported by the most important housing construction subsidy schemes in France. The resources are provided by the state in the form of loans and subsidies. In order to encourage new housing construction, loans were granted at low rates of interest (2 percent per year and a repayment period of 65 years). Moreover, 90 percent of the costs of construction could be financed on these favorable terms. The state in turn determined the maximum level of construction costs and the minimum level of housing quality for subsidized dwellings. Until well into the 1960s, HLM accounted for most new housing. In spite of minimum quality requirements, however, housing construction was mostly assessed in terms of quantity built. During this period, for instance, the grands ensembles were built. The use of rather poorly developed and poorly applied prefabrication techniques resulted in qualitatively poor and unattractive high-rise blocks containing small flats, usually on the periphery of large cities and now characterized by major problems.

THE NETHERLANDS. Partly because of the great housing shortage after 1945, the Netherlands also saw a change in the prevailing opinion that housing construction ought primarily to be attended to by private persons, while the construction of social rental dwellings ought to be only supplementary. According to the Housing Order in force up to then, government contributions for social housing construction could be used only for the rehousing of slum dwellers. In view of the manifest shortages that occurred after 1945, an unusually far-reaching government involvement in housing construction was temporarily accepted.

Government subsidies were extremely broad-ranging in scope and considerable in amount. As much as 95 percent of all housing construction was subsidized. The method of subsidizing was adapted to specific sectors and, as a result of this, important differences emerged in determining rents, costs, and quality control between the various sectors. Despite the private sector's desire to have principal responsibility for housing construction, the government was unwilling to support such a situation. Alongside ideological arguments, pragmatic considerations played a part in its decision not to support such an arrangement. Given the circumstances, the most important aim of the government was to ensure as high a level of housing construction as possible. This required cheap and systematic housing construction, with a considerable proportion being nonprofit, rental housing. By 1959, around 25 percent of housing costs were borne by the state.

GERMANY. After World War II, West Germany faced a housing shortage far greater than that of other European countries, caused by both war damage and the influx of refugees. As in the Netherlands, making up the housing shortage was regarded as an important government task. To eliminate this emergency situation, the first housing act was promulgated in 1950. In this, rent control, housing distribution, and eviction control for both the profit and the nonprofit sector were officially introduced. With regard to social housing construction, the state gave interest-free, long-term loans up to 40–50 percent of the building costs.

Unlike the other six countries, subsidies for the construction of social housing were made available not only to nonprofit organizations but, in an effort to alleviate the housing shortage as quickly as possible, also to others who accepted these conditions. This was an attempt to encourage private investors to invest in social housing, and it largely succeeded. Apart from having the beneficial effect of stimulating housing construction, however, there were certain less desirable aspects to this development. Many problems that currently beset housing in West Germany, such as speculation and the concentration of housing capital in a few hands, can be traced back to this impetuous period of new housing construction. Further, the social housing financed by private investors is subject to the conditions laid down in the housing act for only some twenty-five to thirty years. After that period this housing is no longer subject to rent controls and the government loses control over its allocation. Housing ceases to be part of the social housing sector and becomes part of the private sector.

Since World War II some three million social rental dwellings have been built in West Germany. The pattern has been irregular, however. During the 1960s 41 percent of all new housing constructed was social rental housing. In the 1970s the corresponding figure was less than 30 percent. In the 1980s it continued to fall and by 1987 it amounted to only 25 percent.

SWEDEN. During the first half of the twentieth century Sweden was an unregulated capitalist economy in which the government took little, if any, role in directing industrial development and housing construction. It was only in 1933 that the government recognized the necessity of developing an integral policy for the labor market and the housing market. Sweden was one of the first countries in Europe in which public investment in housing was regarded as an important instrument of employment policy. Until World War II, however, efforts were mainly directed toward coping with only the most serious housing problems, such as overcrowding, and the provision of basic sanitation in dwellings. Government assistance was largely provided through the cooperative associations established by tenants. Such initiatives enabled these tenants to leave the private rental sector and to rent better quality housing more cheaply.

Gradually a unique form of cooperation between the Swedish government and labor market organizations emerged. This ultimately resulted in an agreement in 1938 in Saltsjöbaden and which is generally regarded as the milestone of the Swedish welfare state (the "Swedish model"). All parties aimed at increasing production through among other things strict wage restraint, which then had to be distributed in a fair way. In accordance with the changed general political orientation, in the forties the limited attitude of the central government with regard to housing was definitely a thing of the past.

Although physically unharmed, housing shortages in neutral Sweden were extensive after World War II because of a production crisis during the war and the rapid urbanization after the war. This housing shortage was decisive for the new policy initiatives. The principal objective of the government's housing policy was to expand the housing stock. No less important was its aim to ensure the availability of good quality housing for the whole population. It was therefore considered necessary to limit the profits to be gained from private-sector rental housing and to circumscribe the degree of social segregation (Nesslein 1982). Through a practically continuous period in government by the social democratic party (with the exception of the period 1976–1982), Swedish housing policy was characterized by a high degree of continuity.

Stage II: Increasing Housing Quality

In the second stage, housing policy was more concerned with the quality of housing. The new houses being constructed were more spacious, with more rooms, and the level of amenities was higher. Furthermore, this stage was also characterized in many countries by the switch from new construction to the improvement and maintenance of the existing housing stock. The quality of the housing stock was improved by slum clearance or by renovating poor quality dwellings.

Stage III: Strengthening Private Markets

In the transition from to the third stages, market influences play an increasing role. Often the concept that each household ought to be accommodated according to its needs is steadily abandoned, and housing provision increasingly depends on effective demand. In the third stage much attention is given to the problems of distribution. Because of the decline in public expenditure, the suitability and effectiveness of the various instruments that form part of a government's housing policy are subject to critical considerations. As a result of the reduction in overall subsidies, like general supply subsidies for new construction, and the extension of demand subsidies, the position of less well-off groups in particular is given greater emphasis in housing policy. In this third stage one finds, in general, a decrease in the level of new housing construction in the social sector.

Stage IV: Return of Housing Shortages

In a number of countries one can discern a fourth stage characterized by absolute housing shortages and a shortage of affordable housing for the less well-off. The problem in this context is concentrated notably on the urban areas. In most European cities, low new construction production is accompanied by a strong growth of the owner-occupied sector, often initiated by the government. As a result, exorbitant price increases have occurred in these urban areas, putting the continued existence of the urban economy at risk. Lundqvist (1992) argues in this context that gentrification and good quality for those who can afford that on the one hand, and segregation, decay, and housing shortage for those who cannot on the other, form two well-known sides of the "million dollar coin," as the urban housing problem is now called by some. Some countries (Germany and France) respond to this with a cautious increase in government involvement, both financially and in the field of organization and guidance, whereas in other countries (Great Britain) government concern remains unchanged for the time being (Boelhouwer and van der Heijden 1992:238). However, it is as yet too limited and too early to speak already of an essential adjustment of the advocated market-oriented housing policy in Europe.

Table 7.1 also provides insight into the financing of housing policy and direct government expenditure in 1988. On a cash basis, most of the budget is still spent in the Netherlands, just as in Sweden, on dwelling-linked subsidies (property subsidies). In other countries redistribution problems and strengthening of market functioning have for years formed important policy bases, as reflected in the dismantling of property subsidies and an increase in individual subsidies such as the housing allowance. In Denmark and the United Kingdom the expenditure on individual subsidies in half of the eighties was already greater than that on property subsidies. The continuing investments in new construction and the growth of the number of applications for rent subsidy have led in the Netherlands to an increase in housing expenditure, whereas in other countries it was possible to dismantle property subsidies more quickly, as a result of which the total expenditure stabilized or even fell.

On the strength of this broad-brush description of housing policy, it seems justified to conclude that the development of the social rental sector in the seven countries displays a reasonably large number of similarities. Up to World War II housing production in all countries was still strongly dominated by the private sector. In the first two decades that followed, a change then occurred, in which government influence and the role of the social rental sector increased strongly. With the exception of the Netherlands and Sweden, a withdrawal of the government again takes place from the sixties onward and private housing production again gets the upper hand. However, this general description does no justice to the actual position that the social rental sector occupies in the various countries. In the next section I shall go further into a number of specific characteristics of the sector.

A Further Comparison of the Social Rental Sector

In Table 7.2 a number of important characteristics of the social rental sector in the seven west European countries have been elaborated. First the proportion of the social sector in the total housing stock is shown. The size of the social rental sector proves to vary considerably by country. Three groups may be distinguished:

1) Belgium;

2) Denmark, France, Germany;

3) England, Sweden, and the Netherlands.

In Belgium the social rental sector, with a volume of only 7 percent of the housing stock, is by far the smallest. The explanation for this was already given in the previous section. The Belgian government has always regarded promotion of home ownership as the main objective of its housing policy. The result is that the function of the social rental sector is a very modest one. In addition, lower-income groups are dependent to a large extent on the subsidized owner-occupied sector (notably for large families) and on the private rental sector.

The social rental sector in Denmark, France, and Germany forms about 16–17 percent of the housing stock. In addition to the development of the social rental sector, an important role was also assigned to the private sector in these countries. In Denmark the owner-occupied sector was clearly favored, while in France and West Germany the private rental sector was also considered important.

The largest social rental sectors were created in Sweden, England, and the Netherlands. The period in which this came about differed, however. For England, social rental production was considerable in the first two decades after World War II. In the seventies and particularly in the eighties, however, a great turn-about came, and the proportion of social rental dwellings fell even in absolute figures through the sale of over 1.5 million council houses. Production in Sweden came about in a relatively short space of time (1964–1975)

Table 7.2
Principal Characteristics of the Social Rented Sector in Seven West European Countries

(PRIVATE) Properties	Belgium	Denmark	England	France	Netherlands	Germany	Sweden
Percent of the Housing Stock	7	17	24	17	44	16	21
Owner of the dwelling	Building societies (central government, provinces, municipalities, and private shareholders)	Self-governing associations (53%), corporations (40%), guarantee companies (7%)	Local authorities (98%), housing associations (2%)	Building societies (HLM) (regional government, saving banks, tenants)	Housing associations (86%) and local authorities (14%)	Cooperative housing associations (62.5%), commercial institutions (37.5%)	Municipal housing associations
Way of subsidization	Interest subsidies	Several interest subsidies	Housing revenue account subsidy (central government)/fixed subsidy for housing associations	Subsidized loans and interest subsidies	Annual funding according to certain standards (budgets for: annual payments, extra costs arising from local situations, reduce rents in urban renewal areas)	Interest-free loan, operation costs subsidy, loans to partially cover capital expenditure	Interest subsidies
Body that subsidizes	Region	Central government	Central and local government	Central government	Central government	Central government, federal states	Central government
Control	Strong	Strong	Strong	Reasonable	Strong	Reasonable	Strong

Rent control	Strong	Strong. Via adjustment to wage development	Weak. From attempt to approach market rent	Strong. Government fixes rent increases two times a year, rent pooling possible	Strong. Government fixes rent increases. Since 92 large rent increases to reach cost price	Reasonable. Only upon improvement are extra increases up to 11% possible	Strong. Via negotiations with tenants
Sale of social rented dwellings	Possible. From 1988 more sale than new construction	Possible to small extent via cooperative ownership	Under right to buy from 1980 over 1.5 million dwellings sold	Possible to small extent	Possible to small extent, possibilities extended from 1992	Sale by landlords (tenants obliged to buy)	Sale via co-operative ownership
Accessibility	Problems for lowest-income groups	Great, but growing influx of lower-income groups (no marginalization as yet)	Great, but marginalization of social sector	Housing operation may not be at a loss. Therefore accessibility for lower-income groups a problem	Great. Increasing concentration of lower-income groups. However, through size also middle-income groups	Reasonable, but many lower-income groups in private rented sector	Great
Operating problems	No vacancy problems, but much demand through limited supply	Vacancy from 80s solved	Postwar high-rise. Partly demolition	Postwar high-rise	In postwar high-rise chiefly in easy housing markets	Postwar high-rise, decreasing sharply through increase in demand for housing	Postwar high-rise, decreased through increase in demand for housing
Tenant's influence	Weak	Weak	Weak	Strong, important role in rent bargaining	Weak, lower degree of organization	Weak	Strong

under the successful one-million-dwellings program. Prior to then the role of the social rental sector was limited, the proportion in the Netherlands and England converged. The size of the social rental sector in the Netherlands may be regarded as very high (44 percent). The principal cause of this is that, in contrast to the other countries, up to 1990 there was no question of privatization of social housing. During the period 1945–1990 large numbers of social dwellings for rent were produced every year. Because of strong growth in the number of households, notably after 1970, this relatively high production was not enough to make up the housing shortage. As indicated, in the other countries a state of equilibrium occurred in the sixties or seventies, so that the reason for extensive government involvement disappeared and housing production was left to the market (third phase of government policy).

In addition to the size of the social rental sector, the tenure structure also proves to differ strongly in the seven countries. The first major difference is that between municipal housing corporations (England and Sweden) and associations or foundations. This division has great consequences for the way in which the government was able to put through its later privatization proposals. Thus it was possible for the English government successfully to implement the sale of council houses that it advocated. In other countries, such proposals often foundered on legal restrictions.

The countries also show market differences in the way their social rented sectors are operated. For instance, the government has a strong representation on the boards of the building societies in Belgium and France as well as in the self-governing associations in Denmark. This is not the case in West Germany and the Netherlands (where 86 percent of the stock of social rented dwellings falls outside the purview of government). The organizations that operate social rented housing in these countries can be regarded much more as intermediate parties between the government and market agents.

A remarkable statutory provision for Sweden is that owner-occupied dwellings occur only in the form of single-family houses. As a result a sharp separation has come about between the owner-occupied and the rental sector. Rental dwellings consist in general of small, cheap apartments, whereas the owner-occupied dwellings occur exclusively as single-family houses and may be regarded as belonging to the highest quality parts of the housing stock. Despite the neutrality principle followed in Sweden (equal treatment of the various tenure sectors), there is thus hardly any question of a real choice for various types of households; large, well-to-do households are solely dependent on the owner-occupied sector, whereas small, less well-to-do households obtain housing only in the rental sector. For large, less well-to-do households this of course leads to problems.

With regard to the type of subsidization, the distinction between interest subsidies and annual operating contributions is considerable. Interest subsidies are given in Belgium, Denmark, France, and Sweden. The characteristic of these subsidies is that the government can adjust the subsidization with relative ease when that is considered necessary. In the case of operating subsidies these possibilities are much fewer. In this case, the deficit between rents and operating costs is covered by the duration of the loan. In the Netherlands this happens for every loan separately (up to 1992) and in England for the operation of the whole municipal housing corporation. In the case of long-term agreements, reduction of the subsidy can be achieved only via often unpopular rent increases.

With regard to who provides the subsidy, there is greater similarity. Except for Belgium and West Germany, in all countries the central government acts as the point of issue. In Belgium the region is responsible for this. This is inspired by the regionalization, in which the role of the central state has been greatly driven back. West Germany has a federal structure, in which the Länder account for a considerable part of the subsidization. Finally, until recently the councils in England were able via their housing corporation to make up any deficits, so that it was possible to follow a moderate rent policy. However, recent changes to the law have introduced a stricter separation.

There are two traditions in setting rent levels. One is based on standardization; the other is based on the cost price. In the former, the government determines the rent considered desirable for newly built dwellings and subsidizes the difference via interest subsidies or operating contributions. In such a case strict quality requirements should be laid down and maximum standards adhered to. After all, there is no incentive present for housing managers to keep costs down. However, when the rent is fixed on the basis of the cost price this incentive is present. Higher quality then leads immediately to a higher rent level. Both in the Netherlands and in England recent changes have been introduced by which the subsidization occurs more via standard amounts, and rents form the balancing item of operation.

In all seven countries, security of tenure and rent control are strong in the social rental sector, whereas such regulation is relatively weak in the private rental sector. Except in the Netherlands and Sweden, many liberal regimes apply to the private rental sector. As a result, the rents in the various sectors can vary strongly between one another. Belgium, England, and recently the Netherlands too have the possibility within the social stock of following a differentiated rent policy (rent pooling). In Belgium there is even an individual system, whereby the rent is fixed on the basis of income. In West Germany tenants with a high income in the social rental sector can be assessed via a rent tax (Fehlbelegungsabgabe). The proceeds of this are used for subsidized new construction.

In most of these seven countries, after the introduction of the third phase of housing policy the sale of social rental dwellings is being attempted. However, this policy has been successful only in Belgium, West Germany, and above all England. In England over 1.8 million council houses have been sold since 1979.

In Belgium the promotion of home ownership is a widely propagated objective and local authorities occupy a strong position in the building societies. Here too the ownership of many rental dwellings has been transferred to the occupant. As a result of this and of the limited new construction activities of the building societies, the stock of social rental dwellings has decreased even in absolute terms in recent years, as in England.

In West Germany the sale of rental dwellings is now an undesirable development for the government. As stated above, the obligation to pass on a cost-effective rental for social rental dwellings lapses at the moment when the low state credits that have been used for the financing have been redeemed in full. In this context speculators have the possibility of buying up whole blocks of social rental dwellings. They then redeem the still outstanding government credits, after which they can sell the dwellings. This speculation leads to the indirect tax subsidies provided in the past now being legally cashed in by speculators. The governments of the various Länder are not always against these practices. Through the premature redemption of government credits, the fairly empty subsidy fund is filled again and resources become available for the construction of new social dwellings for rent. Notably in cities like Munich, Hamburg, Cologne, and Düsseldorf the sale of rental dwellings to tenants is regarded as a great problem. In addition to the sale of rental dwellings, the decrease in the proportion of social rental dwellings in the stock is also intensified by the decline in the proportion of social rental dwellings in new construction production and by the fact that the loans of many social rental dwellings from the fifties and sixties have by now been practically redeemed. After this the landlords (including many private persons) are free to rent the dwellings at the market rate, as a result of which a further erosion of the social rental sector occurs.

The reason for the limited success of privatization in the other countries can partly be explained by the relatively strong position of nonprofit landlords. As private organizations it is very difficult for the government to compel them to sell. In Sweden and Denmark the conversion of rental apartments is legally permitted only in cooperative ownership. In Sweden in particular reasonable use is made of this.

The social rental sector, like the private rental sector, is on the wane throughout western Europe. In addition to the sale of social rental dwellings, the strong decline in new construction and the aging of the housing stock play a part in this. This decline and an increase in direct housing expenditure are creating specific problems in this segment of the housing market.

In the eighties, when a shift took place in many regions from a suppliers' market to a demanders' market, practically all countries were confronted with vacancies, most notably in high-rise estates from the reconstruction period. England and France in particular were and still are the most affected in this respect.

As an alternative to demolition (chiefly in England) most countries advocate an integrated approach in which the dwelling, the dwelling's environment, the level of amenities, education, and social problems are tackled (above all in France and, to an increasing extent, also in the Netherlands). In most countries the vacancy problem clearly declined through the increase in housing shortages in half of the eighties.

Because the function and the accessibility of the social rental sector in many countries declined in the eighties, the rise in housing expenditure has become a general problem. This causes difficulties above all for the weakest groups in society. The general rise in housing expenditure occurred because in past decades these governments offered more scope to the functioning of the free-market mechanism (abolition of security of tenure and rent control and reduction of government subsidies), and the price of newly built dwellings rose strongly due to a limited rise in building productivity and stagnation in incomes. Partly because of the decreased accessibility of the social rental sector, it is often necessary to rely on the poor quality private rental sector or face growth in the number of homeless and the number of households that are accommodated in boarding houses (as in France, England, and Belgium). Incidentally, affordability problems occur not only among the lowest-income groups. Thus in both England and Denmark (countries with highly developed owner-occupied sectors) there has recently been a serious crisis on the market for owner-occupied dwellings. Particularly, households that took possession of a home of their own in the mid-eighties were later confronted with payment problems and foreclosure.

In addition to the rise in housing expenditure, the social rental sector is marginalizing in a number of countries (particularly in England and in parts of the poor stock in France). Marginalization leads among other things to an often undesirable spatial distribution of socioeconomic groups, to decay of both the housing stock and the housing environment and to management problems in general.

In countries where an intermediate nonprofit institution is responsible for social housing, this marginalization has up to now been largely prevented. However, in these countries the problem occurs that many middle- and higher-income groups occupy cheap parts of the stock of social rental dwellings, as a result of which less well-to-do house hunters are often forced to take refuge in other segments of the housing market (in many cases the private rental sector), settle for dwellings not geared to their household or even fail to satisfy their demand for housing. As in the Netherlands, Sweden (in the cooperative sector), France and West Germany discussions are therefore being held and measures considered for reducing this skewness in the distribution of the existing housing stock. In West Germany this has led among other things to an expansion of rent tax in the nineties. This measure, which was already implemented on a limited scale in the eighties, is regarded by the federal government as a well-tried and adequate housing instrument. In other countries (like France, the Netherlands, and Denmark), the government is trying to influence the allocation policy of the social landlords. In France in particular there is considerable conflict on this matter between the HLM institutions and the various authorities. Thus the nonprofit organizations in France may refuse tenants who in their opinion are not capable of fulfilling their financial obligations for some length of time. This requirement is made because the housing operation of the institutions may not make a loss. To the central government the fact that the nonprofit institutions do not entirely live up to their primary task, housing the lowest-income groups, is therefore regarded as a considerable problem that is the subject of much political conflict.

To be able to prevent or mitigate the marginalization and stigmatization of the social rental sector, it is important that not only low-income households have to be housed and to have a differentiated housing supply and a differentiated population of renters. Some countries have a better chance of attaining this. Sweden, Denmark, and the Netherlands have more opportunities to do so than countries where the social rented sector has been under pressure for a longer period and where marginalization and stigmatization have already made inroads into (parts of) the sector.

Conclusions

The development of the social rental sector in western Europe displays broad similarity and was in conformity with the housing policy advocated in the various countries. Depending on the period in which the housing shortage was made up, privatization tendencies appeared (or reappeared) in many countries in the sixties and seventies, the influence of the social rental sector on production declined, and home ownership is (again) regarded as the most desirable housing sector.

However, when a more detailed comparison is made, an entirely different picture is formed and it becomes clear that great differences occur in the functioning and the position of the social rental sector in the various countries. Different authors have pointed out that expectations of convergence of the social rental sector in Europe are misplaced (Murie and Lindberg 1991:15; Boelhouwer and Van der Heijden 1992:295). The specific place that the sector occupies in different countries is largely determined by the unique properties of the housing system and the function of the social rental sector in it. Thus the structure of the housing market, which came into being on the basis of a genesis unique to each country, the institutions formed in the course of the years, and the actions of the governments, strongly tinged by ideology and based on traditions, are all too greatly divergent.

In addition to changes from the housing system, factors from outside the development of the social rental sector will also strongly influence the years to come. In particular the dismantling of the welfare state, as has begun in many countries, is of great importance to the social rental sector in this context. Through reduction in the level of social benefits the function of the social rental sector can again change considerably.

References

Adriaansens, Carel A., and H. Priemus. 1986. *Marges van volkshuisvestingsbeleid, naar een flexibeler juridische vormgeving van een marktgevoelige beleidssektor's.* Gravenhage: Staatsuitgeverij.

Boelhouwer, Peter J., and Harry M. H. van der Heijden.1992. *Housing systems in Europe: Part I. A comparative study of housing policy.* Housing and Urban Policy Studies 1. Delft: Delft University Press.

Boucher, Frederique. 1988. "France." *In Between owner-occupation and rental sector.* Hans Kroes, Fritz Ymkers, and Andre Mulder, editors. De Bilt: NCIV 145–82.

Goossens, Louis. 1982. "Het sociaal huisvestingsbeleid in België, Een historisch-sociologische analyse van de maatschappelijke probleembehandeling op het gebied van het wonen." Leuven: Katholieke Universiteit te Leuven, Faculteit der Sociale Wetenschappen, Dissertatie.

Haywood, Ian. 1984. In "Denmark" *Housing in Europe.* Martin Wynn, editor. London : Croom Helm. 178–219.

Lundqvist, Lennart J. 1992. *Dislodging the welfare state? Housing and privatization in four European nations.* Housing and Urban Policy Studies 6. Delft: Delft University Press.

McGuire, Chester C. 1981. *International housing policies, a comparative analysis.* Lexington, Mass.: Lexington Books.

Murie, Alan, and George Lindberg. 1991. *Report of workshop held in Gothenberg February 22nd–25th 1991.* Work group on public and social rented housing. European Network for Housing Research.

Nesslein, Th., S. 1982. "The Swedish housing model; An assessment." *Urban Studies.* 19. 235–46.

Papa, Oscar A. 1992. *Housing systems in Europe: Part II. A comparative study of housing finance.* Housing and Urban Policy Studies 2. Delft. Delft University Press.

Smith, Roger 1984. "Great Britain." In *Housing in Europe.* Martin Wynn, editor. London: Croom Helm. 75–120.

Chapter 8

Do Community Development Corporations
Live Up to their Billing?
A Review and Critique of the Research Findings

William M. Rohe

This chapter reviews empirical literature on Community Development Corporations (CDCs), which are an important subset of the nonprofit housing sector. Numerous favorable claims have been made about CDCs and used to promote their involvement in housing and redevelopment. Descriptive studies are reviewed to profile CDCs in terms of organizational size, funding, activities, and areas served. Evaluative studies are reviewed to address success in securing local support and in implementing projects, efficiency, and impacts on service areas. The studies reviewed lend support to the claims that CDCs follow a comprehensive approach to development, respond to community needs, leverage foundation support, and target low-income and moderate-income areas. The efficiency of CDCs, responsiveness to community priorities, and contribution to community capacity building have been inadequately addressed.

Introduction

The first Community Development Corporations were created in the 1960s to address a perceived failure of public sector programs to adequately address problems of inner city physical decay and economic and social depravation (Keating and Krumholtz 1988).[1] At that time CDCs represented a new approach: they were locally controlled, nonprofit organizations independent of city hall. CDCs, then and now, serve specific low-income or moderate-income neighborhoods by sponsoring economic, social, or physical development projects (Pierce and Steinbach 1987; Zdenek 1987).

Since their initial development, the growth in the number of CDCs has been dramatic. Although there is no exact count, estimates suggest that there are approximately 2,000 to 2,200 CDCs currently in existence (NCCED 1995). This represents a doubling of the number of CDCs in existence ten years earlier (Pierce and Steinbach 1987). As their number have grown, so has their political influence. A number of "umbrella" organizations now represent the interests of CDCs in Washington, D.C., including the National Neighborhood Coalition, the Low-Income Housing Coalition, and the National Association of Neighborhoods. The lobbying activities of these organizations are at least partially responsible for the recent special recognition CDCs have been afforded in federal housing and tax credit programs. There is, for example, a 15 percent set-aside for nonprofit development organizations in both the Low-Income Housing Tax Credit program and the HOME program.

Soon after their appearance on the urban scene, CDCs became a subject of study. Studies of CDCs have examined a variety of topics including the characteristics of CDCs, the activities they sponsor, and their accomplishments. Independent of these studies, advocates of CDCs have made a variety of claims about the advantages of CDC-sponsored revitalization activities. Unfortunately, there has been no review of the research literature to see whether it supports the claims made by CDC advocates. Accordingly, this chapter reviews the claims that have been made for CDCs, critically reviews research literature on CDCs, and assesses whether this literature supports the claims made about CDCs. Special attention will be paid to identifying gaps in this literature. Suggestions for additional research are also presented.

The Claims Made about CDCs

A variety of claims have been made about the advantages of CDCs over the more conventional federally sponsored and locally managed approaches to community development. (See Blakey 1989; Mayer 1990; Reiner and Wolpert 1988; Zdneck 1987). Since they are "closer to the community" and ostensibly controlled by community residents, CDCs are said to be more likely to understand and be responsive to the unique needs of individual neighborhoods. This, in turn, is said to result in greater support from the community.

CDCs are said to adopt a more comprehensive approach to community upgrading. Unlike individual government agencies, they have the flexibility to develop a wide range of programs—from housing rehabilitation to social services to economic development. This, it is argued, leads to better coordinated and more effective community improvement efforts (Blakely 1989).

CDCs are also said to be more concerned with community capacity building. According to Zdenek (1987), the activities of CDCs "are not viewed as an end in themselves but as means for stimulating further development goals" (115). These further development goals typically include the development of both leadership and technical skills among residents and the "empowerment" of the community by developing vertical linkages between residents and the political and economic leaders in the larger community. This capacity building approach is said to foster more fundamental and sustainable community improvement.

CDCs are also credited with being in a better position to leverage private funds for community development projects. Foundations are typically reluctant to provide grants to public agencies since they have access to tax revenue and other sources of support. Foundations have, however, made major financial contributions to CDCs in the form of both loans and grants. Thus, CDCs have access to a substantial source of funding for community development projects that is not available to public agencies (Mayer 1990).

Finally, due to their relatively small size and their lack of bureaucracy, CDCs are said to be more effective and efficient than public agencies. According to Zdenek (1987):

> CDCs are able to link business development projects with benefits to the whole community more effectively than public agencies. Many public agencies dampen implementation by separating the function of economic development planning and comprehensive planning from project development. . . . There should be an advocacy component in planning if the strategies are to be implemented and have an impact. (116)

Is There Evidence for these Claims?

These claims are often made with little or no supporting evidence. Selected examples of successful CDCs are cited but often these do not speak specifically to the claims made, nor do they provide convincing evidence for the general superiority of CDCs over other sponsors of community development activities. Even some of the most ardent supporters of CDCs agree that their effectiveness is sometimes romanticized. Pierce and Steinback (1987), for example, suggest that: "CDCs and their supporters sometimes romanticize the movement's effectiveness. But there are instances enough of 'dream' projects and neighborhood jobs that failed to materialize. Some CDCs are inefficient, poorly managed, plagued by internal tensions, inert, and occasionally—though rarely—corrupt." (9)

The question then becomes, What do we really know about CDCs? What questions have been addressed in the empirical studies of CDCs and what have they found? Moreover, what additional research is needed to allow us to make firm conclusions about the benefits of CDCs? The questions addressed in studies of CDCs can be divided into two categories: descriptive and evaluative.

Some studies focus on one category of question while others have addressed both categories of questions.

Descriptive Questions

A number of studies have sought to provide detailed descriptions of CDCs and their accomplishments. These studies addressed questions such as:

- What are the characteristics of CDCs including staff size, budget, sources of operating funds, lengths of operation?
- What are the major activities sponsored by CDCs?
- What are the characteristics of the neighborhoods served by CDCs?
- What have CDCs been able to accomplish in terms of producing new or rehabilitated housing units, constructing office and retail space, assisting small businesses and creating or retaining jobs?
- How did CDCs fare during the federal funding cutbacks in the early 1980s?

The Characteristics of CDCs

One often asked question about CDCs is simply how many of them are there. Given their rapid growth-rate and the lack of easily obtained data there has been much uncertainty about their numbers. Estimates have ranged between 1,000 and 5,000 and are usually based on little or no data. Three studies commissioned by the National Congress for Community Economic Development (NCCED 1989; NCCED 1991; NCCED 1995) provide the only systematic attempt to estimate the total number of CDCs in the county. The methodology used for these studies involved obtaining list of potential CDCs from a variety of national, state, and local organizations.[2] Each was then sent a survey to see if they fit the study's definition of a CDC.[3] A phone survey of a sample of nonresponding organizations was also conducted to estimate the proportion of CDCs among that group and to assess their organizational characteristics and production. Using this procedure the most recent study estimates the total number of accomplished CDCs to be between 2,000 and 2,200 with an additional 350–400 "fledgling" organizations that had yet to complete a development project. Although there are obvious problems with this estimation procedure—the most significant being uncertainty as to the completeness of the listing of CDCs—this is the best estimate available. Future research should build on the list of CDCs that have been identified to date and strive toward a more complete census of CDCs.

If more reliable estimates of the number and characteristics of CDCs are to be attained, better means of identifying the universe of CDCs need to be developed. One of the main obstacles to this is a lack of a common definition of a CDC. Both "community" and "development" need to be precisely defined before the universe can be identified. Does a nonprofit housing corporation that serves several towns or a region qualify as a CDC? Does a nonprofit organization that focuses exclusively on social development qualify as a CDC? Does a nonprofit have to be controlled by people living in the target area to qualify as a CDC? A second obstacle is identifying the full number of organizations that fit whatever definition is developed. Possibly the most reliable means of doing that is to contact all 503(c)(3) organizations to see if they fit the definition of a CDC. This, however, would be a monumental undertaking.

Researchers have also been interested in the organizational characteristics of CDCs including their average or median age, staff size, and budget size. The more recent NCCED study, for example, found that 24 percent of all CDCs with completed projects were founded between 1986 and 1990. Both Vidal (1992), in a purposive sample of 130 CDCs in 29 cities, and Rohe et al. (1991), in a study of 140 CDCs belonging to the Neighborhood Housing Services Program, report the average age of the CDCs in their samples as approximately twelve years. Together these studies suggest a rapid growth in new CDCs during the 1980s. This growth has been attributed to the increased presence of intermediary groups that provide technical assistance, easier access to project financing, and additional foundation support for operating expenses (NCCED 1995).

The most recent studies of CDCs indicate tremendous variation in the size of these organizations. Some have staffs of twenty or more and multimillion dollar budgets. The typical CDC, however, remains relatively small. Vidal's (1992) study involved CDCs that she describes as "older, larger and more diversified than the typical CDC." She reports that the median number of staff members was seven (five professional and two support), while the median budget was approximately $700,000 annually. Rohe et al. (1991) in their study of Neighborhood Housing Services Organizations found that the typical NHS organization had a staff of four and an operating budget of $134,850. Both these studies, however, found remarkable diversity in the number of staff and in the size of the budget.

FUNDING SOURCES. Research on financial support for CDCs indicates that they receive support from a wide variety of public and private organizations. In spite of the federal cutback in support for housing and urban development programs, the NCCED (1991, 1995) studies and Vidal's (1992) study indicate that the federal government is the most frequently relied upon source of funding. Seventy-eight percent of the organizations in Vidal's study received some federal support, while the most recent NCCED study found that 77 percent of the CDCs received more than $50,000 in federal funds between 1991 and 1993. With the 15 percent set-aside in the HOME program, federal funding is likely to be relied on even more heavily in the future.

State and local governments are also important funding sources for CDCs. The most recent NCCED study reports that 51 percent of the CDCs in their sample received some state funding while 40 percent received some local government funding. Similarly, Vidal found that 45 percent of the CDCs in her sample received state funds, while 36 percent received support from local governments.

Recall that one of the arguments for the advantages of CDCs is their ability to tap the resources of private foundations. Studies consistently indicate that a substantial proportion of CDCs receive at least some funding from foundations. NCCED (1991) found that 41 percent of the CDCs it surveyed had foundation support, while Vidal reports a higher percent (63). Both these studies also indicate about one-third of CDCs receive some funding from local banks.

Intermediary organizations, such as LISC and the Enterprise Foundation, also provide funding for a significant proportion of CDCs. One of the NCCED studies (1991) found that 21 percent of the organizations surveyed received some funding from intermediaries, while Vidal's study found that 30 percent of the organizations in her sample received some support from this source.

MAIN ACTIVITIES SPONSORED. Researchers have also been interested in the types of activities sponsored by CDCs. Recent studies find that CDCs sponsor four broad categories of activities: housing development and rehabilitation; community organizing and advocacy; commercial real estate development; and business development. Housing development and rehabilitation is the most frequently engaged in activity. NCCED (1991, 1995) and Vidal (1992) report that approximately 90 percent of the organizations surveyed sponsor some form of housing program. In the most recent NCCED study, 81 percent of the groups had actually completed housing units between 1991 and 1993. Beyond construction and rehabilitation, CDCs are also managing rental units, providing home ownership counseling, and conducting weatherization programs.

The second most frequently engaged in activity according to both the NCCED and Vidal studies is community organizing and advocacy. This covers a wide range of activities including fighting displacement, lobbying city hall to improve public services, putting pressure on landlords to fix up their units, and fighting unwanted development in the neighborhood.

Commercial real estate development is the third most frequently engaged in activity. Vidal reports that 67 percent of the CDCs she sampled were engaged in some form of commercial development such as building or rehabilitating retail and office space. The most recent NCCED study (1995), however, reports that only 18 percent of the organizations surveyed engaged in commercial real estate development. This difference is most likely due to Vidal's emphasis on older and larger organizations and her use of a more restrictive definition of a CDC.[4]

The least frequent major activity of CDCs is business enterprise development. This involves providing technical assistance and counseling to local entrepreneurs, management training, providing loans to start businesses, and actually owning and managing businesses. Fifty-eight percent of the CDCs in Vidal's (1992) study were involved in some form of business development. Again, however, the NCCED (1995) study found a much smaller percentage of CDCs involved in these activities. Only 23 percent of the organizations in that sample were engaged in business development programs.

The typical CDC is involved in sponsoring activities in several program areas. Vidal, reports that the typical CDC works in housing and two other program areas. They may, of course, sponsor a variety of separate activities in each of these broad program areas.

CHARACTERISTICS OF NEIGHBORHOODS SERVED. Researchers have also wanted to know who is being served by the activities of CDCs. The available evidence, although far from complete, supports the notion that CDCs are effectively targeting their activities to low-income and moderate-income areas and individuals. Rohe et al. (1991), for example, report that the median family income of neighborhoods served by Neighborhood Housing Services organizations is more than $10,000 less than the respective city values. Moreover, the proportion of blacks and Hispanics in the areas served by NHS organizations is substantially higher than the proportion of black and Hispanics in the cities as a whole. The percentage of blacks in NHS neighborhoods, for example, was 34.5 while the percentage of blacks in the host cities was 20.9.

Other evidence of successful targeting of resources comes from the NCCED studies. The most recent of these studies found that 96 percent of all rental units and 91 percent of owner-occupied housing were produced for those making less than 80 percent of the local median income. Similarly, Vidal (1992) estimates that 87 percent of all housing units constructed or rehabilitated went to households with incomes below 80 percent of the area median income. Moreover, the percent of CDC activity targeted to the poorest 30 percent of neighborhoods varied from 22 percent to 75 percent in the various cities included in this study. Yet there is still some question as to how well CDCs are serving the needs of very low-income persons, defined as those making 50% or less of the area median income.

PRODUCTION CAPACITY. Studies have also focused on assessing the production capacity of CDCs. Research typically assesses the number of housing units developed, the number of square feet of office and retail space constructed, the number of businesses assisted, and the number of jobs created or retained. The NCCED studies provide the most comprehensive assessment of the accomplishments in these areas. The most recent NCCED study (1995) estimates that as of 1993, CDCs produced approximately 400,000 affordable housing units, with an additional 30 to 40 thousand units produced in 1994. Moreover, they found that the number of large housing producers (defined as having produced 100 or more units) jumped from 244 in 1988 to 546 in 1993.

The NCCED (1991, 1995) surveys also found that 23 percent of the CDCs studied were involved in small business development and that these organizations reported making 3,512 loans and 242 equity investments in small businesses. The majority of the loans were less than $25,000, while the size of the equity investments was somewhat larger.

Twenty-five percent of the CDCs responding to the NCCED survey were involved in the area of commercial and industrial real estate development. Those organizations report completing 17.4 million square feet of commercial and industrial space during their lifetimes. Finally, CDCs responding to the NCCED survey reported that their combined economic development activities have created or helped retain almost 90,000 permanent jobs.

Vidal (1992) and Rohe et al. (1991) also present recent data on the accomplishments of CDCs. Their samples, however, are not as well suited to estimating the total production of all CDCs in the country. It is interesting to note, however, that Vidal estimates that the annual production of housing units by CDCs nationally is 27,560; the NCCED estimate of the number of units produced in the last three years is approximately equal on an annual basis.

The production estimates presented above are based on figures provided by directors or staff members of the CDCs surveyed. Given their vested interests, these persons may have exaggerated the accomplishments of their CDCs. Moreover, many of the accomplishments claimed are undoubtedly the result of collaboration with other public, nonprofit or private organizations. A CDC may, in fact, have a fairly limited role in producing a housing unit, yet still report it is a unit they "produced." Finally, some accomplishments are simply difficult to determine, such as whether a job was saved. Future studies need to develop a means of verifying the accomplishments claimed and apportioning units of output, such as housing units, to CDCs based on the extent of their involvement.

THE IMPACTS OF FEDERAL CUTBACKS. Several studies have sought to describe the impacts of reductions in federal programs that support the work of CDCs. The first of these was conducted by Cohen and Kohler (1983) shortly after the Reagan administration began making large cuts in the funding of the Section 8 New Construction and Substantial Rehabilitation, CETA, EDA, and other programs relied on by CDCs. In a survey of over 80 CDCs they report that "more than half of the organizations in this survey have already had to curtail programs and services even though the bulk of the federal budget cuts have yet to have their full impacts" (81). Many CDCs reported having to reduce the number of housing units produced and target their activities to higher income groups. Moreover, Mayer (1990) points out that these cuts:

Interrupted and too often reversed growth in the organizations' delivery capacity. Critical expertise and experience were lost, as operating budgets and program funds fell below levels necessary to retain key staff members and provide them with further training and support. (375)

CDCs have not been passive in the face of these cutbacks. Rather they have adopted a variety of strategies to make up for reductions in federal funding. Many CDCs began to sponsor income-generating activities such as housing management or construction projects. Others developed partnerships with private sector developers, financial institutions and corporations. Still others sought funds from foundations and the newly created intermediary organizations such as the Local Initiatives Support Corporation (LISC) and the Enterprise Foundation. CDCs have also turned to state and local governments to provide additional funding. In fact, Vidal (1992) reports that local governments have been the most common sources of replacement funds.

Judging by the increase in both the number and size of CDCs during the last fourteen years, as a group these adaptations have been successful. In fact, Mayer (1990) comments:

The CDCs that survived seem to be more tightly budgeted and managed, better able to assess the true feasibility of planned projects, adept at assembling complex combinations of resources to make projects work, and possessed of greater access to private funds.

Yet the need for CDCs to draw on a complex combination of resources has its drawbacks. Projects often take longer to develop, transaction costs are higher, and the projects are often more difficult to manage.

Evaluative Questions

A variety of studies has gone beyond descriptive questions to ask evaluative questions concerning the success, outcomes, or impacts of CDC sponsored activities. The answers to these questions have particular policy relevance as they provide indications of the effectiveness and efficiency of CDCs, as well as guidance in efforts to enhance their capacities. The evaluative questions that have been addressed include:

- How successful have CDCs been in securing local support for their activities?

- How successful have CDCs been in implementing specific projects or in meeting some predetermined production goal?

- What factors are associated with either successful projects or successful CDCs?

- How efficient have CDCs been in delivering services, producing jobs, or building housing, and how does this compare with other public or private organizations?

- What impacts have CDCs had on their service areas?

SUCCESS IN SECURING LOCAL SUPPORT. As mentioned above, one of the purported advantages of CDCs is their ability to raise funds from nongovernmental sources. Several studies have addressed this issue. In particular, two studies have addressed the success of CDCs involved in HUD's Neighborhood Development Demonstration (NDD) in raising matching funds required by this program. The NDD was introduced in 1983 to provide funding for CDC development projects. A unique aspect of this program was that it required participating CDCs to match the maximum $50,000 HUD grants with funds raised from within their own neighborhoods. Moreover, the match has to be cash, not in-kind or volunteer contributions. The required local match of federal funding varied from one-for-one to one-for-six, depending on the level of distress in the area. The logic of this requirement was to broaden the financial support for CDCs during a time of federal cutbacks, build their fund raising capacities, and strengthen their connections to the communities they serve.

Pratt Institute (1988) conducted an initial evaluation of this program. Among other objectives, the researchers were interested in assessing the success of the thirty-eight participating CDCs in raising the matching funds. They report that twenty-five of the thirty-eight CDCs funded in the first round of grants were able to raise all of the matching funds, while four more have raised more than 85 percent of the funds. They also report that the directors of a large majority of participating organizations felt that having to raise the matching funds within the neighborhood limited their fund-raising abilities. Moreover, all eight groups that failed to raise the required match identified this neighborhood requirement as the primary reason for their lack of success.

A follow-up study of the NDD program conducted by the Urban Institute (1992) included all ninety-four organizations funded from the beginning of the program through 1989. Slightly over two-thirds of the CDCs had raised the full amount of the match and another 9 percent had raised between 90 and 99 percent of the match. The size of the CDC board was found to be positively associated to fund-raising success, while the dollar amount of the required match was negatively associated with success. The authors also report that 70 percent of the CDCs tapped new sources of local funding in raising the match. Fewer than half, however, reported that the new funding sources would continue to support the organizations after completion of the NDDP-funded project. This raises some question of both the efficacy of this program in fostering greater CDC support within the neighborhood and the wisdom of the geographic restriction on fund-raising.

SUCCESS IN IMPLEMENTING SPECIFIC PROJECTS. One approach to measuring the effectiveness of CDCs is to assess the degree to which they successfully implement projects. One of the first studies of the success of CDCs in implementing projects or meeting output goals was conducted by Garn et al. (1976). They studied the performance of the Bedford-Stuyvesant Restoration Corporation, the Woodlawn Organization, and the Zion Nonprofit Charitable Trust over a one-year period. Their method involved working with each of those organizations to set "performance milestones" for all major activities of the CDCs during the coming year. Quantitative goals were set taking into account the funding levels, programs, and community circumstances. The authors then tracked their activities to assess the degree to which these goals were met. The results indicate that these targets were equaled or exceeded in only 22 of 95 instances. They conclude that the CDC managers were learning both to make more realistic milestones and to overcome the obstacles to achieving those milestones.

Eight years later, Mayer (1984) studied 100 CDCs that received support from HUD's Neighborhood Self-Help Development (NSHD) program to see how successful they were in completing projects, leveraging funds, and encouraging volunteer activity. His technique involved comparing the planned outputs as specified in the grant application to the actual outputs. His findings indicate great variation in the ratios of actual to planned outputs depending on the type of project. For example, the ratios for the number of housing units weatherized and the number of units rehabilitated were .971 and .831, respectively. The ratios for the development of new commercial space and for the number of businesses assisted, however, were only .093 and .367, respectively. The number of permanent jobs created was also relatively low at .394. Mayer also reports that the CDC leveraged three dollars for every one federal grant dollar provided.

Vidal et al. (1986) studied thirty-four CDCs sponsoring seventy-two projects supported by the LISC. Among other things, they studied whether the projects funded by LISC were implemented as planned and whether the CDCs received the anticipated financial benefits from their projects. The results indicate that 79 percent of the projects were a success or a "qualified success." Moreover, 50 percent of the projects produced the expected level of return and 70 percent produced at least some financial return. As might be anticipated, projects with "assured demand" such as subsidized housing, had a substantially higher success rate than those classified having "speculative demand," such as new business ventures. Given the lack of a comparison group, however, it is impossible to assess whether projects with LISC support were any more successful than those without it.

Vidal (1992) looked at the "incidence of project failure" among the CDCs in her sample. Three project types were considered: housing development, commercial development, and business enterprise development. Members of the study team were responsible for determining if the CDCs they were assigned had experienced any project failures, including those projects that had completely collapsed as well as those that had major cost overruns, poor quality construction, unrented commercial space, and other major problems. The findings show that 24 percent of all CDCs that had done commercial development projects, 28 percent of CDCs that had done housing projects, and 39 percent that had done business development projects, had at least one failed project.

Using project completion as a means of assessing the effectiveness of CDCs is desirable in that it is relatively easy to measure. However, it says nothing about the cost of the project, its importance to the community, or its impact on the residents of the area served. Overall, it is a fairly crude measure of effectiveness.

FACTORS AFFECTING SUCCESS. Several studies have gone beyond assessments of project implementation to identify the factors that appear to account for the success or failure of individual projects or the organization as a whole. As Mayer (1984) points out, the factors associated with project success are generally the same as those that lead to organizational success. These studies have typically relied on either pure qualitative analysis or a combination of quantitative and qualitative analysis. Mayer and Blake (1981), for example, conducted interviews with the directors and staffs of twelve CDCs and identified nine internal factors, nine factors concerning relationships with the community and outsiders, and eight environmental factors that impact project success. Mayor (1984) expanded this analysis to include 100 CDCs that received grants under the NSHD program. He utilized bivariate analysis to identify associations between a variety of organizational, interactional, and environmental characteristics and project completion ratios. A summary of these factors is presented in Table 8.1.

Rohe et al. (1991), in their study of one hundred and forty NHS organizations, assessed the impacts of a variety of organizational and contextual variables on the overall efficiency of these organizations. They measured efficiency as the total amount that the executive directors claimed had been invested in the target area as a direct result of all NHS activities divided by the total operating budget for that year. The typical NHS organization reported totaling $5.40 for every dollar of operating budget spent.

A multivariate analysis of factors associated with this measure of efficiency found that larger organizations, those with more stable staff, and those that sponsor home ownership promotion and purchase-rehab-sell programs, tend to be more efficient. Qualitative analysis of the results of the interviews with the staff of fifteen NHS organizations suggest other characteristics associated with greater efficiency, including smaller numbers of units owned by absentee landlords; fewer elderly, poor, and minority residents in the area; a smaller target

Table 8.1
Factors in Project Success

Internal Characteristics
- —Leadership by an Effective Executive Director
- —Paid, full-time Staff with Development Expertise
- —Control of Work Levels for Key Staff
- —Doing Homework
- —Flexible Resourceful Planning
- —Clearly Defined Roles of the Staff and Board and Shared Objectives
- —Control Over Spin-Off Organizations
- —Competent Financial Record Keeping
- —A Successful Track Record

Relations with the Community and Outsiders
- —Strong Support in the Local Community
- —Successful Management of Conflicts within the Community
- —Political Clout
- —Working Relationships with Local Business People
- —Working with Private-Project Developers
- —Relations with Key Private Actors
- —Access to Flexible Administrative and Venture Funds
- —Early and from Private Risk Takers, and
- —Access to Technical Assistance

Characteristics of the Economic, Social, and Political Environment
- —Housing and Economic Market Conditions
- —Project Cost Factors
- —Reluctance of Private Lenders to Lend
- —Racism and Sexism
- —Political Attitudes and Timing of Political Events

Source: Mayer (1983).

area; and more favorable economic conditions in the city as a whole. Further-more, staff competence, low rates of staff turnover, the activity level of the board, relations with other organizations, and the effective use of volunteers were also identified as important contributors to efficient organizations.

Schweitzer (1992) studied the factors related to successful projects among 126 neighborhood organizations funded by the Michigan Neighborhood Builders Alliance, a statewide program to support the work of CDCs. Self-reported measures of project goal completion, the impact of the program on the community and several other variables were associated with the characteristics of the organizations, the community, and the projects sponsored. The results indicate that successful outcomes were positively associated with organizational age, experience, and good relations within their communities. Moreover, Schweitzer concludes that major housing development and crime prevention projects were more likely, compared to other projects, to have major impacts on the community.

Focusing on the ability of CDCs to manage rental housing, Bratt et al. (1994) selected seventeen CDCs in six cities and then analyzed their experience with property management. They identified several management problems that pose serious danger to the viability of housing developments if not corrected. Many CDC owned and managed housing developments were not adequately subsidized at the outset, and many buildings were not fully rehabilitated at the time of acquisition. In addition, reserve accounts are often dangerously low, leaving little financial cushion should unanticipated expenses arise. The tenant selection criteria and other regulations associated with federal subsidy programs also added to the management challenge. Bratt et al. recommend a variety of actions to correct these problems including changes in federal programs, additional financial support from foundations, and technical assistance to improve the ability of CDCs to manage their properties effectively.

EFFICIENCY OF CDCs. One of the most controversial questions about CDCs concerns their efficiency in delivering services. Unfortunately, this is also one of the most difficult questions to answer. An analysis of service efficiency requires that the units of output (e.g., housing units built, clients counseled, etc.) be accurately measured and that the full costs of providing each unit of output be assessed. Given the variety of activities undertaken by CDCs, it is often very difficult to apportion operating costs such as staff time and building rent to specific program activities. CDCs, for example, normally do not keep records of the staff time spent on the projects they sponsor. Without this information it is impossible to calculate accurate per-unit costs.

Even when costs can be assessed with relative accuracy, these costs need to be compared to some standard, or to the costs of other organizations sponsoring similar projects. The problem is that finding such a standard or comparison organization is extremely difficult. In addition, the characteristics of the neighborhoods or clients served must also be taken into account when considering program efficiency. The per-unit cost of housing rehabilitation in an area with large, older housing units, for example, is likely to be more expensive than the cost of rehabilitation in an area with newer, smaller housing units.

In spite of these difficulties, several studies have provided assessments of the efficiency of services offered by CDCs. In their study of 140 NHS organizations, for example, Rohe et al. (1991) calculated the number of revolving loans made and the number of housing units rehabilitated per $10,000 in operating budget. They found that on average these organizations made 0.7 loans and rehabilitated 2.21 units per $10,000 of operating budget.

The major problem with this approach is that it does not account for the relative emphasis that the NHS organizations place on providing loans and rehabilitation housing units. Given the lack of data on staff time devoted to specific activities, they assumed that one-hundred percent of the operating funds went for these activities. Thus, the efficiency of NHS organizations that sponsored other programs was underestimated.

Rohe et al. (1991) go on to assess the relative efficiency of each NHS organization by comparing its efficiency rating to a predicted rating that took into account both organizational characteristics (such as staff size, and age of the organization) and contextual variables (such as the median household income and percent of owner-occupied units in the neighborhood). The predicted efficiency ratings were generated by entering each group's organizational and contextual characteristics into a multiple regression equation whose parameters were specified using the data on all 140 organizations. The actual efficiency rating of each group was then compared to its predicted rating to see if it was underachieving or overachieving compared to organizations with similar characteristics.

Robinson and Ferguson (1981) conducted what might be the most ambitious attempt to assess the efficiency of CDCs. They apportioned the operating budgets of NHS organizations to each of five core activities based on executive director estimates of the amount of staff time devoted to each activity. They then used these to calculate the per-unit costs of each activity. The costs of providing rehab assistance, for example, ranged from $176 per person assisted to $2,416 with a mean of $444 for all organizations.

They went on to select fifteen local government programs similar to the NHS program. They collected cost and per-unit output data from these programs and calculated efficiency ratings. The authors caution, however, that the efficiency comparisons were hampered by differences in the clients surveyed by the two types of programs. NHS organizations offer assistance to all neighborhood home owners, while the public programs only serve those with incomes below the moderate-income level prescribed by HUD. Moreover, city agencies received staff services, technical assistance, office space, and other services that do not show up in their program budgets. With these caveats they go on to conclude that:

> The comparisons showed, quite clearly, that other local housing rehabilitation and neighborhood improvement program vary markedly in productivity and efficiency as do NHS. Second, the comparisons suggested that the administrative costs of NHSs in rehabilitation dwellings fall in the same general range as those of other programs. (170)

WHAT IMPACTS HAVE CDCs HAD ON THEIR SERVICE AREAS? Some argue that the ultimate objective of CDCs is to improve the overall living conditions in the communities covered. Accordingly, several studies have tried to assess the impacts CDCs have had on their target areas. Again, some studies rely on subjective measures of impact while others rely on more objective measures.

Cummings and Glaser (1983) examined the perceived effectiveness of CDCs by surveying the executive directors of 119 CDCs across the country. Each director was asked to rate his or her organizations' emphasis on community organization and service, human resource development, and community business and economic development. They were also asked to rate the impacts of their organizations in six areas such as business development and expansions of community service facilities. Not surprisingly, the directors of CDCs that emphasized economic development rated their organizations as more successful in expanding business activities and creating jobs than did organizations with less emphasis on economic development.

Similarly, the Pratt Institute study (1988) of CDCs employed subjective measures of impact. They asked the directors of the CDCs to identify neighborhood impacts. Almost two-thirds of those directors cited improvements in neighborhood conditions since they applied for the NDD grant and two-thirds of them attributed that change to "public and nonprofit efforts" in the area. The reliance on subjective, self-reported measures of neighborhood impact, however, raises serious questions about the validity of these results.

Vidal (1992) relied on a somewhat more objective means of gauging neighborhood impacts. She had study team members assess the extent of overall progress made in addressing neighborhood problems and the magnitude of improvements in specific neighborhood conditions. Overall, team members reported a "moderate level of overall neighborhood improvement." More specifically, she reports that 21 percent of the housing and business development programs had a "substantial effect" on neighborhood problems and an additional 36 percent had a "moderate" impact on neighborhood conditions. Thirty-one percent of programs involving commercial real estate development were rated as having a "substantial effect," while 28 percent had a "moderate effect." The remaining programs only had small impacts.

Vidal also assessed the indirect impacts of CDC sponsored programs on their target areas, although she cautions that these are more difficult to attribute to the activities of the CDCs. Nonetheless, she reports that "only nine percent of CDC housing developers appear to have sparked substantial improvements in non-CDC residential properties, although an additional 56 percent have stimulated small spillover improvements."

In a study of the neighborhood impacts of NHS organizations, Clay (1981) found stronger evidence of significant indirect impacts. He reports that significant investments were being made by neighborhood residents who did not receive direct assistance from the NHS organizations. For example, interviews with residents of a sample of NHS neighborhoods indicate that 56 percent of all respondents had invested in their properties since the NHS was organized with an average investment of $1,058. Moreover, the number and value of building permits increased over the four-year period studied and the number of real estate transactions increased.

Robinson and Ferguson (1981) studied the neighborhood impacts of NHS programs by using windshield surveys and resident interviews. They conclude that "NHS neighborhoods appear to have improved . . . at a moderate pace." The number of housing units with "no observable defects" increased from 80 to 85 percent and the number of blocks without litter increased from 36 percent to 74 percent. They also found that homeowners in NHS neighborhoods are more likely to invest in their homes and to make much larger investments than the average homeowner.

In this study the authors also attempt to assess whether it was the activities of the NHS organizations which are responsible for the neighborhood improvements observed. They argue that "if the NHS works it will bring about the most change in those neighborhoods where it provided the most services, or the most services per dwelling, if other aspects of the neighborhoods are equal." Thus, they calculated correlation coefficients between NHS program activity and changes in neighborhood conditions. The results of this analysis indicate that the total amount of the revolving loans provided per unit is positively related to housing and neighborhood improvement.

Summary and Discussion

The major evaluations of the activities of CDCs provide support for several of the claims made by the advocates of CDCs, while several other claims have yet to be addressed. The findings provide some support for the claim that CDCs tend to adopt a comprehensive approach to community upgrading. They indicate that CDCs are involved in a wide range of activities ranging from the development of housing and commercial property, to the provision of social services, to business development, to general advocacy activities. Remember that Vidal reports the typical CDC is involved in housing and two other major program areas. Many, if not most, public sector revitalization efforts, exclusively focus on housing and infrastructure improvement rather than addressing the full range of neighborhood problems. To some extent this is the result of CDBG program guidelines that emphasize physical development projects over service delivery and other "nonbricks and mortar" activities. Given the interdependence of neighborhood problems the *more* comprehensive approach adopted by CDCs is more likely to lead to greater success in achieving neighborhood revitalization. Moreover, the degree of public agency involvement in organizing and advocacy activities is often severely limited by political considerations. CDCs are in a better position to sponsor these activities, which are thought to be particularly important in the sustainability of neighborhood improvements.

Furthermore, the collective findings of the evaluation studies indicate that the mix of activities varies greatly from one CDC to another, even within the same city. This suggests that CDCs are responding to the unique conditions of their target areas in their choice of program activities. What is not clear, however, is whether the CDCs are addressing the priority needs of the residents of their target areas. More will be said about this below.

A second claim that receives some support from the evaluation studies is that CDCs are able to leverage substantial amounts of foundation and other private funds for neighborhood revitalization. The NCCED study indicates that about 40 percent of all CDCs receive foundation support and Vidal's findings indicate that almost two-thirds of well-established CDCs receive foundation support. In addition, the amount of foundation support for CDCs has been increasing rapidly in recent years. In the early 1970s the Ford Foundation was the only major foundation involved in supporting CDCs. By 1989, however, 165 foundations provided $65 million to CDCs (Council on Community Based Development 1991). Although no comparable figures are available for foundation contributions to public neighborhood revitalization initiatives, it seems safe to conclude that it is far lower. Foundation grants to public agencies for neighborhood revitalization activities are relatively rare.

The studies also suggest that intermediary organizations, such as LISC and the Enterprise Foundation, are playing a large role in channeling foundation support to CDCs. A recent analysis found that 64 percent of all foundation grants are being made to intermediaries rather than made directly to CDCs (Walker 1993). The advantage of relying on intermediaries is that they are in a better position to assess both the overall strength of individual CDCs and the feasibility of specific projects. They can also combine funding with technical assistance, which is likely to lead to more successful initiatives.

A number of foundations are now collaborating through the National Community Development Initiative in developing a national support system for CDCs (Walker 1993). This effort is being administered by LISC and the Enterprise Foundation, and involves the pooling of $62.5 million provided by seven major foundations and one corporation. These funds will be used to build the capacity and fund the projects of CDCs in twenty cities. Clearly, the support CDCs have been able to garner from foundations represents a significant contribution to the revitalization of urban neighborhoods.

The claim that CDCs are effective in targeting their efforts to low-income and moderate-income areas also receives support from the evaluation studies. All the evaluation studies that addressed this issue report very high levels of targeting to low-income and moderate-income areas or individuals. Logically, CDCs would seem to be in a better position to target their activities, since they are better insulated from the political pressures to distribute funds widely. Yet there has been no direct comparison of the areas and population groups served by public agencies and CDCs.[5] Moreover, the degree to which CDCs are assisting the very poor is not known. It may be that CDCs mainly benefit those in the 50 to 80 percent of the median income category and do very little for those making under 50 percent of the local median income. Further research is needed on the specific income groups served by CDCs and public agencies.

The claim that CDCs are efficient sponsors of neighborhood rehabilitation activities has been addressed by several studies, but the results are far from conclusive. Finding appropriate comparison groups and collecting reliable data on both outputs and costs have been difficult. One study did compare the efficiency of CDC sponsored activities with similar activities sponsored by public agencies, yet the authors admit that there were major problems with the comparability of both the cost figures and the clients being served under the two types of programs (Robinson and Ferguson 1981). They were able only to conclude that great variation exists in the efficiency of both public agencies and the CDCs. The other studies on CDC efficiency suffered from the inability to accurately attribute costs to specific program activities. Unless CDCs keep detailed records of staff time allocated to various activities, it will be impossible to calculate accurate measures of efficiency.

Moreover, even if the above mentioned problems could be overcome, quantitative efficiency indicators will be limited to those program activities that can be easily quantified, such as the number of housing units produced or jobs created. Yet, CDCs often undertake community organizing, crime prevention activities, advocacy, and other activities that are important in a neighborhood revitalization effort but very difficult to quantify in meaningful terms. Thus, developing objective, quantitative measures of the overall efficiency of CDCs would seem to be a difficult, if not impossible, task. Qualitative measures will be needed to supplement the quantitative measures if the full range of impacts is to be captured.

Black (1994) and Sullivan (1990) both argue for the use of qualitative research methods, including ethnographic methods, to capture the full range of impacts that CDCs are having on their communities. Sullivan points out that CDCs may have many indirect social impacts, such as strengthening local social control, that need to be recognized and better understood. Black emphasizes the need to assess the performance of CDCs on locally defined indicators of success, not on indicators prescribed by outside organizations or researchers.

Given that CDCs are well institutionalized, more important than their current level of effectiveness is how their effectiveness can be improved. The research on this question (Mayer 1983; Rohe et al. 1991) is possibly the most useful in that it suggests what CDCs can do to increase their effectiveness, even if it can't be precisely measured. Moreover, such research needs to define effectiveness in terms of both the products and the processes of CDC activities. Two organizations may have identical product output, say twenty new housing units, but one may have done so with little community consultation or involvement, while the other may have consulted community residents on location, design, and other issues, and hired local residents to assist with the construction. The community building goals of CDCs should not be ignored in studies of effectiveness.

CDCs have also been said to be more likely to understand the unique needs of individual neighborhoods and to have the support of neighborhood residents. Unfortunately, although this is a researchable topic, none of the studies reviewed addressed this issue. Do the activities of CDCs correspond with the priority needs as defined by the neighborhood residents? Or are CDCs simply responding to the availability of funds for certain activities? What proportion of the neighborhood residents even know of the existence of CDCs and what proportion support their activities by contributing time or money? This is an important area for future research.

Finally, none of the studies reviewed dealt with the degree to which CDCs do in fact result in community capacity building. To what extent is this an active goal of CDCs? To what extent have CDCs cultivated local leadership? To what extent have CDCs led to the enhancement of skills among area residents? And, to what extent has the CDC led to the establishment of vertical linkages between residents and the political and economic leaders in the larger community? These are important questions that need to be addressed in future research on CDCs.

This review of the research on CDCs suggests several obstacles that will have to be overcome before more definitive results can be achieved. First, a common definition of what constitutes a CDC will have to be developed and a better method of identifying the population of CDCs will have to be devised. Second, CDCs, at least the ones under study, will need to keep better records of their costs, of specific program activities, including staff time, as well as their program outputs. An acceptable method of apportioning the outputs of jointly sponsored projects will also have to be developed. Third, comparison projects sponsored by public or private organizations will have to be identified, and the full costs of these projects will need to be carefully calculated. Fourth, better methods of assessing the impacts of the "softer" activities sponsored by CDCs will need to be developed. Finally, more attention needs to be paid to attributing changes in overall neighborhood conditions to the activities of CDCs.

Notes

1. See Zdenek (1987) and Pierce and Steinback (1987) for histories of the CDC movement.

2. These sources included a list of 3,650 organizations provided by the Community Information Exchange. This list was "augmented" during the course of the research.

3. To qualify as a CDC the organization had to meet the following four criteria: (1) be a private nonprofit entity; (2) serve a low-income community or constituency,

(3) be governed by a community-based board; and (4) be an ongoing producer with at least one completed project in housing, commercial industrial, or business development.

4. Vidal (1992) defines CDCs as (1) "non-profit organizations with a community base, i.e., connected to, and somehow considered accountable to, its community (defined in a geographic, ethnic or other sense)"; and (2) "engaged in community economic development, defined as developing housing, commercial real estate, or business enterprises."

5. The available data on the targeting of CDBG funds controlled by local governments does, in fact, show a high proportion of targeting to low- and moderate-income areas and individuals (HUD 1992). The criteria used to define low- and moderate-income benefits, however, makes this figure misleading. For example, if at least 51 percent of the households in an area have low and moderate incomes, then the full cost of any improvement in that area is considered to be benefiting low- and moderate-income people.

References

Black, S. 1994. "Redefining success in community development: A new approach for determining and measuring the impact of development." Medford, Mass.: Tufts University Lincoln Filene Center.

Blakely, Edward. 1989. *Planning local economic development: Theory and practice.* Beverly Hills, Calif.: Sage Publications.

Bratt, Rachel., Langley Keys, Alex Schwartz, and Avis Vidal. 1994. *Confronting the management challenge: Affordable housing in the nonprofit sector.* New York: New School for Social Research, Community Development Research Center.

Clay, Phillip. 1981. *Neighborhood partnerships in action: An assessment of the neighborhood housing services program and other selected programs of neighborhood reinvestment.* Washington, D.C.: Neighborhood Reinvestment Corporation.

Cohen, Rick, and Miriam Kohler. 1983. *Neighborhood redevelopment organizations after the federal cutbacks: Current conditions and future directions.* Washington, D.C.: US Department of Housing and Urban Development.

Council on Community-Based Development. 1991. *Expanding horizons II. A research report on corporate and foundation grant support of community-based development.* New York: Council on Community-Based Development.

Cummings, Scott, and Mark Glasser. 1983. "An examination of the perceived effectiveness of community development corporations." *Journal of Urban Affairs* 5. 315–30.

Garn, Harvey, Nancy Tevis, and Carl Snead. 1976. *Evaluating community development organizations.* Washington, D.C.: Urban Institute.

Keating, Dennis, and Norm Krumholtz. 1988. "Community development corporations in the United States: Their role in housing and urban development." Paper presented at the meetings of the Association of Collegiate Schools of Planning. Buffalo, N.Y.

Mayer, Neil. 1990. "The role of nonprofits in renewed federal housing efforts." In *Building foundations: Housing and federal policy.* Denise DePasquale, and Langley Keyes, eds. Philadelphia: University of Pennsylvania Press. 365–88.

———. 1983. "How neighborhood development organizations succeed and grow: A summary." In *Neighborhood policy and planning.* Phillip Clay and Robert Hollister, eds. Lexington, Mass.: Lexington Books.

———. 1984. *Neighborhood organizations and community development.* Washington, D.C.: Urban Institute.

Mayer, Neil, and Jennifer Blake. 1981. *Keys to the growth of neighborhood development corporations.* Washington, D.C.: Urban Institute.

National Congress for Community Economic Development (NCCED). 1995. *Tying it all together: The comprehensive achievements of community-based development organizations.* Washington, D.C.

———. 1991. *Changing the odds: The achievements of community-based development organizations.* Washington, D.C.

———. 1989. *Against all odds: The achievements of community-based development organizations.* Washington, D.C.

Pierce, Neal, and Carol Steinback. 1987. *Corrective capitalism: The rise of America's community development corporations.* New York: Ford Foundation.

Pratt Institute. 1988. *Evaluation of the neighborhood development demonstration.* Washington, D.C.: U.S. Department of Housing and Urban Development.

Reiner, Thomas, and Julian Wolpert. 1988. "Austerity impacts on neighborhood development organizations." *Policy Studies Journal* 16 (winter) 307–23.

Robinson, Maynard, and Gary Ferguson. 1981. *Neighborhood housing services and the neighborhood reinvestment corporation.* Washington, D.C.: U.S. Department of Housing and Urban Development.

Rohe, William, Sam Leaman, Leslie Stewart, and Barri Braddy. 1991. *Evaluation of neighborhood housing services.* Washington, D.C.: Neighborhood Reinvestment Corporation.

Schweitzer, John. 1992. "Factors related to successful neighborhood projects." Paper presented at the Urban Affairs Association Annual Meetings. Cleveland, Ohio.

Sullivan, Mercer. 1990. *Studying the effects of community development corporations on social control: An anthropological approach.* New York: New School for Social Research Community Development Research Center.

Urban Institute. 1992. *Final evaluation of the neighborhood development demonstration program.* Washington, D.C.: US Department of Housing and Urban Development.

U.S. Department of Housing and Urban Development. 1992. *Annual report to Congress on the CDBG Program.* Washington, D.C.

Vidal, Avis. 1992. *Rebuilding communities: A national study of urban community development corporations.* New York: New School for Social Research.

Vidal, Avis, Arnold Howitt, and Kathleen Foster. 1986. *Stimulating community development: An assessment of the local initiatives support corporation.* New York: Local Initiatives Support Corporation.

Walker, Chris. 1993. "Nonprofit housing development: Status, trends, and prospects." Paper presented at the Fifth Annual Fannie Mae Conference. Washington, D.C.

Zdenek, R. 1987. "Community development corporations." In *Beyond the market and the state*, Severyn Bruyn and James Meehan. Philadelphia: Temple University Press. 112–27.

Chapter 9

Nonprofit Housing
A Study of Costs and Funding

Scott Hebert and James Wallace

Comparing nonprofit and for-profit housing production is very complex. This chapter examines the development costs incurred by nonprofit developers and compares these costs with for-profit industry standards. The authors explain their painstaking efforts to develp an analytic framework based on highly disaggregated cost accounting for fifteen nonprofit developments. They address the relative roles of equity, debt-financing, and non-cash resources in nonprofit development. Given the complexity of the subsidy streams in these projects, it is extremely difficult to know the total subsidy cost. Hebert and Wallace calculate the present value of subsidies both in absolute terms and as a percent of total development cost. They find substantial differences in per-unit costs normalized for size of project, metropolitan location, and date of construction. These differences within nonprofit development appear to be related to local approaches to nonprofit development. The authors find that variation within the nonprofit sector might be as important as variation between the nonprofit and profit sectors.

Introduction

In recent years, the federal government has shown an increased interest in the capacity of nonprofit organizations to produce and manage affordable housing. This interest is demonstrated in the special role created for nonprofits in legislation such as the Stewart B. McKinney Act of 1988, the Financial Institutions Reform, Recovery, and Enforcement Act of 1989, and the Low Income Housing Preservation and Resident Homeownership Act of 1990, as well as in federal programs such as HOME, HOPE, and the Low Income Housing Tax Credit (LIHTC).

Despite the involvement of nonprofits in housing production for more than two decades, and the recent emphasis given to nonprofit housing development, there had been little research on the development costs incurred by these organizations or the financing approaches utilized. One reason for the lack of research was that, until the last few years, nonprofits had been viewed as minor actors in housing production.

Another reason was that a common cost and funding framework for collecting complete data on resources and uses in affordable housing projects did not exist. The significant range of organizational types, populations served, and financing approaches encompassed by nonprofit developers was also seen as complicating the task of structuring systematic and comparative research.

Overview of the Study

As a principal source of funding for such housing, the U.S. Department of Housing and Urban Development (HUD) was particularly interested in examining the issue of nonprofit housing costs and financing. In 1991 the HUD Office of Policy Development and Research contracted with Abt Associates to conduct an exploratory study in this area.[1] The study involved four major tasks.

The first task in the study was the development of a basic analytic framework, in the form of a data collection and analysis instrument, to permit comparative research on nonprofit housing development. The cost and funding framework developed as part of the study has several significant features. First, the framework provides for a complete accounting of development resources and costs, including those attributable to noncash contributions, donations, and subsidies. Second, the framework distinguishes among the various phases of the development process, including the financing phases, to facilitate an understanding of the element of time in the projects and the interrelationship of components. Third, it employs a nested hierarchical structure, which builds up individual expense items into major cost categories for each phase of the development process. This format permits the capture of data on funding sources and uses at both a very fine and an aggregated level of detail. This structure accommodates the variation in data availability from one nonprofit to the next, as well as the varying cost-accounting classifications used by different organizations.

The second major task of the study involved testing the framework on fifteen selected nonprofit development projects, located in five metropolitan areas across the country. The application of the cost and funding framework to fifteen nonprofit multifamily projects was intended to demonstrate the capacity of the framework to capture comprehensive information on sources and uses of funds for a variety of organizational settings, building types, development approaches, and financing packages. The study collected complete data on financing received and out-of-pocket expenses, as well as reasonable estimates of noncash contributions, subsidies, and write-downs by reviewing project files and interviewing key participants in the development efforts. This allowed the build-up of development costs into twelve standard cost categories, permitting crossproject comparisons by category.

A third task was to examine the cost and funding patterns across the fifteen projects for commonalities and differences. Although no statistically valid generalizations can be made from the study properties (given the small number of properties examined and the purposive nature of the selection of projects), a number of preliminary observations emerged about the affordable housing development process, especially for nonprofit developers. The patterns among the sites and their possible implications are discussed later in this chapter.

A final study task specified by HUD was to examine the question of whether nonprofits and for-profits differ in their approaches and the costs incurred to develop comparable housing. Using industry cost standards (R. S. Means) for new construction, the study computed an estimate of the per-square-foot rates for the construction "hard costs" of the six new construction projects in the study, for comparison with the observed nonprofit construction costs. In the broader sense of full development costs, the study also identified the development expense elements where nonprofits and for-profits might be expected to experience different costs. We examine the options available for further exploring nonprofit/for-profit development cost comparisons. At the end of this chapter, we offer some suggestions as to which approaches appear most promising.

The Projects Selected for the Study

This study applied the cost and funding framework, with its supporting data collection methodology, to multifamily projects[2] located in five Metropolitan Statistical Areas (MSAs): Boston, Washington, D.C., Chicago, Kansas City (Missouri), and San Francisco/Oakland. Three affordable housing projects (intended to provide housing affordable to households under 80 percent of median income for at least half of the units) were examined in each MSA.

All of the housing projects selected for examination had been constructed or rehabilitated in the four years preceding commencement of the study, were privately held, and provided family housing. Twelve of the fifteen were rental housing, while three involved cooperatives. Five of the rental projects involved new construction, and seven were substantial rehabilitation efforts. One of the three cooperatives involved new construction, one was concerned with substantial rehabilitation, and the third mixed new construction and rehabilitation. While use of the Low Income Housing Tax Credit was not a selection criterion, it turned out that twelve of the fifteen projects were LIHTC projects.

Projects varied widely as to the development context. Some were in relatively straightforward development contexts, while others faced more challenging environments, such as difficult site characteristics, historic district design restrictions, and neighborhoods requiring heavier security during construction.

The projects selected for the study ranged in size from 15 to 151 units, with a mean of 59.3 units and a median of 43 units. The predevelopment phase (generally, the period from the identification of the site to the start of construction) for these projects ranged from eight months to five years, with an average of 29.3 months and a median of 24 months. The construction periods ranged from five to twenty-two months, with a mean of 11.7 months and a median of 10 months. The overall development period (predevelopment plus construction period) ranged from fourteen to eighty-two months, with a mean of forty-one and a median of thirty-five months.

The nonprofit sponsors for the development projects in these MSAs were incorporated from five to twenty-four years prior to the study. The majority of the nonprofits examined were neighborhood-based organizations (11 of 15), but one nonprofit had a citywide focus and three had a countywide or metropolitan focus. In terms of experience in housing development, there were four organizations with more than fifteen years of production experience at the time of the study, while three nonprofits in the sample had never before undertaken a housing development project.

Methodology

Collection of Data on Development Costs

The study collected data on development costs for nonprofit projects in a variety of forms. Table 9.1 illustrates these data, presented as averages for the projects in each metropolitan statistical area. First, the developers' own estimates of their project costs are listed, as provided in cost certifications, financial statements, or final pro formas. These figures are displayed on an unadjusted per-unit basis in column 1 of Table 9.1. Sponsors differed considerably in their conventions as to what items were included in "cost." Items that were frequently (but not always) excluded from the developers' estimates included interest on bridge loans, prefunded reserves, syndication costs, deferred developer's fees, imputed equity, or the costs of special development features such as underground garages.

Next, to permit crossproject comparisons using consistent expense categories, the study then computed its own figures for cash, or out-of-pocket, costs—that is, the expenses for acquisition, construction, and financing covered through actual cash outlays by the developer, even if some of these costs were financed through loans or grants. These out-of-pocket computations (column 2) in some cases closely reflected the developers' own estimates. In other instances, the study's out-of-pocket figures differed from the developers' estimates due to the inclusion of items such as the expenses covered by syndication proceeds, which the developers had not attributed to the development period. It

Table 9.1
Comparison of Per Unit Development Cost
under Different Methodologies
(Expressed as Averages for Sample Projects
in Each Metropolitan Statistical Area)

Location of nonprofit projects in sample	Column 1 Cost certification/ development estimate (not adjusted)	Column 2 Out-of- pocket cost (not adjusted)	Column 3 Normalized full development cost (w/o land)	Column 4 Normalized full development cost (with land)
Boston MSA	$99,335	$123,136	$144,834	$150,332
Washington, D.C. MSA	$48,488	$49,273	$51,846	$55,233
Chicago MSA	$65,345	$65,345	$54,349	$55,322
Kansas City MSA	$60,089	$61,945	$49,835	$50,946
San Francisco/Oakland MSA	$121,149	$146,487	$126,470	$135,509
AVERAGE	$78,881	$89,237	$85,467	$89,468

Column 1 provides raw costs per unit from the sponsors' records, unadjusted.

Column 2 provides unadjusted cash (out-of-pocket) costs per unit according to the study definition of cash costs.

Column 3 and 4 provide per unit full development cost (including noncash items) normalized for unit size, regional cost variation, and time of development.

Source: Abt study by 15 nonprofit sponsors, 1992.

should also be noted that columns 1 and 2 represent unadjusted or "raw" costs, in the sense that they are not normalized for unit size, regional variations in costs, or time of development.

Because the study was designed to capture a complete accounting of development resources for each project, an estimate of noncash contributions was also derived and added to the out-of-pocket calculations. This combined "full development cost" incorporates the value of all development period resources, such as donated land or reduction in construction loan interest rate, as well as the total amount of any tax credit investor payments. The full development cost was normalized for year of construction, location, and unit size as shown in column 3 (excluding the value of land) and column 4 (including the value of land). The normalization methodology and the implications of the results are discussed in more detail later in this chapter.

A cautionary note is warranted here about comparisons of the costs derived for the study projects with other development projects, whether sponsored by a nonprofit or a for-profit. As noted, the study's cost build-ups include items as project expenses (such as the full value of syndication proceeds regardless of when they are received, bridge loan interest, net worth and partnership operating expenses, prefunded operating reserves, and "paper" developer's fees and builder's profit allowance), which are elements of development cost generally *not* included in published cost profiles of projects. Therefore, care must be taken to avoid inappropriate comparisons of the study's built-up values to raw costs from other projects for which comparable build-ups have not been performed.

Findings

Sources of Funds

A summary of *cash* (whether covered by equity, grants, or loans) and *non-cash* funding for the study projects is provided in Table 9.2. By adding the value of the noncash contributions to that of the cash resources used for the out-of-pocket expenses, a figure for "full development cost" was derived. As shown in Table 9.2, the full development costs (not normalized) ranged from $43,402 to $264,664 per unit, with a per unit mean of $104,520.

CASH RESOURCES. Among the fifteen projects, unadjusted per-unit out-of-pocket development costs ranged from $40,581 to $204,869, with a mean of $89,237. The mean percentage of out-of-pocket project costs covered by cash equity was 28.7 percent, with the remaining 71.3 percent covered through debt financing. Cash equity in the projects ranged from $539 to $122,463 per unit, with an average of $30,505. The most common form of equity in the fifteen developments was tax credit syndication proceeds (investor equity payments), part of the financing of twelve of the projects (80 percent). Only the three Washington, D.C., projects did not use tax credits. In two of the Washington,

Table 9.2
Per-Unit Sources of Funds (Unadjusted)

Source	Minimum	Maximum	Average	Average Percent of full development cost
Cash Equity	$539	$122,463	$30,505	25.3%
Debt Financing	$30,212	$152,411	$58,732	61.6%
Out-of-Pocket Costs	$40,581	$204,869	$89,237	86.9%
Noncash Resources	$2,029	$59,795	$15,283	13.1%
Full Development Cost	$43,402	$264,664	$104,520	100%

Source: Abt study of fifteen nonprofit housing developments, 1992.

D.C., developments, the nonprofit sponsors made use of in-house development funds as a source of equity. In the third, the sponsor utilized cooperative share deposits, a private grant, and net interim income from the project.

The per-unit amount of debt financing (permanent financing) in the developments ranged from $30,212 to $152,411, with an average of $58,732. Thirteen of the developments (86.7 percent) received a letter of credit or loan from a bank or private financial institution for acquisition, interim/construction, permanent financing, or a combination thereof. Eleven projects (73.3 percent) received loans through the city, generally in the form of CDBG or Rental Rehabilitation Program funds. Eight developments (53.3 percent) were awarded loans by their state housing finance agency.

NONCASH RESOURCES. To create a complete picture of the resources entailed in the fifteen developments, data were also collected on noncash contributions received. In cases where the precise value of a noncash contribution was unknown, an estimate was made using local information on prevailing rates. As shown in Table 9.2, the unadjusted noncash contributions realized by the projects ranged from $2,029 to $59,795 per unit, with an average of $15,283.

As a percentage of full development costs per unit, noncash contributions varied from a low of 4.1 percent to a high of 32.8 percent, with a mean for the fifteen projects of 13.1 percent. In terms of mean percentage, the largest source of noncash contributions came in the form of below-market interest rates during development and waived finance fees, generally obtained in connection with debt financing from public sources (such as the state housing finance agency). This category averaged $2,230 per unit or a mean of 26.9 percent of noncash contributions received. The second and third largest sources of noncash contributions were developer's fees and developer's overhead/staff expenses donated by the nonprofit sponsors. On average, these two categories accounted for 21.9 percent and 21.7 percent, respectively, of the noncash contributions received.

Another major category of noncash contributions, averaging 19.1 percent, was related to acquisition. These noncash contributions came in the form of donated land, loan subsidies for acquisition purposes, waived title/transfer fees, and forgiven real estate taxes. In terms of the average estimated dollar value, acquisition-related contributions represented the largest noncash category, with a mean of $4,888 per unit. However, large contributions in this category were limited to just a few of the projects in the sample.

Contributed city infrastructure (such as street and sidewalk repair) also appeared as a source of noncash resources in the sample projects. Such contributions represented an average of 4.2 percent of noncash resources received by the fifteen projects.

PRESENT VALUE OF GRANTS AND CONTRIBUTIONS. As part of the study, a calculation was also made of the present value of all development-period grants and noncash contributions in the fifteen case studies, plus the value of subsidies on long-term loans. The total capital value of these subsidies and contributions ranged from a low of $13,369 per unit to $134,928 per unit. In percentage terms, the present value of these subsidies ranged from 12 to 67 percent of full development costs. In fact, eleven of the fifteen projects received subsidies and contributions whose present value exceeded one-third of full development costs.[3]

Cost Categories and Affordability

USES OF FUNDS: UNADJUSTED COSTS. An overview of the average costs observed in the fifteen nonprofit projects is provided in Table 9.3 for twelve major development cost categories. These cost categories had been defined as a result of a survey of existing accounting frameworks used by nonprofit and for-profit housing developers conducted at the beginning of the study. Again, it is important to keep in mind that these figures represent "raw" costs, in that they have not been normalized for unit size, region, or time of development.

As expected, direct construction expenses (including site preparation and improvements) proved to be the single largest cost category, averaging $61,622 per unit and, as a mean percentage, 60.8 percent of the full development budget. Among the fifteen projects, per-unit direct construction costs ranged from $20,711 to $137,443, or 44.3 percent to 75.7 percent of full development costs.

Table 9.3
Per–Unit Uses of Funds

Cost Category	Mean out-of-pocket	Mean noncash contribution	Mean total	Average percentage
Planning and design	$2,866	$114	$2,979	2.6%
Acquisition	$6,649	$4,888	$11,537	12.4%
Finance/carrying charges	$4,732	$2,230	$6,962	6.2%
Relocation	$311	$0	$311	0.3%
Construction	$61,067	$555	$61,622	60.8%
Real estate taxes	$409	$68	$477	0.5%
Marketing	$393	$0	$393	0.4%
Reserves	$2,559	$0	$2,559	2.2%
Legal and organizational (incl. devel. consultants)	$1,659	$331	$1,989	2.0%
Developer's overhead/staff	$238	$1,942	$2,180	2.0%
Developer's fee	$3,811	$5,156	$8,967	6.2%
Syndication costs	$4,544	$0	$4,544	4.4%
TOTAL	$89,237	$15,283	$104,520	100.0%

Source: Abt study of fifteen nonprofit housing developments, 1992.

Virtually all of the direct construction costs were out-of-pocket costs. The maximum noncash contribution for direct construction costs among the fifteen projects was $5,750 per unit (in the form of donated infrastructure and materials for one of the Kansas City projects). On average, the noncash contributions for this expense category were only $555 per unit. The next largest expense category on average was acquisition, with a mean cost of $11,537 (average percentage of 12.4 percent of full development cost). Among the fifteen projects, acquisition ranged from $745 to $27,381 per unit, and accounted for up to 30.1 percent of the full development budget. An average of 57.6 percent of costs of acquisition was out-of-pocket, with the remainder in the form of contributions.

The third largest expense category was developer's fees. When taken together with developer's overhead and staffing, these combined categories averaged $11,147 per unit (and a mean percentage of 8.2 percent of full development costs). A key finding of the study, however, was that a majority of the "expense" associated with developer's fees and overhead was in the form of noncash contributions from the nonprofit sponsors to the project, generally to cover the equity requirements for financing. On average, the nonprofit sponsors only realized $4,049 per unit as a cash payment of developer's fee and overhead, averaging less than 4 percent of the full development cost.

NORMALIZATION OF PER-UNIT COSTS. To facilitate crossproject comparisons, the full development costs for the fifteen projects were normalized through adjustments for location and year completed (using R.S. Means indices), as well as for unit size (to reflect the equivalent number of standard 844 square-foot, two-bedroom units). Normalization of per-unit costs was performed excluding land costs, as these tended to vary considerably among the projects. However, the available cost indices (R. S. Means) were metropolitan-area wide for all multifamily housing. Therefore, they may not be ideally suited to reflect costs incurred at difficult center-city development sites.

Using the normalization approach described, the resulting adjusted full development costs (without land) ranged from $40,988 to $223,445 per unit, with an average across the fifteen projects of $85,467. New construction projects tended to be the most expensive (with an average normalized per-unit cost of $109,515), particularly those located in center-city sites, those that provide below-grade parking, and those that involved low- or high-rise apartment construction.

A major finding of this study was the large unexplained variation in the costs of nonprofit sponsored affordable housing development, after normalization. Despite adjustments for size differences, locational variations in construction costs, and differences in date of construction, there remain striking differences in per-unit costs. As can be seen in Table 9.1, these differences appear to cluster by metropolitan area and may be tied to the local development and financing models being followed in each metropolitan area.

AFFORDABILITY. The analysis showed that, with the development period subsidies received, the nonprofit sponsors were able to produce units with average rents affordable to households under 80 percent of median income, in all instances but two of the Boston projects. In ten of the twelve non-Boston developments (66.7 percent of the sample projects), the average rents were affordable to households under 50 percent of median solely on the basis of the development subsidies. Further, with the development period subsidies alone, two projects in Chicago and one in Washington achieved rents that could reach households under 30 percent of median income. Thus, the development period public subsidies that were received appear to have been sufficient in most cases to house low-income or very low-income households in a high percentage of the units developed. And, in the two Boston projects mentioned above where the development subsidies were not sufficient to achieve affordability, these subsidies were supplemented with commitments of Section 8 rental assistance in order to house lower income tenants.

Patterns of Development

As noted earlier, one objective of the study was to identify prototype patterns of financing and costs of nonprofit housing development. The limited, nonrepresentative group of fifteen projects that were examined does not permit statistically valid generalizations about the universe of nonprofit housing development, or even about nonprofit behavior in the selected MSAs. However, the observations from the fifteen projects suggest patterns which, if found to be representative, could have significant policy implications. Keeping in mind the speculative nature of these comments, we offer some preliminary observations about these patterns and their potential significance.

MSA DEVELOPMENT SCENARIOS. It is likely that individual MSAs may exhibit their own distinct development scenario (or scenarios), rather than reflecting a standard national prototype for nonprofit development. The site reconnaissance and analysis of selected nonprofit projects suggest that there are local "models" of development, in terms of ownership (whether rental or cooperative housing), construction approaches (whether new construction or rehabilitation), financing mechanism (whether tax credits were syndicated by a local or a national nonprofit and whether the state Housing Finance Agency, CDBG, or private sources provided financing), per-unit costs, and contract rents.

As previously stated, it appears that variations in per-unit project cost are not explained simply by variations in unit size, year completed, or regional labor and material costs. Rather, they seem to be at least in part a reflection of the local approaches to structuring development, with a considerable amount of the variation attributable to the soft costs of development associated with the particular local model. (It should be noted, however, that our preliminary study did *not* attempt to adjust for cost differences in new construction versus varying levels of rehabilitation, or for other special circumstances of each project.)

The local models observed in the study appear to have been created in each MSA by a network of more experienced nonprofit developers, along with support organizations and a few financial institutions. As the several actors involved found a successful strategy, it tended to be repeated. Even when national organizations (such as the Local Initiatives Support Corporation) were involved and brought some standardization to the process, they generally seemed to adapt various financing pieces to a local model. The more experienced developers and support organizations in the MSAs often served as "mentors" to novice nonprofits, so that even these novices were able to undertake ambitious development efforts with complex financing approaches.

If these observations are an accurate indication of the nature of nonprofit development around the country, then to understand the precise ramifications of a policy or program for a particular region, a range of local models and conditions must be identified and understood. This is because the effect of the policy or program will vary with the local development models and local conditions.

Among the study's fifteen projects, the developments in the Boston and San Francisco MSAs were at the upper end of the per-unit cost range. Since the projects in the sample were not randomly selected, and were not necessarily representative of nonprofit development in each community examined, we felt it would be useful for the investigation of patterns of development if the study also included supplementary collection of some "raw" cost information on other recently completed developments in several MSAs. For the Boston MSA, for example, unadjusted cost data were collected from housing officials for nine additional affordable projects (four nonprofit projects and five for-profit projects). The additional group of nonprofit-sponsored projects yielded examples of both higher and lower raw costs than those observed in our formal study sample for the Boston MSA. And it is important to note, so did the for-profit group of projects.

The supplementary Boston information also suggests that there may be changes in the local development models over time. For instance, representatives of Boston housing agencies commented during our supplemental data collection activities that due to changes in the market and in the state's support for housing, developers of affordable housing were shifting to less costly development models.

THE USE OF TAX CREDITS. The prominent use of tax credits and the variation in per-unit costs experienced by the study's tax credit projects suggest that the variation in costs among nonprofit projects may be as important as comparison with for-profit projects. To the extent that a single factor approached being a constant in the fifteen projects, it was the use of Low Income Housing Tax Credits (LIHTC)—present in every project except for the three in Washington, D.C. The tax credit projects are owned by a partnership in which the limited partners have a large portion of the ownership, but the controlling general partner is usually a subsidiary of the nonprofit. Thus, the nonprofit was the initiator and controlling entity in each of these cases. The LIHTC projects also showed great variability in the normalized per-unit costs, from the least to the most expensive project. Therefore, use of tax credits did not appear to make costs more uniform.

The fact that tax credits were not used by the three Washington, D.C. projects in the study may be attributable to several factors. First, reconnaissance suggested that for the period preceding our study the tax credit agency for the District of Columbia had a very modest allocation of credits. Moreover, the limited number of tax credit awards that were made in the time period under consideration went largely to purely for-profit projects. Second, the Washington, D.C., area nonprofit developments frequently involved cooperatives, which do not lend themselves readily to the tax credit program. Third, at the time some of the most active nonprofit developers in the District preferred avoiding the complexities associated with tax credits, choosing to utilize alternate approaches for securing cash equity for projects.[4]

The study also showed that the tax credit projects often used part of their net syndication proceeds (investor payments less costs of syndication) to pay for the soft costs associated with development, such as bridge financing charges, predevelopment expenses, and developer's fees. Other funding sources utilized by the nonprofit sponsors (especially local governments) often did not recognize such expenses as allowable or mortgageable, even if they were crucial to moving the developments forward. Moreover, since the installment schedule for the investor payments meant that reimbursement for these soft costs was often deferred, nonprofits were forced to subsidize the projects themselves during development, through contributions of staff time and other organizational expenses. The nonprofits' frequent inability to recoup the administrative expenses associated with the housing development projects, or to realize significant developer's fees as a mechanism to build up capital, may result in low salaries and limited job opportunities/stability. This in turn may cause high staff turnover, fluctuations in nonprofit organizational capacity, and difficulties in taking timely advantage of development opportunities.

RELIANCE ON MULTIPLE FUNDING SOURCES. The dependence on multiple funding sources, and especially the delays experienced by nonprofits in securing public funding, appears to be a critical element influencing the cost of developing affordable housing. To achieve full funding for their developments, the fifteen nonprofits used multiple funding sources, averaging 7.8 sources per development. Often the financing provided by individual funding sources was modest. Yet this multiple financing resulted in numerous delays in the fifteen projects, especially in connection with public sources of funding. This in turn could delay the closing on private financing.

The need to package numerous small financing components is a common finding of studies on nonprofits regarding the critical and chronic shortage of funds that many such organizations experience. Each private lender apparently tries to minimize risk in such projects by providing only a fraction of the financing needed. Ultimately, the nonprofit developers in this study were relatively successful at leveraging private funds for their projects with the various forms of public subsidy received. Among the fifteen developments, on average, every dollar in public funding or a public noncash contribution was matched on a dollar-for-dollar basis by private financing. However, the delays, the necessity for bridge financing, and the additional settlement and transaction costs associated with the multiple funding sources added to the overall cost of development. Further research would be desirable to quantify these costs and observe whether for-profit developers of affordable housing face similar funding challenges.

Ongoing Property Management and Tenant Services

Although the nonprofit sponsors exhibited a strong continuing interest in how the developments were operated, only eight of the fifteen sponsors actually were managing the completed developments themselves or through closely associated subsidiaries. In the other cases, the sponsors or residents had concluded that management of the properties would be best handled through an outside firm. This was a striking finding. Management fees are a potential source of operating revenues for the nonprofits, yet many were willing to forego this income in the interest of improved property management. However, even when third-party management firms were utilized, the property owner (nonprofit or cooperative) did control the major management policies.

While a majority of the fifteen nonprofits operated various service programs in addition to their development activities, overall the services offered exclusively to residents of the developments were relatively modest. Even those nonprofit sponsors with extensive social services expertise and resources tended to offer the services on a communitywide basis. Sponsors of cooperative projects in the study provided coop training, but generally relatively few other tenant-specific services were provided. These included counseling, tenant organization, and a youth maintenance crew. Services provided to the wider community included social services programs, day care, and elder care programs, and community planning and advocacy work. Although the residents of the developments would not benefit *exclusively* from these services, the common pattern of siting these services in or near the projects increased the tenants' access to them.

Development Costs for Nonprofit and For-Profit Projects

As mentioned previously, one task of the study was to begin to address the issue of comparative nonprofit versus for-profit costs for the development of comparable packages of housing services.

In addition to the small, nonrandom sample of nonprofit projects studied, the research was limited by several constraints in performing a thorough and valid comparison of costs:

- The study made no provision for correspondingly comprehensive data collection for similar actual for-profit projects. Although the data collection instrument did capture information on the physical characteristics of the nonprofit projects, the study did not have the resources for the extensive data on building specifications, construction techniques, and materials that would be necessary to do a *precise* buildup of estimated costs using industry standards (particularly for the rehabilitation projects, which differed dramatically in scope of work).

- Aside from direct construction costs, reconnaissance indicated no industry standards generally applicable to total development cost or its components, such as for predevelopment costs, legal and organizational costs, and marketing.

Nonetheless, as part of the study, a rough comparison with industry standards was made for development "hard costs" for the six new construction projects examined.

ACTUAL CONSTRUCTION COSTS VERSUS INDUSTRY NORMS. For such construction "hard costs," the R.S. Means Construction Cost indices were used to compute the nominal industry costs per square foot for the study projects, using basic information on project location, type and size of building, and type of exterior wall. (Again, note that these metropolitanwide construction cost averages may not reflect typical construction costs for difficult urban affordable housing sites.) The actual per-square-foot construction costs for the new construction study projects ranged from 20 percent above to 20 percent below the nominal industry costs for the specified location, type, and size of building. This variability relative to construction costs is not unlike what one might expect to see from a similar sample of for-profit projects.

Despite the absence of a statistically reliable framework for comparison, the study also utilized observations from the fifteen nonprofit projects to speculate on major cost elements where the nonprofit and for-profit experience might differ. For example, the average predevelopment period for the fifteen nonprofit projects was 29.3 months, or 2 1/2 times as long as the mean construction period (11.7 months). This prolonged predevelopment period was due to the nonprofits' lack of up-front capital and dependence on multiple funding sources (particularly public funding sources where the approval processes were slow), and led to higher development costs. A for-profit (or indeed a nonprofit) project able to secure funding more readily from a small number of sources could be expected to have a shorter and less costly predevelopment period.

The majority of the nonprofits in the study were given property at a discount, which might not have been available to a for-profit counterpart. In addition, because of the distressed nature of some of the nonprofit sites, a for-profit might be more hesitant to undertake projects in these more risky locations unless there were a greater than normal level of financial incentives or guarantees, which might itself lead to added costs.

All the nonprofits in the study also received below market interest rates (BMIR), primarily from public sources of funding. Although these funding sources might be willing to provide BMIR loans to for-profit developers for similar affordable housing efforts, only 51.7 percent of the sampled (primarily for-profit) projects in ICF's 1987 tax credit study reported such below market loans. Therefore, the availability of these BMIR loans might reduce the out-of-pocket financing costs of nonprofits relative to many for-profits. On the other hand, for-profit developers not dependent on public funding sources potentially could experience significantly lower construction costs by avoiding Davis-Bacon prevailing wages or some of the special requirements that come with local public funding, such as hiring targets.

Finally, the fifteen nonprofits in the study realized an average cash payment of developer's overhead/fees equivalent to 3.9 percent of development costs, as compared to the 9.5 percent average for the ICF 1987 tax credit study involving largely for-profit projects. Therefore, it appears that this cost category may be less expensive in nonprofit projects, although whether the actual fees received are sufficient to optimize nonprofit organizational capacity is in question.

In considering the question of comparative costs, it is also important to recognize that while the study focused on nonprofit development, because of the prevalent use of tax credits, most of the projects examined were actually hybrid *nonprofit/for-profit* efforts. The financial profile of these projects was driven in large part by the nature of the tax credit device. As previously noted, the wide variation in the study's per-unit costs for these projects suggests that the structure of the financing may be as important as any cost differentials due to nonprofit versus for-profit development approaches.

Conclusions and Areas for Further Research

The study undertaken by Abt Associates confirmed the feasibility of systematic collection of cost and funding data on nonprofit development projects for both cash and noncash sources. The hierarchical framework developed for the study was found to permit comparative analysis of such projects. However, the preliminary study also suggested a number of areas where the analytic framework and methodology might be refined.

For example, collection of a greater level of detail on the physical characteristics of units would provide a basis for more precise buildups and comparisons with published industry construction cost standards, and the ability to normalize more accurately for special development conditions. There should also be more research on comparable for-profit interest rates and loan conditions for improved estimates of the value of interest subsidies. The issue of how syndication proceeds and expenses are treated in the calculation of "full development costs" under the methodology should also be reviewed, to see if it is possible to construct a financial buildup for development projects that reflects a more conventional view of what is included in "development costs" without excluding the equity generated by tax credits from the analysis.

One factor that complicated the site selection process for this study (and would affect future studies, even with an improved analytic framework) is the lack of a national data-base on nonprofit sponsors and projects. To provide a sampling frame for drawing statistically representative samples of projects for future studies, a publicly available national database on nonprofit sponsors and projects needs to be developed. Examination of a larger group of projects, drawn as a statistically representative sample, would allow a fuller explanation of the variation in the development costs of nonprofit sponsored projects such as that seen in our study.

Although limited by the size and nature of the sample of projects, the study also generated a number of hypotheses about patterns of nonprofit housing development, and reasons for variations among the patterns seen across MSAs. A basic question the study hoped to examine was whether the costs to produce a defined package of housing services differed systematically for nonprofit and for-profit sponsors. The overall pattern of costs among the fifteen projects suggests that variance among the nonprofit project costs might be at least as large as any variance in costs between nonprofit and for-profit projects. Therefore, some of the higher cost levels observed in our study may be more a function of local development conditions and requirements rather than systematic differences in nonprofit versus for-profit comparative efficiencies.

While the development approaches and costs realized varied considerably across the sample, perhaps one of the most significant findings from the study was how reasonable the "full development costs" proved to be for most of the projects, given the challenges faced and the levels of affordability achieved for lower income tenants. As previously noted, the dependence on multiple funding sources (and slow approval processes for public funding) required bridge financing and increased transaction costs that considerably increased development expenses. Many public funding sources were also unwilling to recognize the nonprofits' predevelopment expenses as allowable. To offset such costs (and to meet their equity contribution requirements), nonprofit developers frequently were willing to donate a significant portion of their development fees, or to defer such fees. The nonprofits were also willing to forgo the income represented by management fees if it was felt that management of the completed projects could best be handled by an outside (generally for-profit) firm. Although such decisions may have been advantageous for the specific projects and tenants, they also could be impeding the ability of the nonprofits to build up capital, thereby reducing organizational capacity and opportunities to pursue future development projects. If nonprofit housing production is to increase, these issues of financing and fees must be addressed.

In considering areas for future research, it is also important to recognize that development period finances are only a part of the overall financial picture of housing projects. The other half of the picture relates to the revenues and costs of ongoing operations. Research should address this operating experience, including exploration of the role played by prefunded reserves, syndication proceeds, and operating subsidies in maintaining the viability and affordability of the projects, and of the interrelationships between development costs and operating expenses.

Finally, continuing research is needed on the larger questions of the role of affordable housing production (in comparison with tenant-based assistance) in meeting the housing needs of the eligible population and in contributing to community stabilization and development.

Notes

1. This article summarizes the results of the study on nonprofit housing completed by Abt Associates for the Office of Policy Development and Research of the U.S. Department of Housing and Urban Development under HUD contract DU100C00000-5889.

2. One project, though described by its Kansas City sponsor as "multifamily," actually was a tract development of single-family houses.

3. Note that the value of the subsidies on long-term loans is not included in full development cost.

4. However, one of the Washington, D.C. nonprofit developers in our study did use tax credits in completing a more recent rehabilitation project. This case illustrates both the changes that can take place in MSA development patterns over time, and the dangers in overgeneralizing from the development patterns seen in the study.

Chapter 10

The Tortuous Path
of Nonprofit Development

C. Theodore Koebel

*The complicated network of subsidies and partners involved in the production of afford-
able housing in the United States is further illustrated in this chapter. In many ways the
development profiled should have presented a direct path to the creation of a single-room-
only hotel for the formerly homeless. But even under "best case" conditions, the requirements for multiple sources of subsidy and finance are indeed tortuous. The burdens of
nonprofit development under this housing scheme are so onerous, they limit development
to the most experienced and well connected NHOs.*

Nonprofit Housing Production in the United States

The growing reputation of nonprofit housing organizations in the United
States was significantly enhanced by the Low Income Housing Tax Credit program, under which NHOs have emerged as successful packagers of low-income
housing. The tax credits replaced the Section 8 housing production programs
with a much shallower subsidy, making it significantly more difficult to produce
housing for low-income populations. The increased difficulty of doing low-
income housing development scared most for-profit developers away, except for
developments relying solely on the tax credit as a subsidy and built for a narrow
band of moderate income renters. This has left the production of rental housing
for poorer renters to the efforts of nonprofit developers. Several NHOs gained
national recognition for establishing public-private partnerships in responding to
this challenge. National intermediaries (e.g., LISC and Enterprise) were established to provide technical assistance and syndication services to attract private
equity investment in exchange for the tax credits, lending additional business
prestige to the nonprofit sector.

The nonprofit housing sector was further enhanced by legislative set-asides in such programs as homeless shelters, tax credits, and the new HOME program. The national policy commitment to the sector is reflected in the introduction by Michael Stegman to a recent HUD study of nonprofit housing (Hebert et al. 1993:ii):

> Nonprofit housing developers have become increasingly important producers of housing for low-income people, developing an estimated 20–30,000 units per year nationwide. Projects developed by nonprofits are typically high-risk endeavors in difficult settings for hard-to-serve populations, and often CDCs are the only entities willing to undertake them. Many nonprofit developers provide social or community services in conjunction with physical development, further complicating already challenging efforts. Thus, nonprofit organizations fill a unique and important niche in providing housing for poor people and in rebuilding communities, and they deserve our support.

Interestingly, Stegman was the first to publicly criticize the complexity and cost of the low-income housing development system that has gained praise for the nonprofit sector (Stegman 1990). Although not critical of nonprofit developers, Stegman lambasted the tax credit program and "creative financing" as inefficient and costly. The system is troubled with "high transaction costs, inappropriate targeting of benefits, and insufficient monitoring." The 1993 report authored by Hebert et al. reported on the costs, type of financing, subsidy layering, and development time required for fifteen projects.

These projects typically had seven to eight layers of financing, often required the participation of national intermediaries, and on average took forty-one months to complete. The predevelopment phase accounted for three-fourths of the time required for completing these developments; construction averaged just twelve months. The LIHTC was the primary source of equity funds, with other funds (primarily debt financing) coming from an array of sources for each project: letters of credit or loans from financial institutions, loans from the city (usually with CDBG or other federal funds), state housing finance agency loans, waived fees, donated land, forgiven real estate taxes, and donations of the nonprofit developer's fees and overhead. Similar findings were reported by Slepin (1994) based on a survey of twenty multifamily housing projects developed by NHOs.

Hebert and Wallace in chapter 9 and Hebert et al. (1993) present the most extensive analysis of the costs of nonprofit development completed to date. They concluded that these costs were "generally comparable" to industry averages. However, they did not include predevelopment costs except to the extent these were reflected in the developer's fees charged to the project. This is likely to seriously understate actual predevelopment costs. First, it is highly likely that nonprofit developers do not keep records of all predevelopment costs, particularly staff time. Secondly, even if they know these costs, they are unlikely to pass them on to the development in full if they exceed typical rates for developers' fees. Additionally, the development fees charged to the project are frequently waived or loaned to the project at zero interest as subordinate or unsecured debt. Consequently, the cost comparison presented by Hebert et al. primarily reflects construction costs, which would not be expected to vary widely from industry standards.

The claim of comparable costs notwithstanding, Hebert et al. found that "multiple financing resulted in numerous delays in the fifteen projects, especially in connection with public sources of funding" and recommended increased cost control and fewer funding sources. They also concluded that "the nonprofits' frequent inability to recoup the administrative expenses associated with the housing development projects, or to realize significant developer's fees as a mechanism to build up capital, may result in low salaries and limited job opportunities/stability."

Discussions of the costs of nonprofit development are further complicated by the costs of tax credits. Stegman, in his 1990 article, estimated that the federal tax credit program for low income housing was approximately twice the cost of direct governmental borrowing. Referencing a HUD sponsored study of the cost of the housing tax credits conducted by ICF (1991), Hebert et al. reported that "the ratio of discounted present value of subsidies for tax credit projects was 2.4 times the average discounted present value of the equivalent Section 8 Existing Housing subsidies for the same households." Not only does the tax credit program cost substantially more than direct rent subsidies, the discounted present value of the tax credits (net of syndication costs, which easily take 20 percent of gross investor proceeds) is worth less than half their cost to the federal government.

The complexity of nonprofit development within the current funding system is frequently bemoaned by nonprofit organizations (Slepin characterized NHO development as "deals from hell"), but has received very little systematic study. It is important to document this complexity and the numerous delays and cost increases that it causes. Although the nonprofit housing sector receives well deserved praise for making this system work, its national representatives and intermediaries appear reluctant to criticize this system either because they are part of it or out of fear that criticism, however justified, will lead to further funding cuts and elimination of programs rather than reform.

This chapter tells the story of a single development, the conversion of a vacant hotel to a single-room-only (SRO) facilty for the homeless. A single case study is open to the criticism that it is unrepresentative of other developments and does not present an accurate reflection of the norm. In many ways each nonprofit housing development is unique. But the complexity of the funding system and the tortuous path described here are undeniably common to many nonprofit housing developments. By studying the details of this one case, we can learn more about the problems faced in nonprofit development. As the saying goes, "the devil's in the details."

The Hotel Warwick—Background

The Hotel Warwick was originally built in 1883 to serve as the largest transient residential facility in Newport News, Virginia. As with other older hotels in central cities, many much more splendid than the Warwick, the passage of time was accompanied by progressing deterioration of its market and its physical structure. After a fire destroyed the original structure in 1961, attempts to reopen the Warwick as a hotel were plagued by the advance of urban decline and the exodus of business activity from downtown Newport News. The hotel was rebuilt in the 1960s, but ran into severe operating deficits and closed in the early 1980s. In 1983, one century after the hotel's first christening, a for-profit partnership called Centre Development, Inc., was formed to renovate the hotel. The restoration was to form the cornerstone of the city's Newport Centre downtown redevelopment plan.

Centre Development purchased the hotel for $600,000. At the time, the partners planned to spend $1.75 million for acquisition and renovation in order to bring the hotel up to modern standards. Peninsula Ports Authority (PPA), a state- and city-sponsored economic development agency, agreed to lend the Hotel Warwick partners $1.75 million in tax-exempt industrial revenue bonds backed by a promissory note made payable to the PPA from Centre Development. This promissory note was subsequently assigned to the three banks (Crestar, Sovran, and First American) that had purchased the bonds.

To meet a common requirement of most commercial banks who finance large-scale development projects, the partners had to provide personal equity, in this case $500,000, as evidence of their good faith and commitment to the proposed venture. Additional financing of $500,000 for the hotel renovation was obtained from the Newport News Redevelopment and Housing Authority (NNRHA) based on an Urban Development Action Grant in 1984.

Between 1983 and 1985 renovation costs for the Hotel Warwick skyrocketed from $1.75 million to over $2.3 million, well beyond what the partners at Centre Development had anticipated. Start-up occupancy rates were lower than expected, while operating and maintenance costs were higher. Concurrently, the city of Newport News was experiencing problems with its overall redevelopment strategy. Businesses continued to vacate downtown and crime rates were on the rise. With mounting operating losses, the Hotel Warwick closed again in 1988.

In real estate development, one person's failure is often another's opportunity. The Hotel Warwick had been physically renovated and, despite its failure as a hotel, was still an important piece of real estate, anchoring the downtown's waterfront access. But reuse of the property faced serious obstacles. Centre Development, the participating banks, and the NNRHA wanted to minimize their respective losses without doing unnecessary damage to each other.

The SRO Proposal

In many ways, the Hotel Warwick was the ideal property for conversion to a single room only (SRO) hotel by an enterprising nonprofit housing organization. Shortly after it closed, VMH, Inc., entered the picture. VMH was well suited to take on a hotel conversion as one of the state's larger and more successful NHOs. VMH already owned or operated fourteen multifamily properties throughout the state. Its director of housing management was located in the Virginia Beach-Newport News metropolitan area. The corporation had expertise in applying tax credits to development projects, including state Neighborhood Development Tax Credits as well as federal Low Income Housing Tax Credits. It had earned a solid reputation with the prominent housing organizations that might be involved in this project: HUD, the Virginia Department of Housing and Community Development, the Virginia Housing Development Authority, and the Federal Home Loan Bank of Atlanta.

The executive director was actively involved in the state's housing policy network, serving on the Virginia Housing Study Commission, the Virginia Low Income Housing Coalition, the Nonprofit Advisory Committee of the Virginia Housing Development Authority, and committees or boards of several other state and regional housing organizations. In addition to the executive director and director of housing management, the corporation's management staff included a director of operations and a director of finance and administration. The corporation's legal counsel was experienced with HUD programs and housing tax credits.

By mid-1989, VMH approached Centre Development with a proposition to purchase the old hotel and convert it to SRO use. The plan included the conversion of the vacant structure into 88 single-room units for permanent housing for adults of both sexes, with rent subsidized by HUD Section 8 project-based certificates (Moderate Rehabilitation SRO Program). The plan incorporated the use of state tax credits in lieu of cash for the lenders and tax-deductible gifts from Centre Development for the equity needed in the purchase of the building and Section 8 Mod-Rehab SRO certificates to subsidize postconversion rents. Additional financing to cover necessary conversion costs would be leveraged through federal tax credits. The proposal was the first glimmer of hope the Warwick partners had seen since its closing in 1988. Centre Development was enthusiastic with the offer, but the three lenders were cautious and needed to be convinced that tax credits and tax deductions had the same value as cash.

The Tortuous Path to Purchasing the Property

During the first half of 1991, a possible development agreement emerged. Modification agreements, indemnity contracts, and deeds of assumption were drafted by the parties' attorneys. In the deal, VMH agreed to pay the $1.75 million obligation of Centre Development to the three banks holding the Peninsula Ports Authority bonds, as well as the $500,000 rehabilitation note held by the NNRHA, the balance of which had increased to $612,000 due to unpaid interest. VMH would transfer state tax credits in three or four annual installments to the banks for the $1.75 million used to retire the debt. VMH convinced NNRRA to defer payment on its loan until the year 2007.

The tax credits used for the acquisition came from the Virginia Neighborhood Assistance Act Tax Credit program, which provides state tax credits of 50 cents per dollar contributed to nonprofit corporations benefiting neighborhoods. The donation is limited to a maximum of $350,000 per donor corporation per year. Coupled with the federal and state tax deductions allowed for gifts to charitable organizations (which applied to the half not covered by the state tax credit), the banks could cover the cost of approximately 70 percent of their contribution. The balance was essentially contributed by Centre Development, the cost of which was only partially offset by the federal and state tax deductions for a contribution to a 501(c)(3) organization.

The use of the state tax credits was limited by the annual maximum contribution allowed, by the donors' annual tax liability, and by the annual allocation of tax credits to VMH. (Although a five-year rollover of unused credits is allowed, the banks were not interested in that option, since it involved some risk that the full amount could not be used.) The combination of factors influencing the use of the tax credits required retirement of the bonds over three tax years. A closing would be held with each installment, transferring contributions, tax credits, and property rights in stages. VMH would gain title to the hotel and assume the obligation to retire the bond debt with the first closing. To reduce VMH's exposure to potential losses, Centre Development agreed to purchase the building from VMH and reassume the debt obligation in the event the debt could not be retired through future installments of tax credits, deductions, and contributions.

As the plan to transfer the property and debt obligation to VMH progressed toward a settlement, the project ran into its first major setback. Right before the first scheduled closing in June 1991, one of the participating banks, First American, was purchased by another bank (First Union). Complications surrounding First Union's ability to make use of the tax credits and changes in corporate leadership resulted in its decision to withdraw from the agreed settlement. The "deal" appeared to be dead.

Resuscitating dead deals requires a deal-maker with either "deep pockets" (a rarity among nonprofit housing corporations) or a strong network of business and government associates (the social capital equivalent of deep pockets). VMH turned to Signet Bank, which was known to be both profitable and civic-minded. Signet agreed to step in and purchase the bonds held by First American. Even though there was nothing to gain from the deal financially, VMH managed to convince Signet that it would have limited risk exposure and should salvage the deal as part of its community reinvestment responsibilities.

The deal was back on track and the closing was rescheduled for December 1991. An initial payment was made to retire bonds from the combination of tax credits, deductions, and the contribution of uncovered losses by Centre Development. VMH assumed title to the property along with the obligation to repay the remaining bond debt and the deferred NNRHA loan. Implementing a complex purchase agreement based entirely on state tax credits and federal and state tax deductions for charitable contributions, plus uncovered donations from the previous owner, was a heady success. Two years had elapsed since VMH started working on the project. The near disaster in June had been averted and the property transfer was completed. The nonprofit developer now owned a vacant hotel but still needed to obtain funding for the conversion of the hotel to an SRO for the homeless.

The Tortuous Path to Redeveloping the Property

Property development under the Section 8 assisted housing program was relatively easy to finance. The federal subsidy commitment in essence guaranteed a rent-roll sufficient to retire the property debt and cover maintenance costs and other nondebt operating costs (as well as provide a profit). The subsidies underwriting the rents were committed to the property for fifteen to twenty-five years, ample time to cover permanent financing. The Section 8 program was substantially overhauled in 1986. Its housing production program was replaced with the Low Income Housing Tax Credit, which provides much shallower subsidies and requires much higher rents and incomes of tenants.

The development of housing for tenants who were formerly homeless cannot rely significantly on rental income from those tenants. Debt service (usually the amortized cost of property acquisition and development) and other operating costs for anything other than a fleabag, skid-row hotel would require substantially higher rents than could be afforded by the homeless. In light of this and in recognition of the substantial loss of SRO hotels to urban renewal and other downtown redevelopment projects, Congress enacted the Section 8 Moderate Rehabilitation Program for Single Room Occupancy Dwellings for Homeless Individuals. The program provides a renewable ten-year commitment of rental assistance. Although construction and permanent financing must be obtained outside the program, the rental subsidies are supposed to cover debt service sufficient to retire the cost of moderate rehabilitation during the initial ten-year commitment. Maximum rents are set at 75 percent of the Fair Market Rent for an efficiency apartment. The rental subsidy is not designed to pay for support services.

A Section 8 commitment was received in September 1992, but the Housing Assistance Payments Contract wasn't executed until December of the next year. The HAP required occupancy by the end of 1994. The annual contributions contract was for $352,700 per year, equivalent to $345 monthly rent per unit or 75 percent of the Fair Market Rent for an efficiency apartment (effectively a similar size unit to the SRO units). VMH, however, expected that SRO units for the formerly homeless would be significantly more expensive to operate and maintain than a standard efficiency unit for "regular" tenants and feared that rental income would be insufficient to support adequate maintenance and replacement reserves. Consequently, the building renovation was designed to provide a facility with as little maintenance and replacement as possible. Prevented from covering what were considered reasonably anticipated costs out of the annual rent subsidies, the developer decided to shift these costs to the construction budget.

Although the conversion of a recently renovated hotel to SRO use would seem to be relatively straightforward, such was not the case. Building codes for residential use are predicated on standard building types: single-family homes and apartment buildings. A transient hotel does not meet many of these requirements. Additionally, an SRO hotel for the homeless needs a security system that will guard against entry from fire exits without interfering with the protections of the fire code.

Delays in acquiring the vacant building indirectly contributed to escalating costs. Plumbing lines burst and the boiler was damaged during a rare winter freeze. In addition to fixing the plumbing and replacing the heating system, the conversion included new flooring (replacing carpet with linoleum), a new roof, new wiring, replastered walls, and a $100,000 security system. Throughout the nonprofit developer's five-year process to acquire and redevelop the property, conversion costs (net of acquisition, operating reserve, developer's fee, and LIHTC syndication fee) climbed from the initial estimate of $1.0 million to $2.3 million. Fixing or replacing damaged systems, rising materials' costs, changes in code requirements, and modifications in the scope of work to accommodate a tight operating budget played major roles in this increase.

Cost escalations of this magnitude reflect the numerous delays and complications that push a seemingly straightforward project into a five-year saga. It also reflects the peculiarities of the programs used to pay for such housing. Almost as important as the escalation in construction costs is the escalation in so-called soft costs—particularly the fees and reserves associated with obtaining money to support the project beyond the level sustained by the Annual Contributions Contract (Section 8 rent subsidies). The need to seek out additional funds was costly, in time, administrative overhead, and fees.

The effort to obtain additional funding reads like a virtual history of contemporary housing programs, some of which did not even exist when the acquisition process was started. The HOME program was tapped for a Congregate Housing loan of $350,000 through the Virginia Department of Housing and Community Development and a $163,350 loan from the Newport News Redevelopment and Housing Authority. The HOME funds in turn required the creation of a Community Housing Development Organization to be the eventually owner of the property. The nonprofit developer also applied for and received a $300,000 loan through the Affordable Housing Program of the Federal Home Loan Bank of Atlanta. This required negotiations with yet a fourth bank, which had to apply for the funds on behalf of the nonprofit developer.

Yet another application was made for a Low Income Housing Tax Credit allocation and a Historic Tax Credit allocation after Congress liberalized these programs' subsidy layering restrictions, which previously prohibited the combined use of subsidy programs with tax credits or made it impractical to do so. A net investment of $1.9 million was made in March 1994 by the "limited partners" in exchange for housing tax credits of $217,756, taken annually over ten years, and a historic tax credit of $487,744 taken in the first year. The tax credits required an $80,178 syndication fee, plus substantial legal and administrative overhead. Additionally, the tax credit program reinforced the pressure to "front-end" costs by rewarding more tax credits for a larger eligible basis, which is created by doing more construction.

The federal tax credits also required a commitment to maintain occupancy by tenants meeting the program's low income criteria for fifteen years. Extreme penalties are assessed limited partners receiving tax credits for properties that violate the program's occupancy standards. Consequently, these investors demanded that sufficient up-front operating reserves be established to carry the project for years eleven to fifteen in case the ten-year Section 8 rental subsidy was not renewed. Since there was no anticipated excess cash flow to repay the nonprofit developer's equity and loans to the project, any distribution of reserves to the investors would further enhance their rate of return and would diminish the nonprofit's recovery of principal.

In April 1993, the nonprofit developer retired the original bond debt with a final exchange of state tax credits for contributions from the three banks and virtually owned the hotel "free and clear" (except for the deferred NNRHA loan). A year later the three additional loans through the HOME program and FHLB Affordable Housing Program were closed, along with the LIHTC limited partnership agreement. To enhance the financial attractiveness of the project, particularly to the limited partners, the nonprofit developer committed $627,072 to the project from deferred payment of its developer's fee and its contractor's overhead and profit, along with two zero-interest loans from its own resources. This liability on the part of the nonprofit developer was virtually mandated by the operating reserve required by the LIHTC investors to protect their tax credits in case the Section 8 subsidy is not renewed. This commitment by the nonprofit developer of a substantial reserve fund required additional negotiations over the distribution of these funds after year fifteen or upon sale of the property.

In March 1994, with permanent financing in place, the developer was ready to obtain a construction loan. Construction loans typically require firm commitments for permanent ("take-out") financing to be in place. Since the equity raised by the housing tax credits would not be firmly committed until the establishment of the limited partnership, the construction loan became virtually contingent on the partnership closing, which didn't occur until well after construction was initiated. Delaying construction until a construction loan could be closed would have threatened the Section 8 commitment, which needed two extensions in any case. Initiating construction without a construction loan would expose even larger, for-profit firms to serious risk of financial failure due to cash flow problems. A nonprofit corporation starting without a construction loan is an invitation for disaster. Nonetheless, the developer faced another possible unraveling of years of work. Consequently, construction was initiated in September 1994 through juggling a line of credit, drawdowns from the state and city HOME grants, the Federal Home Loan Bank Affordable Housing Program loan, and VMH's internal resources. With construction underway, the developer was liable for payment of subcontractors working on the conversion. These payments presented an ongoing strain on the nonprofit corporation's cash flow and required periodic attention from the director and administrative staff to avoid financial failure. But by the time the construction loan could be closed, it was superfluous. With just a few weeks to go to the opening of the Warwick SRO in September 1995, the developer had managed to finance construction through the time-consuming juggling of other commitments.

The various applications for funding the Hotel Warwick SRO required a great deal of staff time, with some programs demanding more attention than others. The coordination of the tax credit exchange with the three banks was the hardest element of the project, according to the developer. This wasn't due to the complexity of the state tax credit program, but to the time consuming and difficult process of convincing the participating banks that the combination of tax credits and tax deductions along with gifts from Centre Development to the new owner would be adequate to retire the bonds held by the banks. The developer rated the applications for the Low Income Housing Tax Credit and HOME Congregate Housing funds as the next most difficult step. The state's HOME process was complicated by the appraisal process, which took nearly nine months to complete. (Not surprisingly, appraisals which rely on "comparables" would not be completed readily for an SRO hotel.) The applications for the Section 8 commitment and the Federal Home Loan Bank loan were substantially less difficult, and the Community Housing Development Organization (CHDO) application required the least amount of staff energy, but did not involve any financial commitment to the project.

Conclusion

The nonprofit housing sector in the U.S. has been praised for mastering the complexity of tax credits, complicated financing, and subsidy layering. National and state intermediaries have been established to help make the low-income housing system work. But the system itself is a Rube Goldberg contraption that only an insider could defend and only a masochist could enjoy. The current system is overcomplex and expensive. Significant costs are hidden. Transaction costs are outrageously high. Delay and inefficiency are commonplace.

The system itself is a significant barrier to the development of the nonprofit housing sector. Only a few organizations can acquire the skills required (skills that should have little to do with producing low-income housing). The level of complexity makes it difficult to repeat the process in any given neighborhood. Successful NHOs are likely to find it necessary to look for workable deals across a larger geographic scale than a neighborhood and are thus pushed into communitywide, regional, or state roles. For others, one experience with the system is enough to last a lifetime.

The complexity and waste involved are likely to contribute to burnout and turnover in the personnel attracted to nonprofit development. These dedicated individuals deserve a system that can reward success and can promote the long-term development of the nonprofit housing sector. The current system requires substantial social capital along with financial capital. It taxes the trust and reciprocity that are essential elements of social capital. Transaction costs and network maintenance costs are high. As noted earlier, successful implementation and generation of social, political, or economic benefits to participants are necessary to the continuation of partnerships. When transaction costs are high, there is probably little tolerance of failure. High transaction costs and high costs of failure are likely to pressure NHOs into blind commitment to making a project work, at least on the front end. This may bode ill for the future stability of NHOs and their properties.

The first step toward reform is to simplify and combine federal housing programs. Federal tax credits are too costly and inefficient to be the system's primary building block. A single, direct subsidy program (grant or loan) could readily replace the multiple programs now required and could do so with less cost. With a workable program, subsidy layering rules could be established that would bar combinination of federal subsidies, although leveraging of state and local subsidies might be encouraged (if they are not simply disguised federal subsidies).

At the moment, the nonprofit housing sector is praised for making this system work. This might not last. Having a pivotal role in an inefficient and wasteful system can lead to being branded as inefficient and wasteful, rather than being praised as resourceful. There is a real danger that honest criticism will lead Congress to repeal rather than reform current housing production progams. That danger must be judged against the dangers of continuing to support the current system.

References

Hebert, Scott, et al. 1993. *Nonprofit housing, costs and funding, final report: Volume I—findings.* Washington, D.C.: U.S. Department of Housing and Urban Development, Office of Policy Development and Research.

Slepin, Matt. 1994. "Analysis of Project Financing," in Community Information Exchange, *Case studies on affordable multifamily rental housing.* Washington, D.C.: Community Information Exchange.

Stegman, Michael A. 1990. "The Excessive Costs of Creative Finance: Growing Inefficiencies in the Production of Low-Income Housing." *Housing Policy Debate* 2,2: 357–73.

Part III

Policy

Chapter 11

Restructuring the Nonprofit Sector: On Lessons Learned from American and European Experience

Robert B. Whittlesey

This chapter critiques current housing policy in the United States based on past successes and failures, the capital requirements of housing production, and the much deeper experience in Europe with nonprofit housing. The U.S. scheme of tax credits for low-income housing production are inadequate and inefficient compared with direct capital subsidies. Whittlesey promotes a broad and diverse nonprofit housing sector as the centerpiece of American housing policy. Production would be subsidized primarily through capital grants, which would reduce rents and over time capitalize the nonprofit sector. The composition of the sector would be diverse, but entry and eligibility for subsidies would be regulated. Vertical integration and representation of the sector nationally would be required. Local housing partnerships might be the initial building blocks of the institutional framework for a revitalized low-income housing system.

Introduction

The current system for providing government subsidized housing for low- and moderate-income households in the United States is inordinately complex and wasteful of both public and privates resources and energy. We are asking providers to do more with increasingly reduced or at least more unpredictable funding. Community development corporations (CDCs), for example, are being asked to undertake programs such as resident organizing, day-care, job training, youth, and security programs with little assurance that there will be adequate revenue to pay for such services. CDCs are frequently dependent on grants rather than program fees and earnings on assets to cover their overhead. At a time when we want to see initiatives come from the neighborhoods themselves, the system stands as a significant impediment to such local community efforts. It is likely to defeat the goal sought by many of building an effective community-based non-profit sector in cities and towns across the country (Giloth et al. 1992).

This chapter looks at the American and European experiences with non-profit housing and sets forth proposals for developing the American nonprofit housing sector as the first step in establishing a sound institutional infrastructure for providing low-income and moderate-income housing. Although in Canada and Europe the term *social housing* is used to describe housing that has received government funding, for Americans the term brings with it negative political connotations. Consequently, *community housing* seems to be an appropriate substitute for the United States. I suggest that it cover housing that has received direct or indirect financial assistance (i.e., tax credit subsidies, interest rate reductions, etc.) from government.

Community housing would not include owner-occupied housing except where there is public funding and there are restrictions on use or sale to maintain the housing as affordable for low-income and moderate-income families. Americans need to keep reminding themselves that home owners receive the majority of all federal housing subsidies in the form of income tax entitlements with no associated social obligations. We are, however, now doing a better job including such tax expenditures in national housing planning. We can look to the day when the allocation of housing resources will be more equitable between home ownership and rental housing, which is the only housing that the majority of poor families can afford.

This paper stems from the author's thirty years of experience in Boston with government subsidized housing including extensive work with community-based groups as well as five years as the court-appointed master in a tenants' class action case seeking reform of the Boston Housing Authority. In addition to work in Boston, this paper is also based upon the author's knowledge of nonprofit housing in some twenty cities acquired as part of a survey of local public/private housing partnership that led to the formation of the National Association of Housing Partnerships, Inc.

As the former executive director of the Metropolitan Boston Housing Partnership (then the Boston Housing Partnership, Inc.), I became interested in the United Kingdom's Housing Corporation and national housing institutions in other western European countries. The Housing Corporation, the primary funding source in the United Kingdom of nonprofit housing organizations (called housing associations), has awarded grants to NHOs that over the last five years have averaged in total more than 1.5 billion pounds per year (about 2.4 billion U.S. dollars). The Netherlands, Denmark, Sweden, Germany, and France, in addition to the United Kingdom, have well established social housing sectors and a variety of institutions and programs from which we can learn a good deal. The system in the Netherlands is particularly significant in its reliance on nonprofit housing organizations.

Background

In the sixty years since the depression, the United States has undertaken a number of major housing initiatives with mixed results. We built a home mortgage system centered around level payment, self-amortizing, fixed-rate, long-term mortgages insured by the government. Home ownership became a reality for a majority of Americans. The insured mortgage led to the development of a vast secondary market that recapitalizes loan-originating institutions and provides access to a variety of nonbank sources of capital through mortgage backed securities.

We built 1.4 million units of federally funded public housing owned by local housing authorities, which have demonstrated both the good things that can be accomplished through government as well as things to be avoided. We learned to our sorrow that large high-rise projects do not work for concentrations of poor families. Public housing continues to fight the political difficulties associated with large troubled projects, even though high-rise projects are only 17 percent of all public housing units (Council of Large Public Housing Authorities 1988). The good projects, and there are many, receive little attention and hundreds of thousands of families wait for the limited number of vacant apartments that the authorities can afford to renovate.

We carried out several large federal housing programs through private developers, a majority of which were for-profit organizations, the traditional producers of American housing. While more than a million units were built or rehabilitated, the majority of which were successful, it took large financial incentives from the federal government through mortgage loan insurance, interest support, rental assistance contracts, and tax concessions from the government to gain developers' participation. Legislative and regulatory requirements, problems associated with site acquisition and local approvals, and hassles with the public bureaucracies made the programs difficult and of interest only to companies that learned the systems and were willing to pursue the necessary approvals and suffer the time delays and risks that were involved. Costs were high and it was argued by many that much of the housing was not adequately targeted to those in greatest need. Program funding and tax incentives for these programs were largely withdrawn during the seventies and eighties. More recent budget reductions and program consolidations have further diminished interest on the part of private for-profit developers in government assisted housing development.

Federal housing programs of the sixties and seventies were financed with government insured mortgages and subsidy contracts with covenants that the owners operate the projects as subsidized housing for a period of years, frequently twenty years. These agreements are now expiring and the Congress has decided not to provide the new subsidies required to keep rents in these projects affordable. Much of this housing will be converted to market rate housing and lost from the subsidized housing inventory. It is not surprising that long-term affordability has emerged as a primary criterion for future housing subsidy programs.

Long-term affordability has a major impact on the liquidity of real estate assets and residual values, and is more readily achieved through nonprofit ownership. For-profit corporations frequently have need to refinance properties for tax purposes and other business reasons. The absence of residual value could result in indifference on the part of owners for ongoing maintenance. However, for NHOs, both their social purpose and their need for equity in sound real estate should be incentive enough for good management and maintenance.

One of the early and successful HUD programs that still continues is the nonprofit housing program for the elderly. Over 250,000 units have been created through NHOs across the country with very few failures. Under the program the federal government has provided capital funds for construction and long-term operating subsidies. This program has enhanced the capabilities and asset base of numerous nonprofit housing providers, has helped develop social services for the elderly, and provides a model for future programs.

Successful community development requires local initiative and leadership. The large federal urban renewal and public housing programs of the fifties and sixties encountered the difficulties inherent in programs managed from Washington. Community redevelopment is now seen as an activity to be planned and implemented by local agencies.

All of these factors—disfavor with public housing, difficulties with regulations, the impermanence of for-profit development, targeting to those in greatest need, and local community control—have led to an increased interest in nonprofit housing organizations, particularly where the organization is community-based or has broad institutional support. Current NHOs are for the most part more sophisticated than the church and neighborhood groups that sponsored housing under the HUD programs of the sixties and seventies. Further, there has been a significant increase in local government and private philanthropic funding of nonprofit housing and new private and quasi-public institutions have emerged that support NHOs.

While there has been significant growth in the number and capacity of nonprofit housing corporations over the last decades, we should take care not to overstate this progress. Most of these organizations are small and operate on very limited budgets, as shown by the surveys conducted by the National Congress of Community Economic Development (reviewed in chapter 8). Small property portfolios have meant that few community-based nonprofit organizations are in a position to profitably manage their own properties and receive the fees for doing so. In a recent study of CDC developments, the authors found that of twenty-eight developments, fifteen were spending more than they were taking in, and fourteen of twenty-three developments had no reserves at all (Bratt et al. 1994).

Small housing organizations are viable if appropriate technical assistance is available and satisfactory arrangements made for property management and other professional services. In the United Kingdom, for example, of the 2,700 registered housing associations, approximately eighty percent have less than 100 units (Cope 1990). Most small housing associations do not presume to be housing developers. For the United States, many NHOs will be devoted to a single project and neighborhood. As discussed later, these small NHOs need to be linked to other organizations through contracts, partnerships, and affiliations with umbrella agencies.

While CDCs are getting most of the attention today, we must not overlook the potential for major NHOs that operate on a regional and national basis. They develop and manage significant numbers of housing projects, particularly for the elderly and special-needs households. Currently, these include organizations such as Volunteers of America with its 8,000 units, or Common Bond Communities in the Minneapolis/Saint Paul area, which has developed and successfully manages 2,500 units, or BRIDGE, which has developed and manages 6,000 units in the five-county San Francisco Bay area. These larger organizations frequently act in partnership with neighborhood-based organizations and on projects in which a local board or residents' association participates in management.

In the United Kingdom, which is one-fifth the size of the United States, there are sixty nonprofit organizations that own more than 2,500 units and eighty-four more with over 1,000 units (Housing Corporation 1993). The 850 or so NHOs in the Netherlands own on average nearly 2,500 units (Boelhouwer and van der Heijden 1992). Nearly all of these larger NHOs manage their own properties and earn fees to support their organizations.

There are institutional reasons why community housing is best achieved through nonprofit organizations. Programs frequently center on resident ownership or direction and this is best implemented through nonprofit entities in which residents can have significant participation. Community housing is predominately targeted to low-income families and households. These households need services and services cost money. NHOs have access to philanthropic funding for which for-profit entities are not eligible. NHOs are more accountable to the public and less likely to abuse subsidy programs.

The impetus for establishing a restructured nonprofit sector stems both from the trends outlined above and the substantial funding reductions and program changes now proposed by the Clinton administration and the Congress. Simple reform of old programs is not an option. We need new concepts that are consistent with predictable change, restore political support, and set long-term goals. Building a significant nonprofit housing sector is a major undertaking that requires targeting resources and coordination among its participants.

Achieving distinct and important roles for the nonprofit sector should have only marginal impact on the for-profit housing industry, which will continue to

be the primary producer of housing in the country. Many NHOs will be owners only and will obtain real estate development and management services from
others. Additionally, for-profit firms will provide most of the professional services. They may be able to participate under modified conditions in some of the
same programs utilized by the nonprofit sector.

Guidelines for Developing the Nonprofit Housing Sector

I suggest the following guidelines for the nonprofit sector in the United
States based on lessons learned from our own past experience as well as the experience of other countries with advanced community housing sectors. These
guidelines are discussed under five headings: housing allowances, the nature of
community housing, financing community housing, asset management, and supporting institutions.

Housing Allowances

Poor families cannot afford the cost of standard housing (Joint Center for
Housing Studies 1990; Stone 1993). Shelter costs are the largest and the most
fixed expenditures in low-income family budgets and the most difficult to meet.
The inability of many families to obtain standard suitable housing has devastating impact on families, particularly children, creates personal insecurity and
domestic conflicts, fosters deteriorated housing, and leads to concentrations of
the poor in depressed neighborhoods. The most direct solution is some form of
income assistance to make up the difference between an appropriate percentage
of the family's income for housing and a reasonable market rent for a suitable
standard unit. It is not surprising that most advanced societies have such programs. The difference in America is that rental assistance is awarded to only a
third of those families that need them. Often rental assistance has been assigned
to developers under long-term contracts to help secure project financing. These
long-term commitments have significant impact on the government's budget
and both the Clinton administration and the Congress are proposing to shift
project-based subsidies to tenants and to limit contacts to one or two years.
Under the circumstances, rental assistance in the form of housing allowances
will be less important in housing finance. However, housing allowances,
because they are an important factor in building family responsibilities and self-
sufficiency, and have a direct impact on housing conditions and neighborhoods,
should remain separate from welfare payments and be restricted to meeting
shelter costs.

In any future community housing system for America, an expanded and
more generalized housing allowance program is seen as a basic component. In

the near term, housing allowances will be primarily issued to homeless and special-need households, to families where project-based subsidies are withdrawn, and to families displaced by demolition of public projects or by other government action. Unlike some European systems, housing allowances in the United States will continue to be restricted to housing that meets prescribed health and other standards. Housing allowances, subject to maximum limits and reasonableness of rents, should cover the costs of suitable housing for each family and allow housing choice as dictated by job location and other appropriate family needs. The allowances would be granted directly to eligible families except for elderly and special-needs housing where appropriate facilities need to be developed. They would be administered by local government directly or through an administering agency that is not a direct provider itself, preferably agencies serving metropolitan areas or regions.

The Nature of Community Housing

With a housing allowance program in place, community housing can be and should be a marketable good at rents that do not exceed market rents in the neighborhood and as often as possible are below such rent levels. Its physical design should be compatible with other adjacent housing. It should be economically and socially integrated to the degree possible. Mixed-income housing means that some portion of the project's subsidies are devoted to lowering housing costs for moderate-income families, thus using resources that might otherwise be targeted to the "most needy" (Nelson and Khadduri 1992). Experience has demonstrated, however, that concentrations of low-income families in separate and distinct projects is ill-advised, with the exception of small buildings in scattered locations. Mixed income occupancy would gain more public acceptance and support. Ownership by residents, exclusively or in conjunction with others, would be frequent and resident participation in management, either through ownership or resident associations or councils, would be the norm. Limited equity cooperatives, which function much like rental housing, would be a possibility. In each of these, resident interest in minimizing occupancy costs should be demonstrated through their acceptance of responsibilities to conserve utility use and to care for, repair, and repaint their apartments.

Community housing should also foster individual home ownership in a variety of forms from separate fee ownership to forms of shared ownership, possibly as occurs in the United Kingdom. Under shared ownership, the residents buy a portion of their unit with a nonprofit development corporation owning the balance. Residents finance their share through their own individual mortgage loan, pay rent on the portion that is not owned, and have a right to purchase the balance of the unit when they can afford it. Each development of more that thirty or forty units should have some individual ownership units, either at the onset or over time. This would test the marketability of the housing and create diversity among residents.

Owners and developers of community housing would have to meet established qualifications and be approved by an authorizing agency; development costs would be held within prescribed limits; and sound management that meets performance standards would be assured. Marketing of units would have to meet fair housing standards, and the tenant selection and leasing requirements of the primary program under which the development was funded. Redundant leasing and occupancy regulations of multiple agencies should be avoided. A proportion of available units would be allocated to local government for families that were on its waiting list.

Community housing would bear no unusual development or building costs that are not ordinary to the industry as a whole. Where government requirements introduce additional above-market costs such as specific wage levels or job training, supplementary grants or funding should be available.

The absence of long-term operating subsidies should allow flexible project operations and minimize the need for regulations. There should be fair housing requirements and minimum goals for low-income occupancy. Profits on the sale of residuals would be controlled; instead, the objective would be for NHOs to accumulate financial equity.

Financing Community Housing

With the withdrawal of federal support for housing production in the eighties, a larger percentage of project costs has been funded from state and local government sources, equity raised through syndication, and grants from foundations and corporations. Financing equity and debt from multiple sources has become the norm. A typical project will have seven or more funding sources— two or three lenders, several kinds of local government grants or junior loans, five or ten tax credit investors, money from a state or local trust fund, and foundation grants—with each party trying to establish where it is in the pecking order if the project should fail (Hebert et al. 1993; also see chapters 10 and 11).

There is little evidence that much is gained by having multiple lenders and plenty of evidence that it confuses underwriting, clouds responsibilities, and introduces reporting and legal requirements that add to the cost of the housing. Aggregating funds from half a dozen sources takes time, introduces risk, and is beyond the capabilities of many sponsors. A developer starts with one or two commitments, then chases after several others, all of which depend on some action by either a legislature, an allocating agency, an administrator, or a committee of private or corporate investors. All have their own time cycle. Some will delay action pending a decision by others. Frequently, when a developer gets it all together, the first commitments have run out or the terms changed. All this costs money and everybody pays.

In 1968 South End Community Development developed a twenty-four-unit rehabilitation project, received a 102 percent construction loan, and permanent mortgage take-out for the project, and the legal costs—including both the initial and final loan closing—were $1,400. All the documents with the exception of the attorney's comprehensive opinion and the title opinions were prepared by SECD's administrative staff using standard FHA forms. The Urban Edge Corporation in Boston recently spent about eighty times as much for legal fees on a fifty-unit project they have just completed.

The Local Initiatives Support Corporation's demonstration rehabilitation program in New York City substantiated the advantages of a program with simplified funding. Under the demonstration, projects were financed through a combination of deferred mortgage loans from the city and investor contribution based on low-income housing tax credits.

The growth of social housing in Canada, the Netherlands, Denmark, and France demonstrates the contribution that readily available financing can make. In the United Kingdom, housing associations can look at a chart and pick out the proportion of development costs that the Housing Corporation will provide as a grant (currently about 55 percent of total development costs). Bank financing makes up the balance. In the Netherlands, local government has guaranteed project loans in the past under a relatively simple contract. More recently, loans are guaranteed by a fund established by the NHOs themselves. Ready mortgage financing allows development to occur in an orderly and cost effective way, and permits the developer to concentrate on the job of designing, building, and managing the housing.

Funding applications for housing grants in the United Kingdom are relatively straightforward. Nonprofits are allowed 2.5 percent to 4 percent of development costs for administrative overhead and this seems to cover their costs. In the project described earlier, Urban Edge spent three times as much for administrative overhead under the funding system operating in the United States.

Project financing can be and must be simplified. The goal would be to limit financing to three sources: (1) a single first mortgage loan from a lender; (2) capital subsidies from government through a single agency (which would coordinate funding from other public sources); and, (3) owners' equity primarily for working capital and reserves.

MORTGAGE LOAN FINANCING. Nonprofit housing finance should be based upon a single first mortgage, as done under earlier HUD programs. In the future, the feasibility of projects will depend on grants or secondary loans from local government using federal block grants or special local funds and investor contributions based upon federal and state tax benefits. Although loan to value ratios will be low, significant risks will be associated with completion of construction, projections of rental income and operating expenses, and debt service coverage. We can presume that local governments will press developers to seek maximum loans from lenders in order to conserve their grant funds. In the longer term, NHOs will have significant equity in real estate to secure lines of credit to partially finance new projects and repair their existing stock.

Mortgage loan financing needs to be readily available from banks and other financial institutions skilled in community lending. Public grants or loans to projects must not create barriers to conventional mortgage financing. Without long-term, project-based subsidies from HUD, NHOs may have to turn to consortium lenders such as Massachusetts Housing Investment Corporation in Boston, Community Preservation Corporation in New York, or Community Investment Corporation in Chicago, the state housing finance agencies (SHFAs), or special lenders. In time, experience will allow the general lending community to participate.

The state finance agencies might play a particularly significant role. FHA coinsurance with SHFAs should be continued. This would produce lower interest rates for SHFA financing and allow the SHFAs to underwrite projects and monitor ongoing management.

For the banks to fully participate, there must be a secondary market and this will require reordering much of the "creative financing" now going on. Subordinate debt documents that cities originate need to be standardized. Model documents can be designed and at least offered to local jurisdictions. Leaders in this effort would logically be the Federal National Mortgage Association and the Federal Home Loan Mortgage Corporation as well as HUD and the state housing finance agencies.

The standard financing of HUD subsidized housing has been with nonrecourse mortgage financing. This means that the owner is only putting up the mortgaged property as security and is not personally responsible for a default on the mortgage loan. Under HUD regulatory agreements, projects were operated as separate financial entities. Nonrecourse financing and separate operating entities facilitated both the syndication of property ownership through limited partnerships as well as the sale of mortgages on the secondary market. With changes in the way community housing is financed, community developers may have to offer guarantees or letters of credit to secure project financing. In some cases these may have to be supported by the local government. A variety of guarantees may also evolve through local and national intermediaries and mortgage insurance companies.

In the Netherlands there are now two funds that support their nonprofit housing associations. The first is the Social Housing Guarantee Fund that guarantees capital market loans for new developments, improvements, and maintenance programs. It is a private fund, although it did receive 60 million guilders (about $25 million) as initial capital from the government. It operates now on loan discounts and a loan back to the fund of 1.25 percent of each guaranteed amount. The second is the Central Fund that supports housing associations that cannot meet the financial requirements of the Guarantee Fund and provides financial assistance to associations and projects that are in financial difficulties. The Central Fund, for example, is financing in partnership with the government the renewal of the famous 12,000-unit Bijlmermeer development in Amsterdam. Now with the funds established, housing associations in the Netherlands have multiple sources for project financing—borrowing on their own net worth, using loans provided by local government, borrowing with loans guaranteed by local government, and borrowing with loans guaranteed by the Guarantee Fund. The national government seeks to have most loans guaranteed by the fund.

PUBLIC SUBSIDIES. New community housing projects depend on public subsidies to make projects affordable. With the elimination of most long-term rental subsidies, public subsidies will be increasingly through capital grants from government. In the last decade, local government and states have increased their involvement in community housing. With federal funding of community housing through block grants, the focus on state and local government will increase dramatically. They will have the primary responsibility of seeing that community housing projects are feasible, both during construction and over the long term.

Subsidy funds should be provided in the simplest way possible, namely as direct grants, or in limited situations as deferred interest and principle subordinate loans repayable only on discontinued use of the project for community housing. Currently, the greater part of public subsidies for housing production are the tax credits provided to private investors. Investor contributions based upon low-income housing tax credits should be thought of as a pass-through of public funds even though investors assume risks and administrative burdens. Tax credits have been a major source of funding of low-income housing although alone these credits rarely permit rents that are affordable by lower income families (those below 50 percent of the median income). Tax credits have proven to be valuable in attracting corporate participation in community housing. These private investments are important in paying for items that the public agencies do not fund, such as operating reserves, more reasonable developer's fees, and consulting and resident services. Tax credits also reward the financial intermediaries that manage the syndication process and provide investor services. Tax expenditures such as low-income housing credits have recently proven to be politically more assured than annual appropriations for housing. But tax credit investments come at a very high cost to the government, have significant operating complexities, and high costs to the producers of low-income housing. Additionally, tax credits are a significant barrier to housing development by small organizations and a serious administrative problem for local government.

In the future capital grants and investor contributions to projects will have to be in amounts that reduce mortgage financing, so that debt service along with operating expenses can be covered by rental income at local market rents. Occupancy by families with housing allowances could occur, as well as occupancy by families without such assistance. Because public funds are limited, resources may have to be concentrated on fewer and smaller projects, and projects in which costs approach those supported by the local market rents.

The federal government has learned that up-front capital grants save money and are more efficient than long-term financing arrangements under which the federal government pays interest and retires debt over a period of years on project bonds. Financing of both the public housing program and the nonprofit elderly housing program were changed to grants raised through general federal borrowing.

Public grants, subordinate loans, and allocations of tax credits should be coordinated. All of these subsidies should be obtained through a single application to the appropriate state or local funding agency. The lead agency should coordinate funding from other public sources. One set of regulations and procedures should govern the transaction. One of the practices that needs to be stopped is partial funding from multiple organizations or agencies to allow each to claim that it "funded the project."

Unusual funding is required in certain areas where operating expenses for standard housing, even excluding debt service, still exceed rental income. This occurs in depressed neighborhoods where building and operating costs are high in relation to rents. These situations require subsidies for operations, possibly from investor contributions, augmented housing allowance payments, cross-subsidies from other properties or philanthropic grants, as well as large capital subsidies to cover development costs. While these subsidies may appear to be excessive, they are needed in areas where many low-income families reside.

The practice of using private philanthropic grants to shore up inadequate government financing should be discouraged. These funds should be reserved for items that the public agencies cannot fund, such as special community facilities and resident organizing and services.

OWNER'S EQUITY. Housing grants should be seen as a strategy not only to subsidize rents for residents and save money for the government, but also to provide net worth to nonprofit owners to make them financially stable and independent. In the United Kingdom, it was the straightforward Housing Assistance Grants from the Housing Corporation that allowed the Paddington Churches Housing Association to go from owning a few hundred units at the end of the sixties to owning more than 8,000 units at the end of the eighties. It allowed the Sanctuary Spiral Housing Group to buy its first units in 1965 and have 13,000 units by the end of the eighties. Much of this housing was in two-story and three-story terrace houses often developed in small clusters. The housing grants established the housing associations' equity that now allows them to finance part of the development cost of new development and the renovation of their existing properties.

NHOs must operate as businesses, have operating surpluses, and accumulate real estate property assets. Nonprofit developers should have the right to retain savings achieved within cost limits. In the United Kingdom, once a development budget is approved, savings in such items as construction interest go to the developer. NHOs must also be able to raise rents to cover maintenance and other operating expenses, and set aside adequate replacement reserves.

Much of the present nonprofit family housing in the United States is burdened with deferred maintenance and requirements to pay off subordinate debt and investors. Little equity will materialize for these owners. This is an unfortunate result of past programs. The limited financial resources of most nonprofit developers means that predevelopment advances will still be necessary, as well as bridge loans in connection with syndication. Currently, local and national intermediaries are addressing this need but this response is far from universal. As NHOs build their assets, they will be increasingly in a position to have their own lines of credit to cover preclosing development expenses and eventually some proportion of development costs.

Well established organizations such as those created through our elderly program or potentially established through public investment in NHO projects will make a percentage of our housing permanently affordable. This is a significant social goal that will have beneficial impacts on our social welfare system and might indirectly contribute to lower market rents.

Cost Limits

Community housing developers are confronted by difficult trade-offs between creating good housing and staying within prescribed cost limits. Such limits are understandable in publicly supported programs but must be realistic and not micromanaged by remote regulators. Enforcing inappropriate cost constraints can result in inappropriate designs, inadequate operating budgets and reserves, and failed projects. Developers should have flexibility to adjust budgets within limits, taking into consideration expenditures made to reduce lifetime costs, energy use, and other operating expenses.

There are factors present in projects built in depressed areas that must be recognized by funders. Costs associated with security, vandalism, employment of less skilled workers from the neighborhood, use of less experienced subcontractors, reuse of urban sites, and old utility services are frequently high and difficult to explain. Each project has its own irregularities and problems. The lack of experience of many community-based developers means that costs will have to cover learning on the job, consulting fees (to the degree these are not funded by HUD or local government), little or no equity, and other exceptional conditions. Cost limits will be controversial until a more orderly production system and more reliable cost information are available. In the interim, it is important that cost limits not be applied arbitrarily and there is sufficient flexibility to accommodate projects in high cost areas.

Asset Management

If current initiatives prevail, community housing will be less burdened by public regulations and will be more market-oriented. NHOs that acquire multiple properties will find not only that they must have effective property management of individual developments, but sound management of entire portfolios. They will be confronted with decisions about investing to protect their equity, cross-subsidizing to maintain project incomes, refinancing projects, selling unfeasible projects, and managing reserves. Many NHOs will require training and technical assistance.

A subset of asset management is project management itself, either through the NHO's own staff or contracted out to others. If there is one lesson that we should take to heart it is that management must not be treated as an afterthought to development. Even for NHOs contracting out property management, supervising the contract manager can be a challenge.

The size of portfolio required for effective property management is debatable. Under the earlier HUD programs, projects of 200 units were considered feasible as a separate operating unit. While this is possible in selected situations, the experience of successful NHOs such as Community Builders in Boston with 3,500 units under management and the Common Bond Corporation in Saint Paul with 2,500 units, or successful for-profits firms like Maloney Properties in Boston with 4,000 units suggests that a portfolio of at least 2,000 units or more, including elderly and low-density family housing outside the inner city, is well advised.

An issue facing owners and managers in depressed urban areas is the need for special security and other services that are hard to include in standard budgets. A lesson learned in Boston and elsewhere is that residents need to be involved in management and local community concerns. The Metropolitan Boston Housing Partnership has funded a Resident Resource Initiatives program that provides training to residents and engages them in resident associations and community issues. It has been a demonstrated success.

NHOs frequently find that they cannot hire good property managers, particularly for inner-city properties. Six of the ten CDCs in the Metropolitan Boston Housing Partnership's (MBHP) initial program employed outside management firms. Five have been replaced, some twice. While there are some very good property management firms, there clearly is a need for more. Individual firms hesitate taking on too many projects in difficult urban areas. Experienced management companies will also avoid owners who do not make decisions in an orderly way, do not set clear goals and performance standards, or are likely to interfere inappropriately in the management company's work.

In some European countries, management costs are separated into components such as administration, maintenance, services, and utilities. This allows billing for services and analysis of costs and performance. Residents are generally responsible for utility costs including heat and are charged for most services. In the United Kingdom, such things as special staffing in elderly housing and ground maintenance in family housing are treated as services for which extra charges are made. In the Netherlands where NHOs are the major providers of rental housing, they invariably manage their own properties. In fact, a number of for-profit developers build housing which they then turn over to NHOs to manage. Consequently, management fees are a substantial part of the NHOs' revenues in the Netherlands.

Institutions

There are three groups of private institutions that have special roles to play in any future nonprofit housing sector: NHOs; organizations providing technical and professional services; local and national nonprofit housing intermediaries.

NONPROFIT HOUSING ORGANIZATIONS. NHOs vary in purpose, size, and organizational structure. Some will be community-based (ranging from a single neighborhood to a metropolitan region), others will not. Some will be major businesses and others will be resident owners of a single project. Frequently, the large NHOs will provide services to other NHOs. It is clear from the experiences in the United Kingdom, the Netherlands, and Scandinavia, the nonprofit housing sector can be organized to accommodate both small and large organizations.

Many of the current NHOs in the United States will experience difficulties in the foreseeable future as federal funding is reduced and programs are modified and deregulated. Small NHOs will be hard pressed to cover overhead. Those associated with financially sound developments and capable leadership will do better. Several limited equity cooperatives in Boston are demonstrating that modest costs of maintaining the ownership corporation can be covered within the management budget of a project. These projects also demonstrate the advantage of operating housing where there is only one mortgage loan and the budget is limited to rents in and operating expenses out. Residents find this a lot easier to understand than complex financing involving investors.

In Bratt's 1992 study of CDCs, the largest percentage of administrative income received by CDCs is from local government, but there is keen competition for these funds. Many state programs that support CDCs are being cut back. Foundations and corporations were the second largest source of administrative funds, but private funders tend to put time limits on funding of operations in connection with public programs such as community housing.

The federal government began funding community development corporations in the mid-sixties under the Special Impact Program of the 1964 Economic Opportunity Act. In the late sixties, CDCs and community action agencies received funding through the Office of Economic Opportunity. By 1968 the Nonprofit Housing Center was created in Washington with Ford Foundation funds to provide technical assistance to NHOs. Annual production under the federal subsidized housing programs reached 200,000 units in 1969 and over 400,000 in 1970 and 1971. Approximately 40 percent of the projects were sponsored (not necessarily owned) by NHOs and cooperatives. Subsequent federal government funding of CDCs occurred in the seventies through the Community Services Administration and the HUD Office of Neighborhood Development. However, during the seventies, the HUD housing programs were curtailed. There were substantial failures among the projects with nonprofit sponsors under the HUD programs; the Nonprofit Center was closed; and NHOs turned to advocacy rather than housing production. Even though the HUD housing programs were further reduced in the eighties, the number of NHOs actually increased during this time (Bratt 1992:36).

Much is now expected of NHOs even though few have demonstrated that they can survive on income generated from their housing and related activities. Most depend upon grants to cover a significant percentage of their core operating expenses. This will not improve as there is little likelihood of substantially increased funding of housing programs in the next few years. Federal legislation has now authorized local government to use block grant (HOME) funds for funding core operating expenses of CHDOs. It remains to be seen how effective such top-down assistance will be in building the capacity of local NHOs in the absence of a more rational environment in which to build and manage housing. Nonprofits that succeeded well under the earlier HUD programs were those that had substantial institutions behind them, developed elderly housing or middle-income housing, or those that were able to implement a series of projects and thereby attain a critical size for self-sufficiency. In a majority of the latter cases, implementing a series of projects was made possible through an urban renewal designation, a program that no longer exists.

Maintaining organizational stability and an experienced staff requires a consistent level of activities. Few cities in the United States allocate funds so that housing development organizations have a steady level of work. The city of Amsterdam negotiates annual allocations of funds with twenty NHOs as a group to ensure that all have work in process. As mentioned earlier, the United Kingdom had the steady flow of Housing Corporation funding to housing associations from 1974 on that made possible the substantial growth of its nonprofit housing sector. Housing associations now own about twenty-seven percent of all private rental housing in the United Kingdom (Boelhouwer and van der Heijden 1992:175). The Housing Corporation now has a program under which it allocates production funds for a three-year period on the agreement that the housing association will produce a specified number of units that meet the corporation's design and cost standards, and will guarantee to pay for cost overruns.

Some NHOs in the United States have their own construction operations, which is a potential source of income. However, it is difficult maintaining a steady level of work when funding is so unpredictable. CDCs are now undertaking a variety of social service programs and some of these will provide net revenues to these organizations. But these specialized nonhousing programs generally require skills and experience that most NHOs do not possess. There are local planning roles that CDCs can undertake, but these depend on governmental funding, which is in short supply.

Community-based organizations are frequently limited by charter and community interests to a service area. Development of the organization may require modification of this focus. Community Builders in Boston was once a community-based CDC. In response to requests for technical assistance, it expanded its service area from a neighborhood to a metropolitan area, and subsequently to its current service area of New England, New Jersey, Pennsylvania, and Delaware. It has done this to allow it to utilize its skills and experience in new situations consistent with its mission of assisting community-based housing organizations. This has been the pattern of many of the housing associations in the United Kingdom.

TECHNICAL AND PROFESSIONAL ASSISTANCE ORGANIZATIONS. The second group of players in the nonprofit sector are firms that provide technical and professional assistance. Federal legislation has recognized the need for such technical assistance and there is a growing number of such organizations in the United States. Since 1992, HUD has funded organizations to provided technical assistance to Community Housing Development Organizations (CHDOs) on an as-requested basis.

Experienced NHOs can provide assistance to others. In the United Kingdom, the Netherlands, and Denmark, large NHOs provide development and management services to small organizations. The growth of the nonprofit sector in the United Kingdom to 700,000 units of rental housing could not have been achieved without larger NHOs providing services and technical assistance to the smaller ones. In Denmark, KAB Building and Management Company, which is owned by the nonprofit organizations it serves, has assisted other NHOs in developing over 50,000 units of housing and now manages over 33,000 units, none of which it owns. In the United States, Community Builders has assisted other organizations in developing over 6,500 units of housing.

Providing competent consulting in all parts of the country is difficult in the United States because programs and procedures are different in each state and locality. The need for competent consulting will be further increased when federal funds are administered through local government. Successful community development requires support from and involves extensive negotiations with local government and frequently out-of-town consultants do not have the necessary familiarity with local officials and programs. Partnerships with non-profit and for-profit firms and contracted professional services will be the answer for most NHOs.

INTERMEDIARIES AND PARTNERSHIPS. The third group of institutions are local and national intermediaries or public-private partnerships. A key element in these new organizations is leadership from business corporations and major institutions. Business willingness to become involved varies in different areas but there are successful models where such participation has been crucial in programs dealing with job training, education, and affordable housing. There is a growing realization on the part of business that a lack of affordable housing and the problems of depressed neighborhoods can be a drain on the local economy, limit the available labor force, and increase the cost of local social services paid by the general taxpayer.

The primary role for local public-private partnerships is as a catalyst for programs with specific goals and as an intermediary between community developers and the variety of other organizations on which they must rely. Local public-private housing partnerships are driven by local goals and reflect the local political environment. Affordable housing programs cannot succeed without capable administration by local government, and the help and participation of the private sector. There are a number of ways in which the private sector can assist local governments in carrying out their community housing responsibilities. The private sector can initiate programs with specific goals that respond to local needs; build political coalitions for program approval and implementation; provide private investment; intervene when programs or projects are in difficulty; and give local community development institutional continuity and recognition.

Many local public-private partnerships are now connected through the Neighborhood Reinvestment Corporation, with 140 affiliate Neighborhood Housing Services organizations across the country, and the National Association of Housing Partnerships, Inc. These and similar organizations help foster the best programs and practices. There are also major national intermediaries, including the Local Initiatives Support Corporation, the Enterprise Foundation, and others, that influence national policy and bring resources and other assistance to local organizations. The eventual roles for these intermediaries is still unclear, but they will be important in the growth and support of any significant national nonprofit sector.

Although public-private partnerships might add to the complexity of the housing development system, there is little direct evidence of this. Many NHOs are determined to make the system more efficient and rational. What is evident from the more established systems in Europe is that either government itself or some government-recognized agency needs to serve as a focal point of a national nonprofit housing system. The Housing Corporation in the United Kingdom and the Nationale Woningraad in the Netherlands are examples. Local public-private partnerships affiliated through national organizations may be the key to the further development of nonprofit community housing in the United States.

The Future

Housing programs will be in transition for the balance of the nineties and funding will be both reduced and its administration changed. There are numerous concerns about how the changes are affecting vulnerable populations and what can be done to help them. Housing allowances will be a frequent expedient in meeting low-income housing needs. This may further establish housing allowances as the primary housing protection for the poor.

There are serious questions as to how changes can be brought about, particularly if most practitioners are frantically trying to save their organizations as funds are cut and programs eliminated. Structural changes will become mandatory as federal budget reductions take effect. Local government will have to accept increased responsibility for both program implementation and effective use of funds. Lenders will need to be assured that public commitments are genuine. Nonprofits will have to say no to projects that lack adequate funding or are subject to unknown conditions. More housing activity will have to be predicated on what is possible within the market. New business practices and decision-making will be necessary for organizations to survive. Housing authorities will have to appraise their properties and make judgments about how to use their net worth. They will have to set rents and provide services that are competitive in the market, an entirely new experience.

In all of this, important opportunities exist for NHOs. These include the transfer of a significant number of existing subsidized private and public housing projects to nonprofit ownership. As mentioned earlier, many privately owned, subsidized housing developments have requirements for use as low and moderate income housing that will expire. As these projects are deregulated and the funding modified, many owners will be prepared to sell. Acquisition costs may be very modest in low-rent areas and, subject to the condition of the property, may be feasible for purchase by a nonprofit organization. Other projects will be owned or taken over by the government and made available at a nominal price. Many privately and publicly owned developments could be transferred at a low sales price and without debt. Nonprofit ownership would be appropriate in view of the required public subsidies and negotiated sale prices. The federal government might provide funds from the FHA insurance fund for repairs to make apartments marketable or local government might provide funds from its block grants. Large sums are now authorized for public housing modernization and might be used in these transactions, particularly where the new owners are resident organizations.

An alternative for public housing would be to use already appropriated modernization funds as a guarantee fund for new mortgage loans. In both subsidized and public housing, tax credits might be utilized in projects where investors could be assured that apartments could be feasibly operated at the projected market rents. These low cost sales would be equivalent to the capital write-down discussed earlier to allow rents at local market levels.

In the case of public housing, large authorities could be divided and transferred to several nonprofit entities and smaller authorities merged to achieve economies of scale. Residents should be favored as the new owners, with or without partners. In some cases, the complexity of the transaction and repair program would require the resources and skills of a major organization. A model for such a program is the two-thousand unit Demonstration Disposition Program in Boston being implemented by the Massachusetts Housing Finance Agency.

The above transfers would create several hundred major NHOs and make a significant impact on the nonprofit sector. There are examples of public housing transfers in both the United Kingdom and the Netherlands. All of the government owned social housing in the Netherlands has now been successfully transferred to nonprofit ownership. In the United Kingdom, where council housing dominates the rental housing stock, the program to convert council housing to private ownership continues.

Building a restructured nonprofit housing sector is a timely strategy to help save existing housing and to build for the future. It must start with initiatives that allow for predictable change, accommodate reduced funding, and conform to sound long-term goals based upon experience here and abroad. Changes are inevitable; but if not managed skillfully, these changes will further exacerbate the affordable housing shortage that still plagues the United States.

References

Boelhouwer, Peter, and Harry van der Heijden. 1992. *Housing systems in Europe: Part 1.* Delft: Delft University Press.

Bratt, Rachel G., et al. 1994. *Confronting the management challenge: Affordable housing in the nonprofit sector.* New York: New School of Social Research, Community Development Research Center.

Cope, Helen. 1990. *Housing associations: Policy and practice.* London: MacMillan Education Ltd. 28.

Council of Large Public Housing Authorities. 1988 (Revised). *Public housing today.* Washington, D.C.

Giloth, Robert, Charles Orlebeke, James Tickell, and Patricia Wright. 1992. *Choices ahead: CDCs and real estate production in Chicago.* Nathalie P. Voorhees Center for Neighborhood and Community Improvement.

Hebert, Scott, et al. 1993. *Nonprofit housing, costs and funding, final report: Volume I—findings.* Washington, D.C.: U.S. Department of Housing and Urban Development, Office of Policy Development and Research.

The Housing Corporation. 1993. List of the largest 200 housing associations by size of stock.

Joint Center for Housing Studies. 1990. *The state of the nation's housing: 1990.* Cambridge, Mass.: Joint Center for Housing Studies, Harvard University.

Nelson, Kathryn P., and Jill Khadduri. 1992. "To whom should limited housing resources be directed?" *Housing Policy Debate* 3(1).

Stone, Michael. 1993. *Shelter poverty: new ideas on housing affordability.* Philadelphia: Temple University Press.

Vidal, Avis C. 1992. *Rebuilding communities: A national study of urban community development corporations.* New York: New School for Social Research, Community Development Research Center.

Chapter 12

Responding to the Crisis
in Nonprofit Housing

C. Theodore Koebel

This concluding chapter argues that there is a crisis in nonprofit housing in the United States that is independent of current funding levels. A more fundamental crisis is rooted in a misunderstanding of the role of nonprofit housing. The partnership between government and the nonprofit sector should be based on the sector's ability to produce superior quality services, not on its ability to subsidize those services through contributions of time and money. Government funding is not the only problem facing the sector. The sector faces serious challenges through commercialization, dominance by executive directors, loss of mission, loss of voluntarism, and co-optation. Responses to this crisis must be rooted in greater understanding and promotion of mission, boards of directors, trust, voluntarism, diversity, primacy, and partnership.

The Crisis in Nonprofit Housing

There is an emergent crisis in nonprofit housing distinct from the current crisis in housing policy. Reduced funding and the inordinate complexity of housing programs are important elements of this crisis, but in many ways these problems are secondary or symptomatic of more fundamental problems unrelated to funding levels. The more fundamental problems reflect unresolved misunderstandings of the nonprofit sector as a whole and of nonprofit housing in particular, both in the perspective of government policy-makers and the perspective of many nonprofit housing advocates.

Nonprofit housing is part of the broader nonprofit sector, but has remained largely outside the current debate on the sector's role and relevance, where attention has focused on health, education, and social services. But housing is unlikely to be exempt from the challenges facing the broader sector, now under

255

attack on a number of fronts. To a great degree, the entire nonprofit sector faces a crisis of legitimacy that is reflected in the breakdown of its partnership with government, and in the sector's increased commercialization (Hodgkinson et al. 1989).

The breakdown in the government-nonprofit partnership is twofold: first, it involves a fundamental misunderstanding of the nonprofit sector on the part of policy-makers; second, various strategies to introduce market discipline on the nonprofit sector have resulted in a commercialization of the sector that undermines its distinctiveness and threatens its future. This crisis of legitimacy increases the potential for nonprofit failure, which would seriously erode the potential for building a sounder, more effective, partnership between the sector and government. At the same time, developing a vigorous nonprofit sector may well be the necessary ingredient for a sustained, responsive, and responsible American housing policy.

In the ongoing battles over the federal budget deficit, the nonprofit sector has been wrongly perceived as a source of revenue rather than as a source of services for which government, largely, has to pay. While the sector's ability to leverage both charitable donations and volunteers is important, these are not substitutes for government funding of social services provided for the public good. The nonprofit sector does not have the capital necessary to pay for large portions of the nation's social service requirements, nor should it be expected to transfer public funding obligations from universal taxes to voluntary contributions. A social welfare system that depends on voluntary contributions will inevitably fail, due to the same free rider problem that prevents market provision of public goods.

Partnership between government and the nonprofit sector should be based on the sector's ability to produce superior quality services, not on its ability to subsidize those services through contributions of time and money. This is not to say that the latter are unimportant. Philanthropic and voluntary support provide important evidence that communities value and support the goals and activities of specific organizations. They might also be important avenues of expressing community commitment and leadership. But they are not substitutes for tax-supported services.

Misunderstanding the role of competition in the nonprofit sector is as damaging as misunderstanding the role of the nonprofit sector as an alternative public revenue source. Inefficiency in the nonprofit sector is a legitimate concern and pricing should always be a matter of some tension between government and the sector. But competition between for-profit and nonprofit firms erodes the distinctive features of the latter and ultimately the justification for special public treatment and respect. Under open competition, nonprofit firms are forced to commercialize, adopting the same bottom-line criterion as for-profit firms. Forced to provide the same output and cost relationship as a for-profit vender, NHOs risk losing their orientation to serving the most needy. For example, under the Low Income Housing Tax Credit program, one would expect the same performance from nonprofit and for-profit firms, except for the preferential treatment of NHOs under part of the program.

Closely associated with open competition is the shift to consumer subsidies rather than producer subsidies. This shift has been very pronounced in housing, where housing certificates and vouchers have gained favor at the expense of site-based, producer subsidies. The shift to consumer subsidies is also a major factor in the continued growth of the nonprofit sector despite government retrench-ment (Salamon 1993). Although the 1980s witnessed significant reductions in social services spending (except for health and pensions), nonprofit sector rev-enues increased significantly. Salamon (24) attributed this growth to "service fees and other essentially commercial income, including sales of products."

At the same time, for-profit participation in social services also increased, furthering the "marketization" of the American social welfare system "as non-profit organizations have been sucked increasingly into market-type relations and for-profit firms have steadily expanded their market niche" (36). Not only has this contributed to the commercialization of the nonprofit sector, it could have implications for the quality and availability of social services to the poor. Smith and Lipsky (1993) have identified problems associated with the contract-ing regime dominating much of the nonprofit sector, several of which are par-ticularly germane to nonprofit housing: commercialization; dominance by executive directors; changes in scale; loss of voluntarism; dominance of market norms; and co-optation.

Commercialization

Commercialization represents the shift in nonprofit organizations from small, informal, voluntary organizations to professionally administered corpora-tions emphasizing corporate norms. NHOs responding to the contracting regime adapt readily to corporate norms. After all, property development is a business and success requires business skills and practices. These aspects of corpo-ratization are potentially beneficial. Property development projects can provide short-term rewards to sponsors and tangible evidence of success, which in turn contribute to the development of future funding relationships and partnerships. Increased professionalism and attendance to business practices are essential ele-ments of successful development. NHOs should be run like businesses, but the problem arises when this is "at the expense of their responsiveness to clients and their capacity to foster unique community values" (Smith and Lipsky 1993:25).

For example, organizations created to promote community development in a particular neighborhood often respond to government contracting oppor-tunities by shifting attention from their most pressing needs (e.g., community organizing, job training, and education) to those needs for which contracts are available (e.g., housing). Once established as a successful housing developer, the organization is faced with a dilemma. In order to continue to succeed as a housing developer, it has to pursue opportunities outside its initial territory of focus, since government is unlikely to provide sufficient support for continued development in a single neighborhood. The organization may become very successful, but not at its original intent.

Dominance by Executive Directors

Increased demand for professional expertise and the complexities of government contracting and of property development contribute to a shift in decision-making authority away from voluntary boards of directors to executive directors. Board members find it increasingly difficult to understand the requirements of successful development and to challenge the perspective of the executive director. If the latter is successful in the government contracting game, the board is likely to become even more deferential. Over time, the composition of the board might be adjusted to provide the professional guidance that the director needs in accounting, finance, personnel, or other corporate functions. As board composition changes, few board members know the original mission of the organization. Constituent representation on the board from neighborhood residents or from clients is increasingly difficult to maintain. The vision and mission of the organization become the domain of the executive director and the rest of the professional staff, who understandably are interested in pursuing the funding opportunities that are most likely to maintain their jobs. Thus corporate success can be accompanied by mission drift.

Changes in Scale

Many NHOs originate in response to the problems of a specific low-income community or neighborhood. They start as voluntary, grassroots efforts. Although participation might be high and board members relatively numerous, the size of the organization as measured by staff and budget is small. However, successful government contracting and successful property development require staff with diverse skills. Extremely small organizations will find it difficult to demonstrate the proposal development, contracting, and implementation expertise expected by government agencies. Income under the contracting regime is primarily generated by additional development projects, which brings the aforementioned press to broaden the organization's geographic scope. Broader scope requires greater organization.

Once NHOs have achieved success in multifamily property development, they must address property management. Since managing property can be a good source of fee income for NHOs, there is inherent pressure to enter the property management business. With continued success in multifamily development, they assemble a portfolio of properties and possibly a property management division.

Increased scale is not inherently a problem, but it does significantly change the organization. Again, this is a question of mission and purpose. If the original goal was to be an advocate for a particular neighborhood or to provide leadership in its redevelopment, success under the contracting regime is likely to push the organization away from that goal.

Loss of Voluntarism

Increased professionalization, scale, and attendance to corporate norms present many NHOs with a dilemma. Although initiated with a high level of voluntary effort, many NHOs achieving success in government contracting find that volunteers are less of a corporate benefit and may even be a liability. Organizing and managing volunteers requires administrative support, which might be more costly than the savings achieved through voluntary labor. The use of volunteers for tasks requiring professional expertise or building trade skills could expose the NHO to potential embarrassment if the necessary expertise is not demonstrated and to legal liabilities for inadequate work and accidents. Funding sources are more likely to value the commitment of staff resources, which are easier to supervise than volunteers. Consequently, voluntarism gets pushed to the periphery of the organization's activities and might even be abandoned as a distraction. One of the defining characteristics of the nonprofit sector (often referred to as the "voluntary sector") is diminished or extinguished.

Dominance of Market Norms

Successful NHOs often pride themselves on their commitment to market norms such as entrepreneurship, efficiency, competition, and the "bottom line." These market norms can be at odds with nonprofit norms, such as the commitment to mission, charitable purpose, and voluntarism. This is an area where it is necessary to understand the importance of maintaining ongoing tension, rather than jettisoning either set of norms—aptly termed the "double bottom line" by Bratt et al. 1994. Organizations that ignore the financial bottom line do so at the risk of bankruptcy. Administrative ineptitude and inefficiency are obviously not virtues. At the same time, enhancing the corporate balance sheet can easily eliminate any distinctive characteristic of an NHO other than its tax treatment and undermine the rationale for favorable treatment.

Co-optation

Government funding sources, as well as private sources of capital including philanthropy, expect vendors or grantees to perform in acceptable ways. This includes implementing the agreed upon objectives or tasks; managing funds according to government regulations and normal business standards; and generally attending to business. Although the goals to be pursued are often influenced by the vendor (in some instances this influence can be substantial), nonprofit organizations face co-optation by conforming to the envelope of acceptable goals and means. This includes accepting the prevailing democratic and market norms. Radical assessments of community problems that are rooted in other norms are not likely to be accepted. Additionally, political protest and demonstrations are not likely to be seen as acceptable to government funding sources.

This presents a challenge to NHOs promoting community development in neighborhoods where community organizing is as needed as physical development. To maintain a commitment to political activism, Stoecker (1996) recommends that two different types of community development organizations are needed: one for community organizing and mobilizing, and one for physical development. CDCs specializing in physical development would comply with and benefit from the strictures of the contracting regime, whereas grassroots community mobilizing groups would specifically address political action. Although this would clear up some verbal ambiguity surrounding CDCs, the funding of overt political action would remain problematic and might further erode support for public funding and favorable tax treatment.

Responses to Commercialization

The experience of nonprofit health care providers suggests that increased commercialization reduces the public legitimacy of the sector. If nonprofit providers have no distinguishing characteristics other than their tax treatment, Congress is likely to be pressured to eliminate their favorable tax status. A commercialized nonprofit sector is also likely to be criticized for failing to achieve its broader public purpose mission, increasing the potential that the sector will be identified as a failure relative to its mission. The nonprofit sector's political liability for such failure is not likely to be diminished because the root cause was government's misunderstanding that altered its relationship with the sector. The sector's response to the pressures of commercialization must address seven critical areas: mission; boards and policy; trust; philanthropy and voluntarism; organizational diversity; subsidiarity (primacy); and partnership.

The Fundamental Importance of Mission

In nonprofit housing, mission is everything. Lose sight of your mission and you lose the very thing that justifies your existence. Needless to say, the mission of NHOs is unrelated to "profit" or corporate growth. (Making money or at least not losing it is important, but it cannot be the mission of nonprofit housing.) NHOs need to carefully craft their mission statements to identify their public purpose. For the most part, the purpose of NHOs is to respond to housing problems that are inadequately addressed by the for-profit market, such as low-income housing production, neighborhood revitalization, promotion of fair housing, emergency shelter, and transitional and group housing. Some NHOs have more particularized missions than others in respect to geography or population served. But all need to keep a focus on their mission and strive to embody that mission in everyday tasks.

Although executive directors and other staff often do a commendable job in demonstrating their commitment to mission, it is primarily the responsibility of the board of directors to imbue the organization's mission into its operations. Executive directors are much more likely to respond to current payroll needs and thus ignore mission drift for the sake of funding. The board's responsibilities for overseeing the implementation of mission go beyond the choice of "what to do" to "how do we do it." For example, most NHOs have a mission of improving housing and living conditions for low-income households. Boards must address and periodically review the organization's performance in serving the targeted population (with sober recognition of the pressures to skim off the top of eligible incomes).

Boards and Policy

Boards need to be visible and active. NHOs as well as other nonprofit organizations tend to become "director driven" rather than "board directed." NHOs need to establish a creative tension between the board and the executive director. Founding board members might have a clear understanding of the NHO mission, but as organizations mature, more and more board members are selected for particular skills rather than their understanding and commitment to the organization's distinctive mission. Additionally, board selection can become more the domain of the executive director than the board or the membership. (Most NHOs do not have a membership of quasi-stockholders or trustees who elect the board. Instead, the board elects its own members, often at the recommendation of the executive director.) New directors might have limited exposure to the NHO and little understanding of its mission. Unless the NHO establishes procedures for educating new board members on their responsibilities, their oversight is likely to be limited to fiscal and management practices rather than overall purpose.

Client and neighborhood participation on NHO boards is often recommended as a way of maintaining a focus on the organization's service mission. Certain federal housing set-asides for NHOs are limited to those with numerical control by clients or low-income neighborhood residents. Nonprofit theory and research identifies the importance of trustworthy performance whenever the client has no effective contract or market influence. Many NHO services are in this category. However, it is not known if board representation improves trustworthy performance, or if such performance might be better achieved through other administrative means. Regardless of client representation on boards, the implementation of mission and trustworthy performance are issues that NHO boards should regularly address.

Trustworthiness

One of the strongest rationales for nonprofit housing is their trustworthiness in protecting the interests of the clients served and in providing public goods. Given the potential for opportunistic behavior by profit-motivated firms in the delivery of publicly assisted housing, NHOs would be expected to deliver higher quality services and to protect the interest of low-income clients. Although this is presumed to be the case, it has not been addressed through research so far. Evidence of higher quality services would include the physical quality of properties, responsiveness to maintenance requests, a greater range of tenant services, lower tenant turnover, higher tenant satisfaction, and more property amenities. Evidence of protecting the interests of low-income clients would include soliciting the input of tenants (and other clients), greater responsiveness to tenant needs, and more tenant-centered selection and eviction criteria.

NHOs should not only be expected to be trustworthy relative to clients, they should be trustworthy relative to their government funding sources. Programs should be implemented as agreed and moneys accounted for in conformance with professional norms. Open and honest communication with government sponsors is essential to the development of trust. Pushing the bounds of advocacy to conflict and political protest tears the fabric of trust.

Philanthropy and Voluntarism

NHOs have to demonstrate community support for their work. Local contributions of time (voluntarism) and money (philanthropy) are important evidence of community support. The temptation is to become solely an arm of government, implementing public programs on a contract or fee basis, and forsaking efforts to raise donations and supervise volunteers. Government contracting is a critical source of support for NHOs, but it is a mistake to rely exclusively on this. Some NHOs see donations and volunteers as returning little to the bottom line. That can be the case, but it misses the point. Community support reflects that the NHO is doing something worthwhile, something that resonates with people who agree with its mission. It does not mean that the NHO can survive off it.

Organizational Diversity: Not Every NHO Needs to be a Developer

There is a tendency in discussions of nonprofit housing to focus on one particular form: community development corporations. Even more specifically, the focus is on CDCs engaged in housing production. This ignores the diversity that exists in nonprofit housing in several ways. Many NHOs are not involved or have only a limited involvement in housing production. They run homeless shelters, group homes, transitional housing, and a variety of service programs. Additionally, some CDCs are much more oriented to community organizing and political action. These are important functions of the nonprofit housing sector and should not be ignored despite funding difficulties.

The focus on housing production has a more pernicious effect than just overlooking the diversity of nonprofit housing. It also tends to legitimize housing production as the proper role of NHOs and their primary measure of performance. This encourages expectations that NHOs should be engaged in housing production. Elevating housing production to a norm for NHOs has important negative consequences. Housing production is enormously capital intensive, thereby making NHOs largely reliant on federal housing production subsidies and accentuating the negative aspects of commercialization of the sector. Small, neighborhood NHOs have less chance for survival, for if they succeed in becoming housing production corporations, they are likely to look beyond their original service area for new markets. If they don't succeed in expanding their housing production, they are viewed as failures or are maintained as inefficient producers. Public maintenance of inefficient producers denies opportunities for larger NHOs specializing in housing production, thereby diminishing the overall impact of the sector.

Housing production should be seen as one niche, albeit an important one, in the range of services properly offered by NHOs. Only a few efficiently organized NHOs operating as housing producers and managers are required in a given city or region. These NHOs can achieve economies of scale and staff expertise that would enhance production performance and can provide housing production services to other NHOs when needed on a contract basis. This would free other NHOs to pursue their missions without having to divert resources and energy to housing production. It could also concentrate commercialization with housing producers where the impact of commercialization would be more compatible with the organization's mission.

Subsidiarity (Primacy)

The principle of subsidiarity underlies government-nonprofit relationships in western Europe. It stresses the central importance of human dignity rooted in the person and the family. The role of public policy is to support the individual and the family when needed. When individuals and families need additional assistance, it should be delivered by those closest to them—churches and associations (i.e., the nonprofit sector), then local government. More remote levels of government should be directly involved only when the capabilities of those closer to the family prove inadequate. Although there are parallels between grassroots democracy and subsidiarity, the latter is distinct in its emphasis on the social proximity of caretakers and service providers.

The nonprofit housing sector (and the nonprofit sector as a whole) could be well served by embracing and promoting the principle of subsidiarity in the United States (Wolfe 1995). This would reinforce the sector's commitment to a mission of service and its role as counterbalancing the impersonal and coercive power of the state. The connection of subsidiarity to Catholic tradition and the lack of popular understanding of the term suggest that another term would potentially be more acceptable. "Primacy" or the "principle of primacy" might be more appealing in the United States, since it more readily implies the primary importance of the individual and family, with declining priority as one moves away from the family. The conflict between the particularism of the nonprofit sector and the universal access promoted by government must be addressed through cultivation of broad involvement in nonprofit provision. Parallel provision directly by government might be necessary where the nonprofit network is not comprehensive.

The Partnership Paradigm

Salamon (1993) described the pre-1980 relationship between government and the nonprofit sector as the paradigm of partnership. The prevalent preferential contracting relationship provided the nonprofit vendor substantial influence over implementation of public programs, transforming the contracting relationship into a weak partnership. The diversity and complexity of these relationships proved difficult to manage and was in need of reform, but the wrong reforms were made. Instead of preferential contracting with nonprofit suppliers, the relationship shifted to the market model of competitive contracting and consumer subsidies. A strict vendor relationship replaced an implicit partnership.

This failure at the national level was due in part to the lack of a readily understood model or metaphor of the partnership paradigm. The lack of an easily communicated partnership metaphor, which reflects the funding responsibilities of the state and the service delivery responsibilities of the nonprofit sector, has seriously damaged the paradigm's continuation. NHOs have established national level public-private partnerships, but these have mainly been resource partnerships built around the Low Income Housing Tax Credit program or the franchise partnership of the Neighborhood Reinvestment Corporation. Development of a national public-nonprofit housing partnership will be further constrained until the sector is sufficiently integrated to allow effective national representation.

Partnerships

Given the dominance of contracting partnerships in the United States and the lack of a vertically integrated nonprofit housing sector, it appears doubtful that a full partnership between the national government and the nonprofit housing sector will emerge in the near future. American housing advocates look longingly on the full housing partnerships that exist in Europe, but the historical, ideological, and organizational underpinnings of those partnerships are not likely to be repeated in the United States. Instead, more attention to the contracting model is needed. The threat of convergence on for-profit behavior within a competitive contracting scheme points to the potential loss of nonprofit identity and further marginalization of low-income tenants. Nonprofit housing corporations become increasingly "entrepreneurial" and thereby risk becoming lost. More refined contracting schemes at the national level need to be studied, ones that reward social benefit as well as competitive costs.

Partnership is more likely to be established at local levels and much work is needed to understand how local partnerships can be nurtured. Establishing trust and a record of accomplishment are essential to the development of interorganizational cooperation and partnerships (Kramer and Tyler 1995). Trust is the language of partnerships. Without it the maintenance costs of partnerships are likely to exceed the benefits of participation. Trust is "faith in the moral integrity or goodwill of others" (Ring and Van de Ven 1994:93). It not only involves goodwill in process but also outcomes, the "fair dealing" that establishes a sense of equity in exchanges (Ring and Van de Ven 1994:95). As trust builds, uncertainties over the partnership are reduced and the process of negotiation, commitment, and implementation is simplified as personal and organizational congruence are confirmed.

Trust, reciprocity, indebtedness, "log-rolling," and cooperation play important roles in developing collaborative relationships between organizations. Trust is developed in a delicate interplay of personal and organizational interactions. Trust builds from the personal level and is confirmed by institutional commitments. Over time trust is solidified by institutional norms and informal and formal policies. Given the reliance on personal interactions in the initial establishment of trust, the development of partnerships requires continuity among negotiators and decision-makers. NHOs and cities interested in creating partnerships need to attend to the development of the personal and organizational requirements for establishing trust. Since trust is enhanced by congruent expectations and norms, differences in social status and organizational roles of participants—common to housing partnerships—could act as a deterrent to partnership unless addressed forthrightly.

If trust is the language of partnerships, accomplishment is their currency. An action orientation is necessary. Two of the fundamental reasons for collaboration are resource mobilization and implementation authority. If an individual organization independently had both sufficient resources and sufficient authority to act, there would be virtually no reason for collaboration. Projects requiring substantial resources and the authority (or expertise) of numerous organizations are more problematic for the initial establishment of partnerships, but small successes can provide the organizational experience and abilities required for more substantial projects. Small accomplishments confirm and build trust, as well as return benefits that help solidify the partnership. Successful and lasting partnerships depend on "collaborative advantage"—

> the creation of synergy between collaborating organizations. Collaborative advantage will be achieved when something unusually creative is produced . . . that no one organization could have produced on its own and when each organization, through the collaboration, is able to achieve its own objectives better than it could alone. In some cases, it should also be possible to achieve some higher-level "meta-objectives"; objectives for society as a whole rather than just for participating organizations. (Huxham 1993:603)

It is not surprising that most housing partnerships have been created in response to the current complexity of low-income housing production. NHOs bring much needed resources to these partnerships as packagers of deals. But there are serious liabilities to building partnerships around an inherently flawed funding scheme. Rather than silently acquiescing to or supporting the complexity of current production subsidies, NHOs and their local partners would be better served by continuing to critique the system and making recommendations for reforms. Additionally, housing partnerships should develop "metamissions" beyond resource mobilization for tax-credit developments in order to broaden their base of support.

NHOs should understand clearly the resources they bring to partnerships. With limited access to capital, they primarily bring their implementation expertise and trustworthiness. Coalitions among NHOs and neighborhood interests would enhance the ability of NHOs to deliver on neighborhood redevelopment projects. NHOs should be careful to limit their commitments to the boundaries of their expertise. They should establish a record demonstrating the trustworthiness of their operations and the quality of their products.

Successful local housing partnerships could establish the basis for participation of NHOs in local governing regimes—"the informal arrangements by which pubic bodies and private interests function together in order to be able to make and carry out governing decisions" (Stone 1989:6). Often these governing regimes are heavily influenced by business interests and business-dominated governing regimes have tended to give short shrift to equity concerns in favor of implementation ability. Stone (1989) and Fainstein (1994) have suggested nonprofit organizations and community groups as a much needed counterbalance to business interests in the public-private partnerships implementing large-scale urban redevelopment projects. Astute political leaders could enhance their own leverage in favor of equity goals by including NHOs in governing regimes. At a minimum, empowering NHOs within housing partnerships would help broaden the social agenda.

At the national level, a strong coalition of NHOs and local housing partnerships is necessary to establish the political support for a housing partnership between government and the nonprofit sector. It is important that a national coalition include the diversity of the nonprofit housing sector and promote a clear rationale for a national housing partnership. Greater vertical and horizontal integration will be required to achieve the national representation of nonprofit housing similar to that in western Europe. It will also be necessary to regulate the sector. If NHOs ever gain close to exclusive prominence in the provision of assisted housing services, regulating entry into the field will become even more important. It is naive to think that greed and profiteering will be eliminated as human traits simply because an organization meets the current requirements for NHOs.

The argument for a national partnership must be rooted in the distinctive contributions of nonprofit housing and the principle of primacy. A clear understanding of the relationship between government and the nonprofit sector is fundamental to broadening the current contracting relationship into a partnership. The theory of nonprofit housing needs to be refined beyond the rudimentary elements presented here to create the basis for workable models and norms. Many of the contributions of nonprofit housing remain undocumented assertions. A national research agenda is needed to clarify and support a broadened role of the nonprofit housing sector.

Research Directions

This book represents a starting point in developing a theory of nonprofit housing and in placing nonprofit housing squarely in the realm of nonprofit sector research. It is also a call for the nonprofit housing sector to broaden its attention and to engage the debates surrounding the nonprofit sector as a whole, in the U.S. and abroad. Without a theory of nonprofit housing and research demonstrating the nonprofit housing sector's distinctive contributions, the future is likely to continue the pattern of sporadic waxing and waning of government support noted by Rachel Bratt in chapter 6.

The theory presented identifies several areas of distinction for nonprofit housing that point to the broad elements of a nonprofit housing research agenda: mission and trust; boards and policy; philanthropy and voluntarism; primacy;

partnership; and political economy. Nonprofit housing research needs to move beyond counting units and resources to developing a richer understanding of this sector. Comparative studies between NHOs and for-profit housing providers are needed. Both sectors provide assisted housing under the Section 8 program and the Low Income Housing Tax Credit. It is frequently claimed that nonprofit housing is permanently committed to low-income use, whereas for-profit providers commit to low-income use only through the term of a contract and until a use with a higher return presents itself. However, nonprofit housing could be made less permanent by financial failure and inadequate maintenance.

Answers to the following questions would help move our understanding and our expectations to a new level.

Mission and Trust:

- What is the impact of mission on NHO-decision making and operations?

- What is the impact of mission on quality of services and characteristics of clients?

- What evidence of trustworthy behavior can be found in policies and procedures for tenant selection, representation, and eviction?

Boards and Policy:

- How does mission affect the deliberations and decisions of NHO boards and executives?

- What constituencies do NHO boards represent? How are board members selected?

Philanthropy and Voluntarism:

- What roles do philanthropy and voluntarism play in nonprofit housing?

- What impact do philanthropy and voluntarism have on the public perception of NHOs?

- What impact do philanthropy and voluntarism have on NHO goals?

- What impact do philanthropy and voluntarism have on quality of services?

Primacy:

- How has the principle of subsidiarity affected nonprofit housing in western Europe?

- To what extent is primacy valued by NHOs in the United States?

Partnership:

- How is interorganizational trust established?

- What personal and organizational attributes enhance the development of trust?

- Does preferential contracting promote greater NHO influence on implementation decisions compared with competitive contracting between NHOs and for-profit firms?

- How does competition among NHOs for government contracts affect NHO-government relationships?

- What influence do national representatives of nonprofit housing have on government policy in the U.S.? What impact does vertical and horizontal integration have on the influence of national representatives of nonprofit housing?

- How are local housing partnerships formed? What resources do NHOs bring to local partnerships?

Political Economy:

- How do local governing regimes affect housing partnerships? How do NHOs influence local governing regimes?

- What impact do political affiliations have on perceptions of nonprofit-government relationships?

- Under what conditions do NHOs engage in political protest and community organizing? Does government contracting restrict organizing activities? How do government funding opportunities and policies encourage NHOs to become housing producers? What impact does housing production have on the commercialization of NHOs?

Conclusion

Recent theoretical and empirical work on urban governing regimes has made it clear that politics matters. A corollary to this is that ideas matter. The liberal conceptualization of the welfare state that guided social policy after the depression has floundered. At the same time, the conservative challenge that promotes markets as the sole solution to public problems is too draconian to last. The left promoted the nonprofit sector as an extension of the state and in doing so transformed it into government. The right embraced the nonprofit sector to mask its fiscal goals as redemption of the human spirit and in doing so will starve the sector. Perhaps it is folly to cry pox on both houses. But in order for the nonprofit sector to become the centerpiece of a new consensus about the welfare state, we must advance our knowledge of the sector and the norms that can sustain it. Otherwise, the sector will volley between state and market depending on the tilt toward liberal or conservative political dominance and its potential will be lost.

References

Bratt, Rachel G., et al. 1994. *Confronting the management challenge: Affordable housing in the nonprofit sector.* New York: New School of Social Research, Community Development Research Center.

Fainstein, Susan S. 1994. *The city builders.* Cambridge, Mass.: Blackwell.

Hodgkinson, Virginia A. et al. 1989. *The future of the nonprofit sector.* San Francisco: Jossey-Bass.

Huxham, Chris. "Pursuing collaborative advantage." *Journal of Operational Research Society* 44 (6)599–611.

Kramer, Roderick M., and Tom R. Tyler. 1996. *Trust in organizations: Frontiers in theory and research.* Thousand Oaks, Calif.: Sage Publications.

Ring, Peter S., and Andrew H. Van de Ven. 1994. "Developmental processes of cooperative interorganizational relationships." *Academy of Management Review* 19 (1) 90–118.

Salamon, Lester M. 1993. "The marketization of welfare: Changing nonprofit and for-profit roles in the American welfare state." *Social Science Review* 67 (1)16–39.

Smith, Steven R., and Michael Lipsky. 1993. *Nonprofits for hire: The welfare state in the age of contracting.* Cambridge: Harvard University Press.

Stoecker, Randy. 1996. "The political economy of the community development corporation model of urban redevelopment." Revised version of a paper presented at the 1995 American Sociological Association annual meeting.

Stone, Clarence N. 1989. *Regime politics: Governing Atlanta, 1946–1988.* Lawrence: University Press of Kansas.

Wolfe, Christopher. 1995. "Subsidiarity: The 'Other' ground of limited government." In *Catholicism, liberalism, and communitarianism.* Kenneth L. Grasso et al. Lanham, Md: Rowman & Littlefield Publishers.

Contributors

Peter J. Boelhouwer is a researcher with the OTB Research Institute for Policy Sciences and Technology at Delft University of Technology, The Netherlands. His research focus has been privatization, the sale of public housing, housing allowances and comparative housing research. Dr. Boelhouwer is co-author of *Housing Systems in Europe: Part I, A Comparative Study of Housing Policy* (Delft University Press, 1992), as well as articles and reports on Dutch and European housing policy.

Rachel Bratt is professor of Urban and Environmental Policy and chair of the department at Tufts University. Her research interests are in the areas of housing and community development, particularly the needs of low-income households and the role of community-based housing organizations. She serves on several Massachusetts boards and advisory committees and is a former member of the Federal Reserve Bank Board's Consumer Advisory Council. She is a co-editor of *Critical Perspectives on Housing* (Temple University Press, 1986), author of *Rebuilding a Low-Income Housing Policy* (Temple University Press, 1989), and co-author of *Confronting the Management Challenge: Affordable Housing in the Nonprofit Sector* (New School for Social Research, Community Development Research Center, 1994).

Peter Dreier is the E. P. Clapp Distinguished Professor of Politics and the director of the Public Policy Program at Occidental College in Los Angeles. From 1984 to 1992 he served as director of housing for the Boston Redevelopment Authority and as senior policy advisor to Mayor Raymond Flynn. He served on the Advisory Board of the Resolution Trust Corporation from 1993 to 1995. Dr. Dreier writes frequently on American politics and urban policy for professional journals, magazines, and newspapers.

Robert Dyck is professor of Urban Affairs and Planning at Virginia Polytechnic Institute and State University. His research focuses on domestic and international issues of urban and regional development, including organizational and institutional changes implied by the transition to post-modernism, and the urban design contributions of Joze Plecnik and other central European architects. Dr. Dyck is co-founder and director of the Virginia Center for Organizational Innovation. He is currently at work on a book entitled Self-Transformation of the Forgotten Four-Fifths, which includes case studies of self-reliant, community-based, innovative development.

Scott Hebert is a senior associate at Abt Associates in Cambridge, Massachusetts. At Abt Associates, Mr. Hebert has directed policy studies and evaluations for a wide variety of housing, community revitalization, and economic development efforts. Prior to joining Abt Associates in 1991, Mr. Hebert served as an administrator for affordable housing, community development, and anti-poverty programs at the local and state levels.

Harry van der Heijden is a researcher at the OTB Research Institute for Policy Sciences and Technology at Delft University of Technology, The Netherlands. His research focus has been housing policy, building market and comparative housing research. Dr. van der Heijden is co-author of *Housing Systems in Europe: Part I, A Comparative Study of Housing Policy* (Delft University Press, 1992), as well as articles and reports on Dutch and European housing policy.

C. Theodore Koebel is director of the Center for Housing Research and associate professor of Housing and Urban Planning at Virginia Polytechnic Institute and State University. He has published widely on housing and development issues, including public-private partnerships. He is a past editor of the *Journal of Urban Affairs* and recently edited a special issue of the *Journal of Urban Technology*. He has been a founder and board member of several nonprofit housing organizations.

William M. Rohe, Dean E. Smith Professor in the Department of City and Regional Planning at the University of North Carolina at Chapel Hill, is director of the Center for Urban and Regional Studies. Dr. Rohe has been a visiting scholar at the U.S. Department of Housing and Urban Development and a member of the Chapel Hill Planning Board. He is the author of numerous journal articles reflecting his interest in low-income housing programs and social impacts of homeownership on low-income people.

Bishwapriya Sanyal is associate professor and department chair of Urban Planning at Massachusetts Institute of Technology. Dr. Sanyal has served as a consultant to the Ford Foundation, World Bank, International Labor Organization, the United Nations, and the United States Agency for International Development. He has research experience in India, Bangladesh, Zambia, Kenya,

Jordan, Brazil, and Curaco. He is the author of numerous articles on planning and development and of *Cooperative Autonomy: The Dialectics of State-NGO Relationships in Developing Countries* (Geneva: International Institute for Labor Studies, 1994) and editor of *Breaking the Boundaries: A One-World Approach to Planning Education* (Plenum Press, 1990).

Richard Steinberg is professor of Economics at Indiana University/Purdue University at Indianapolis. He is a past president of the Association for Research on Nonprofit Organizations and Voluntary Action and a deputy editor of *Nonprofit and Voluntary Sector Quarterly*. He has written extensively on the economics of the nonprofit sector, the relationship between government spending and private donations, the role of incentives in nonprofit performance, and public policy towards the sector. He wrote *Economics for Nonprofit Managers* with Dennis R. Young (Foundation Center Press).

James Wallace is a principal associate and vice president at Abt Associates, Inc. Over the last twenty-five years he has performed policy research on virtually all of the assisted housing programs of the Department of Housing and Urban Development (HUD) and has published extensively in the field. He was Chief Policy Analyst for the President's Commission on Housing in the early 1980s, and the principal investigator to develop a national database on low-income housing tax credit projects.

Robert B. Whittlesey is the founder of the National Association of Housing Partnerships. He is past president and director of the Metropolitan Boston Housing Partnership, Inc. Mr. Whittlesey has over thirty years of experience in the provision of affordable housing, including service as executive director of the Boston Housing Partnership, founding executive director of The Community Builders, and court-appointed master responsible for reforming the Boston Housing Authority. He has authored several reports on housing policy and programs and is a long-standing advocate of progressive housing policy.

Index